♥ Hope's Wish ★

To Ella Grace! ★

Spirit of Hope 2017!

Shelly Stout

HopeMom :-)

Hope's Wish

How one girl's dream made others' come true

Stuart and Shelby Stout

THOMAS NELSON
Since 1798

NASHVILLE DALLAS MEXICO CITY RIO DE JANEIRO

Published in Nashville, Tennessee, by Thomas Nelson. Thomas Nelson is a registered trademark of Thomas Nelson, Inc.

Thomas Nelson, Inc., titles may be purchased in bulk for educational, business, fund-raising, or sales promotional use. For information, please e-mail SpecialMarkets@ThomasNelson.com.

Unless otherwise noted, Scripture quotations are taken from HOLY BIBLE: NEW INTERNATIONAL VERSION®. © 1973, 1978, 1984 by International Bible Society. Used by permission of Zondervan Publishing House. All rights reserved. Scripture quotations marked NLT are from Holy Bible, New Living Translation. © 1996. Used by permission of Tyndale House Publishers, Inc., Wheaton, Illinois 60189. All rights reserved.

Library of Congress Cataloging-in-Publication Data

Stout, Stuart, 1957-
  Hope's wish / Stuart and Shelby Stout.
      p. cm.
  ISBN 978-1-59555-158-0
  1. Stout, Hope Elizabeth—Health. 2. Osteosarcoma in children—Patients—North Carolina—Biography. 3. Make-a-Wish Foundation. I. Stout, Shelby, 1958- II. Title.
RC280.B6S76 2008
362.196'994710092--dc22
[B]

2007049516

Printed in the United States of America
08 09 10 11 12 QG 7 6 5 4 3 2 1

QG 01-07-16

This book is dedicated to God
who continues to be our strength and hope.

To our beautiful daughters Austin and Holly
who are our everything and especially to our sweet Hopie
who taught us all what it truly means to love one another.

Contents

Foreword

I became familiar with Hope Stout and her inspiring wish during my very first week as president and chief executive officer for the Make-A-Wish Foundation® of America. I traveled to Charlotte, North Carolina, to attend the second annual Celebration of Hope, a fund-raising gala in memory of Hope Stout. During that evening, I met hundreds of caring people who were moved by the life of this remarkable young woman. I also had the opportunity to meet Hope's parents, Shelby and Stuart. Their remarks that night were the highlight of the evening for me: they poignantly talked about Hope's ordeal with cancer and her decision to help others while in the midst of it.

Four years ago, Hope's unique wish left a lasting mark on the hearts of everyone involved with the Foundation. At first, Hope wished to become famous. However, after learning more about the Make-A-Wish Foundation's work and the fact that 155 children in North Carolina were waiting to receive their wishes, she changed her wish into one of the most selfless acts I have ever known. She wished to raise enough money to grant the wishes of those 155 children: more than one million dollars.

I never had the privilege of meeting Hope, but I feel like I know her because of this book. Since this book was published, I have shared it with numerous people. I have given it to prospective employees, new donors, and people not familiar with the Foundation's work. I believe it is simply one of the best portrayals of what families go through when a child becomes seriously ill. It also demonstrates the power of a child's wish: in this case, a wish to help others.

I am privileged to be in the position to hear so many amazing stories about the courageous children we serve. Last year, thirteen thousand children with life-threatening medical conditions received their heartfelt wishes. These wishes were sometimes as simple as having a computer, a pet, or a shopping spree; sometimes, they were as complex as restoring an old car, taking a trip to another country, or becoming a superhero. Every forty-one minutes, the Foundation grants a child's wish somewhere in the United States, and since 1980, the Foundation has granted the fondest wishes of more than 153,000 children, including Hope.

It has often been said that trials bring out the true character of a person. Readers will have an inside look at the character of not only the Stout family but also the Charlotte community.

Shelby and Stuart, thank you for sharing Hope's story with us. I am convinced it will bless and encourage so many people to look for God in the details of their lives. You raised a remarkable young woman.

Finally, Hope, you did more to impact our world in twelve years than many of us will in a lifetime, and your legacy lives on. On behalf of the thousands of children with life-threatening medical conditions who will have their heartfelt wishes granted because of you, thank you.

David Williams
President and Chief Executive Officer,
Make-A-Wish Foundation of America®

Life Is Precious

Writing this book about our amazing daughter has largely been a blessing for Shelby and me. It is also without question what we feel God wants us to do. Hope was a wonderful child, and her story has inspired thousands. Naturally, we want to share it.

But it has not been without its moments.

Almost every morning on the way to work, I pass by a particular bus stop. This bus stop is for younger kids and during cold or rainy weather, the children sit in cars with their moms, waiting for their bus to come and take them to school. It is a routine occurrence, a scene that knits itself into the background of everyday life during the school year. Most folks ride by these bus stops, not giving them a second glance other than to slow down and be cautious.

But I notice something more. I see it almost every day and prior to Hope's journey, it would have gone unnoticed by me as well.

I see the precious gift of life.

I see a mother putting her daughter's hair up or laughing in the car with her when the rain falls outside.

I see a father kiss his daughter good-bye and high-five his son as they head to the bus. To them, it's just another day in their lives. Just another day of school and work with nothing out of the ordinary.

But to Shelby and me, it's another day without our Hope.

I am writing this book, which is based on my wife's journal during our daughter's illness. Shelby will add "Reflections of a Mother" at the end of some chapters. Then when Hope nears the end of her journey, our roles will reverse. Shelby will carry the narrative for these critical chapters because she spent a great deal of time with our daughter, helping her with the ordinary processes of life. And I will add "Reflections of a Father." I will resume the narrative in the last two chapters.

Our purpose for this book is simple. We want to make sure everyone realizes how important, and how precious, is the gift of life. How precious is a moment as ordinary as waiting for the yellow school bus.

This book is not limited to parents who have lost a child or have a child with cancer; instead this book is for anyone who is suffering a difficulty—a job loss, family problems, financial woes, divorce.

It is for anyone who might be facing tough times in the future.

We now know that God wants us all to have the childlike faith Hope possessed, a faith that refuses to be overcome by doubt or fear. This is the confidence that God is there with us and will take care of us. If this lesson is learned before a storm hits (and in this human pilgrimage rest assured that trials and tribulations will come in some form), you will be prepared to weather the storm and come out blessed because of it.

When Hope was interviewed by Charlotte radio personality Keith Larson about her wish, she matter-of-factly said, "We're just giving it to God, and He's gonna take care of it. Have a 100 percent faith in God, and anything is possible."

And she was right. Hope's wish to fulfill the wishes of the 155 children in North Carolina who suffered from life-threatening medical conditions was realized on January 16, 2004, less than three weeks after Hope's passing. The vast majority of the one million dollars was raised in the month between December 19, when Keith Larson and other media began to tell Hope's story, and January 16, which was the first Celebration of Hope, a gala event to raise donations to Make-A-Wish.

And her faith in God, and in people, made this happen.

The Bible tells us that "a little child will lead them."[1] We found that Hope's voice as a twelve-year-old led us in our struggles and prompted the entire city of Charlotte to fulfill the wishes of these children.

Michael Yaconelli says in his book *Dangerous Wonder*, "Deep within all of us, there is a voice. It speaks to us continuously, knocking on the door of our consciousness. When we are children the voice is loud. Its loudness is not like a train or jet engine. It shouts to us with a whisper. This voice of our childhood is the voice of wonder and amazement, the voice of God, which has always been there speaking to us, even before we were born."[2]

Yet as adults, we try to control life and the voice becomes much softer because we think we know best. We grow up and healthy doses of life's realities bog us down.

We forget that childlike faith.

We hope that this book will help anyone who reads it to regain a childlike faith. That's what we learned from Hope Elizabeth Stout in her twelve short years.

1

"My Leg Really Hurts."

We don't remember exactly when Hope first said the words, "My leg really hurts" to us. Given the events as they have unfolded, we would have taken Hope right then and there to the hospital and insisted on every medical test known to man: CAT scans, PET scans, MRIs. Maybe that would have changed our journey. But Hope, having shot up four inches in less than a year, was constantly experiencing growing pains. Almost every night, she asked her mother or me to rub her legs, arms, and calves, much in the same fashion as our other daughters had when they were going through puberty. Hope's occasional complaint seemed to be nothing out of the ordinary. Most kids have growing pains and their parents don't give them a second thought.

We just wish we had.

From March through May 2003, Hope did pretty much what she wanted. Occasionally she would say that her knee was bothering her, but then she wouldn't mention it for a while and we would forget about it. Finally, in mid-May, after complaining about the knee hurting for several days in a row, Shelby took Hope to our pediatrician.

He put Hope through a strenuous exam, poking and prodding the knee area, asking her to do deep knee bends and stretches.

He did everything but take an X-ray of the knee.

The doctor, who has been the girls' pediatrician for their whole lives, indicated that he felt nothing in either the bone or the ligaments and that most likely Hope had just strained her knee. That seemed logical, given all the basketball, cheerleading, and tumbling she had just completed. He recommended that she wear an elastic brace to immobilize the knee somewhat and take it easy for the next week or so. If there was still pain after two weeks, he recommended seeing an orthopedist.

As school was winding down, Hope continued to engage in all kinds of physical activities including her cheerleading routines. We went down to the beach for Memorial Day Weekend and rode jet skis, went swimming, and enjoyed the fun of being at Holden Beach. That weekend in May 2003 a humorous incident involving the jet skis took place.

This was the first summer Hope was old enough to ride the ski solo, and I was riding along, showing her how to safely operate the watercraft. Since it was the first big boating weekend of the summer, the Wildlife patrol was randomly pulling boaters over to see if their watercraft had all the required equipment. We had just gotten started when they promptly waved me over.

Upon seeing her father stopped by the Wildlife officers, Hope zipped off in the opposite direction. The officers made a routine check of my jet ski, and after seeing that I had all the required paperwork and gear, appeared ready to let me go.

Or so I thought. As I was about to push off, one officer asked me a question. "Is that girl riding that jet ski down there with you?"

"What girl"? (I figured it was worth a shot; maybe he would forget about it and move on.) "That red headed girl riding the same ski you are. She is with you, right?"

"Oh, that one. Yep, she is my daughter," I said reluctantly.

The officer did not seem amused. "Can you ask her to come over here?"

"Certainly, Officer," I replied, and after a minute of waving my arms wildly, I managed to finally get Hope's attention.

This could be bad, I thought. *Hope hasn't been driving the ski for very long.* I could see her driving up at top speed and crashing into the Wildlife boat. The thought of ending up in jail occurred to me.

But to my surprise, Hope drove the jet ski up expertly, well under the No Wake limit, and pulled alongside the officer's boat like an old pro.

After a check of her ski, the officer asked Hope how old she was.

"Twelve," she answered.

The man turned toward me and said, "She either needs to be sixteen years of age and have a valid driver's license, or she needs to have a Water Safety certificate to ride a jet ski solo."

I pleaded ignorance of this requirement and asked for a break on getting a ticket. The officer agreed to let us off with a warning, telling us to head straight back to the dock.

We thanked him and headed that way. When we got to the dock, I asked Hope why she had taken off.

"Well, Dad, I figured it was better if only one of us got busted. Since he had you pulled over, I just skedaddled."

I was never more proud of my daughter than at that moment.

She knew her dad could take care of the situation and turned it over to him. She totally trusted me to get us out of trouble. As we would see with the events that were about to unfold over the next six months, she again trusted her Father to take care of things; she just turned it all over to Him.

And so did Shelby and I.

2

A Torn ACL?

On Saturday night, June 21, 2003, the night before our middle daughter, Holly, and I left for a mission trip to Tennessee, our family went out for a seafood dinner at Joe's Crab Shack, where our oldest daughter, Austin, was working as a waitress. One of Hope's best friends, Emily Rutherford, went with us. It was a fun evening, with lots of laughter as Hope teased her older sister as she waited on us. When we were walking to the car, I noticed Hope limping worse than ever before.

"Shelby, she really is limping," I said softly to my wife. "Have you noticed that?"

Shelby nodded yes. "Hope told me a couple of days ago that her leg was really hurting, and so I called the pediatrician's office to tell him she was still in pain. They made an appointment for her on Monday with an orthopedist," Shelby said as we approached the car. "They think it is probably just growing pains or stress, but at least we can find out why it is hurting."

We drove home from the restaurant and nothing more was said about it. Later that night after packing for the trip to Tennessee, I went in to say good-bye to Hope because we were leaving very early the next day.

After I kissed her goodnight and cut the light off, she said, "Dad, my knee is really hurting bad."

"Yeah, I saw you limping tonight at dinner. Let me take a look."

Hope pulled back the sheets as I switched the light back on, and for the first time I noticed that her knee was indeed swollen. I gently felt around the knee, mainly in the areas where the ligaments were. Using my hand, I applied some very light pressure around the swelling, and Hope reacted immediately.

Seeing her reaction to the slightest pressure, I quit rubbing her knee and assured her that she would be okay, knowing that she was seeing an orthopedist on Monday. I again kissed my youngest daughter goodnight and went into our bedroom.

Shelby was in bed, reading a book. She looked up when I walked into the room.

It's funny how you remember words you say in certain situations. At this particular moment, I said something to my wife that still haunts me to this day.

"Have you checked out Hope's knee?" I said. "It is really swollen. You know what, I bet anything that she has torn some cartilage or worse yet, maybe an ACL with all the flipping and flopping from cheerleading. We will probably be facing some surgery, and with our luck, it will have to be done just in time to screw up our vacation at the beach next week."

"I know, I wouldn't be surprised either," Shelby replied. "She was tubing at the lake a couple of weeks ago, and that leg was bouncing on the water—and with all that other stuff, she probably did something to it. I hope it doesn't mess things up next week either, but if it does, it does."

As the next few days and months unfolded, this moment shows

just how shallow and self-centered our lives were. Here we were, worrying about some possible knee surgery screwing up *our vacation*. It was all about us. Life was all about us.

The next morning, on Sunday, June 22, Holly, a rising high school sophomore, and I left for Oliver Springs, Tennessee, to participate in a REACH Work Camp. REACH is a ministry that brings in youth groups from all over the country for a week of refurbishing homes in rural communities, in this case Oliver Springs, which is located north of Knoxville. A typical small town in America, Oliver Springs has all the accoutrements you would expect: a Wal-Mart, several fast-food places, and movie theaters.

There is also quite a bit of poverty in the area. And that is what REACH focuses on: getting to the people in need and providing them with basic, necessary construction on their homes, which is unaffordable for most of these folks. REACH pays for all the construction materials, and the youth groups provide the labor. This wonderful ministry ends up blessing the building teams even more than the residents.

As Holly and I began our trip, we could not have imagined that this week would become one of the most difficult of our lives.

3

REACH Week

R EACH week is a very special time for our church youth group. Young people who go on this trip don't just sign up; they have to raise money to pay their way and do a set number of hours of service work prior to the trip. All of the kids who attend REACH are committed Christians who want to be there and make the necessary sacrifices to do so. This is a fun week of fellowship and hard work, but one that provides an opportunity to meet people from all over the country.

The trip took about four hours, and after getting situated in the high school where we were staying, the entire group of around 350 gathered for the opening ceremony, during which the work teams get to meet each other.

As one of the crew leaders, I was assigned a group of kids from Michigan, Maryland, South Carolina, Ohio, New York, and two girls from our Matthews United Methodist Church. We were allowed about an hour to get to know each other, and during this time I met Tommy who was from a suburb near Ann Arbor, Michigan.

As we sat on the gym floor talking and getting acquainted, Tommy's shorts slid partially up his leg, revealing a nasty scar that ran from the top of his knee up to his thigh. "Tommy, what happened to your leg? How did you get that scar? That looks like a nasty football injury."

After seeing the swelling in Hope's knee the night before, the concern had begun to gnaw at me, and I could not resist asking Tommy about the scar on his leg. What was causing her knee to swell up like that—and to be so very painful? Could this be serious, more serious than just an ACL? But after arriving in Tennessee, with the excitement of meeting my team and the anticipation of the week ahead, I had managed to forget about Hope's knee. Until now.

Tommy's answer to my question brought these thoughts all back to me—and chilled me to the bone.

"No, Mr. Stout, I got this scar from surgery. I had a tumor removed from my knee when I was a sophomore. I had some knee pain, and *boom!* there was this tumor on an X-ray. Fortunately it was not cancerous, but it took me about a year to get back to where I could walk normally again. The surgery left me with this nasty scar . . . But I am fine now and the chicks really dig the scar!"

His answer brought a smile to my lips, but the words I had spoken to Shelby the night before all of a sudden came rushing back to me.

Could this really be serious—not some ACL or knee injury that might inconvenience us, but possibly a *tumor?* Could Hope's knee pain really be cancer? Despite the heat in the gym, that thought made me shiver. And very soon, I began to rationalize. This couldn't possibly happen to us. It happened to Tommy, but he is fine. His tumor wasn't cancer.

The next day was Monday, June 23. After breakfast and devotions, my building team headed to the job site for the week.

Another team of eight was assigned to work with us on a house for a resident who needed wheelchair access throughout her property. The teams were given a list of assignments to be accomplished during the week, and we started to work immediately upon arriving at the site.

One of the biggest assignments was removing the flooring in the bathroom and replacing it entirely, along with new handicap accessible bathroom fixtures. The problem was, the bathroom was only big enough for two people to work in, and one of them had to be me.

Abby, a petite eighteen-year-old from Michigan, got the lucky job of helping me in the cramped, hot quarters. We began taking measurements to see how much flooring would be required, so I could give a daily order of supplies to the troubleshooter/supplier who came by early in the day.

After giving the troubleshooter our order, Abby and I started the nasty, hot job of removing the old flooring. Thankfully the work took my mind off Hope's upcoming doctor visit at eleven o'clock that morning; I knew that Shelby would call me on my cell phone as soon as they found out anything.

By eleven forty-five or so, the lack of a phone call actually made me feel better.

Just before noon, my cell phone beeped, telling me I had a voice mail. After walking outside, I dialed the number and retrieved the message. As I began to listen, the sounds of hammers pounding nails, electric saws zipping wood, and laughter coming from the kids blended into the words I heard.

Shelby and I have been married for over twenty-four years, and when I heard her voice, it immediately revealed a tone that was not good. Because we were in the mountains, the reception was spotty and the call broke up in places. Yet I knew that my wife sounded very scared, and I heard enough to realize she was telling me to call her as soon as possible. Then the call went dead.

But not before I heard these words.

. . . possible tumor . . . oncologist . . . biopsy on Friday . . . very scared . . . please call when you get this.

The words that I heard over the crackle of the static took the breath out of me. I managed to stagger over to a pile of lumber stacked in the yard and sat down heavily. The seriousness of the situation began to hit me with full force. *Possible tumor . . . oncologist . . . biopsy.* What did all that mean?

Despite the twenty or so youth and adults around me, I began to cry for the first time in years.

One of my co-leaders, Ann, an emergency room nurse from Baltimore, immediately came over, concerned that I was having a heat-related attack. She knelt down in front of me, and after reassuring her that I was all right, I told her what I had just heard. She gave me a hug and then her nursing instincts took over.

"Okay, Stuart, here is the deal. I am going to take you where I know your mind is heading: that what they see on the X-ray is cancer. Well, if it is, she is young and there are so many new treatments now—really amazing stuff. I know. I have seen them!"

She paused for a moment to let her encouraging words have full impact. Then she said, "Now, I have just taken you to the worst place you can go. So let's move back from there. It could be *so many* things other than cancer."

Knowing Ann's nursing background, her words calmed me quite a bit. We talked a few more minutes, and I soon felt in control enough to call Shelby back.

To make the call, I had to get in the van and drive about a half mile up the mountain to get decent reception.

At first Shelby was very upset with what was crashing down on her and Hope, but after a few minutes, she began to calm down and focus on what the orthopedist had told her and all that had happened since she had left the message.

The X-rays at Carolinas Medical Center (CMC) had, in fact,

revealed something abnormal. The orthopedist said it could be an infection—or it could be a tumor. But there was something "suspicious," and that was enough to have the orthopedist recommend seeing an oncologist on the next floor of the Medical Center.

Immediately!

Hope had been taken upstairs where the oncologist reviewed the X-rays. He recommended that they schedule a biopsy as soon as possible and some other tests prior to that.

Shelby went on to tell me that an appointment for the biopsy had just opened up for Friday morning, something that practically never happens. She said the doctors were amazed, because it usually takes weeks to get a biopsy scheduled but a cancellation had taken place that morning.

Looking back now, we wonder about that. Did a cancellation "just open up" or did these doctors know what they were dealing with—and that this biopsy needed to happen *now*.

Shelby and I spent some more time on the phone comforting and reassuring each other, and then I asked to speak to Hope.

"Hopie, I am coming home tonight. I want to be with you and Mom to go to these tests."

"Dad, that's crazy! . . . You just got there. Stay up there with Holly. I am fine. This is nothing. Me and Mom and Austin can handle this."

A second earlier, I had been ready to charge back to Charlotte, but I was so comforted by the strength in Hope's voice that I immediately began to calm down.

And she was right. Hope Stout was a very healthy kid, so healthy that it did not seem possible that there could be anything wrong with her. She had never been sick and had only had one major calamity requiring medical attention. That had occurred the previous summer in the now-infamous scooter wreck.

Hope and her buddy Emily had gotten the popular battery-powered scooters the previous Christmas. On August 11, 2002,

Hope and Emily were riding their scooters when one *zigged* as the other *zagged* and a collision occurred.

Emily hit her head and face hard, and Hope tore open a gash in her right knee, resulting in twelve stitches. Now, almost a year later, there was something showing up on an X-ray very near where Hope had gashed open her knee.

I told Hope that I loved her and would see her on Thursday night, and then Shelby got back on the phone. She told me that she had told the orthopedist about the scooter accident, and he said it was possible that what was showing up on the X-ray could be an infection from that accident. And that did seem logical. Cancer did not seem logical, so naturally we began to hope that this was just an infection, a small piece of sand that had not been flushed out and was now causing problems. Still serious but much better than the alternative. The C word.

After getting assurances from Shelby that she and Hope would be fine, I returned to my work crew as they were breaking for lunch. During our midday devotions, I told the group what was going on with Hope and asked them to lift up Hope and my family in prayer.

After the prayer, one of the kids assigned to the team helping us, a young man named Chris, asked to speak to me privately. This seemed odd to me, but I said, "Sure," and the two of us walked to the edge of the property.

"Stuart, I really don't know how to tell you this, but during my junior year, I was playing soccer and another kid ran into my leg. I felt something pop and we thought my ACL or MCL was torn.

"I was taken to the hospital and they did an X-ray. When the doctor came back in the room, I could tell by the look on his face that something was bad wrong. What he told my parents and me still shakes me up.

"The doctor said, 'We see something on the MRI that looks

really bad . . . You do have a torn ACL as we thought but we see something else. You also have a growth coming out of your knee and frankly we are about 100 percent sure it is cancer.'"

For the second time this week, I began to feel light-headed. First there was the experience of seeing Tommy's scar the night before and now Chris's story. The two young men had never met each other or me until this morning.

Chris continued. "The doctor made immediate arrangements for us to go to Duke University Hospital, and less than twenty-four hours later, I was admitted. It all happened so fast, my mom and dad were wrecks, but before we went to the hospital, our church quickly organized a prayer service, asking for God to be with us and to heal whatever I had.

"We checked into the hospital and I had a bunch of tests during the next few hours. The next day my parents and I were waiting in my hospital room. The same doctor walked in. The dude who looked like he had seen a ghost the day before now had a smile a mile wide.

"He told us, 'Folks, I cannot explain it. We have looked at the MRI from two days ago, and now have a battery of tests to compare it to. There is not a tumor! Whatever was there, and I emphasize there *was* something there yesterday, is gone! The only thing we have to fix now is the ACL.

"'But one thing is for sure, Chris. You do not have cancer!'"

Chris's words completely stunned me. And what he said next still means so much to me.

"Stuart, I want you to know that God will take care of Hope and your family. That you are my group leader is not a coincidence."

As I took in Chris's words, my mind began to calculate the chances of two guys being in my group, both with knee injuries that looked at first to be cancerous but turned out fine. God had surely placed these two young men on my team for a reason.

Reflections of a Mother

Before I talked to Stuart that day I knew I needed help. When the doctor left to check on getting the tests scheduled, I went outside to place a call to our pastor, Ken Lyon. I told him what was going on and Ken said a prayer on the phone. Then I went back into the room with Hope. Apparently I had forgotten to tell Hope where I was going, so our daughter lit into me. "Gee, Mom, I thought you had left me."

I heard the fear in Hope's voice. "No way, Hope. I just went to call Pastor Ken and we said a prayer together."

"Okay, then that's a good thing." Hope paused a second or two, and then she asked me, "Uh, Mom, what if this *is* cancer?"

I took a couple of deep breaths and then answered as positively as I could. "Hopie, if it is cancer, we will fight it.

"But let's not get ahead of ourselves. Like the doctor said, it could be a lot of other things. Let's wait and see what happens."

However, I suddenly realized I didn't have control anymore.

As a mom I had been able to fix most every boo-boo for my girls. Now all that had changed: this could not be fixed with Bactine and a Band-Aid.

4

Hope Thou in God

Word quickly spread throughout the whole camp about Hope. Each evening, the individual youth groups would gather separately after the main session. To accommodate our large group, we met in the football stadium, which was located just behind the school. Every night the whole group would offer up prayers: for the residents we were working with, for the success of the projects we were working on, and most especially for Hope and our family. Each evening Holly and I felt the love and support of these wonderful kids and adults.

Back home in Charlotte, Hope began a week of tests. Shelby, along with help from my cousin Wendy Reeder, took Hope to several clinics where she went through a battery of tests, the results of which would be needed prior to the biopsy scheduled for Friday. Everything went very smoothly—except for one slight faux pas.

As they headed out for the various tests, Hope forgot her shoes. Not once or twice but three times!

As a result, she ended up with a complete line of new summer footwear, compliments of her forgetfulness.

Really, who forgets their shoes when going to a doctor visit?

Only our Hope.

Despite all that has happened since the summer of 2003, that memory remains as a cherished reminder of Hope's uniqueness. And we would see plenty more of her personality traits as the next six months unfolded.

As the week wore on, I began to get more and more anxious as Friday approached. Mike Schaefer, a good friend of mine who lives in Knoxville, made arrangements for a rental car so that I could drive back to Charlotte on Thursday night. We had decided that Holly would remain at camp until the closing on Saturday, June 28. As I was preparing to leave, all of the guys in my "C" group helped me load the car, and we had a prayer to send me on my way. I left Oliver Springs at around 6:00 p.m.

The drive between Knoxville, Tennessee, and Asheville, North Carolina, on I-40 is one of the most scenic in the country. Normally when I travel, the radio is set to either a talk station or news. But on this journey, I kept the radio off.

The week at REACH was a spiritual high for me, but as soon as I left the camp, the "what ifs" started. I felt the world closing in around me again, just as I did when I got the news on Monday that something was wrong. So I did what many of us do: I began to pray—very hard.

Actually, that is not true. Praying isn't exactly what I was doing. Instead I was telling God how I wanted this to turn out. His will did not cross my mind—only my wants and needs mattered. Naturally I began to make deals with God: I asked for His forgiveness; I promised to live my life better—the entire standard stuff you say when you are desperate. And then I did one other thing, something Shelby and I have been doing our whole married life whenever we are facing a challenge or crisis.

I asked God for a sign.

Nothing dramatic like the Red Sea parting—just something that would let me know that Hope would be okay.

Literally minutes later, somewhere in the North Carolina mountains, just as the sun was setting on a beautiful summer evening, I rounded a curve as I headed east on Interstate 40. A billboard that was built high up into a mountain caught my eye. When the words on the billboard began to register, they felt like a slap upside the head.

The sign contained four words written in bold red letters: Hope Thou in God.

That was it. No accompanying words to indicate what Bible verse it came from or even the company that was providing the advertising; only those words in big, red block letters on a snow-white background.

Gee, God, is that the best You can do? I asked. I even chuckled at my own feeble attempt at humor. However, the peace that suddenly came over me was unmistakable. I called Shelby and told her about the sign. We did not realize it at the time, but this would be the first of many occasions when God would comfort Shelby and me with a sign from above.

After that remarkable experience, the rest of the trip home was uneventful; I continued to pray and to thank God for everything He had done for us. And I felt so much better.

And why not?

I had my sign.

The sign said: Hope Thou in God.

And that is exactly what we did, starting the next morning at eleven thirty.

Reflections of a Mother

A bone scan occurs in two different procedures: the injection and then the actual test. On the day Hope got the injection, I decided to take her for a manicure in between appointments to calm her nerves. Hope was at that age where getting manicures and proper hair-styling was becoming important, but remembering her shoes was not high on the priority list.

Going somewhere without your shoes might sound odd to some people, but for Hope Stout this was a fairly normal occurrence. One time in particular stands out.

Every summer, my family went on a canoe trip that was followed up with a visit to Shatley Springs, one of those wonderful places you find in the North Carolina mountains, to eat dinner. The town of Shatley Springs is actually a restaurant; that is all there is to the town. They serve family-styled country cookin', and because this is one of our family's favorite places, we eat there several times a year.

We were planning to meet up with my mom and dad and my brothers and their families and ride up together. When we were about fifty miles up the road, we stopped for a bathroom break. Everybody piled out of the car and headed toward the fast-food restaurant. Hope was leading the way—barefooted.

"Hope," I said, "you need to have your shoes on to go in there. Go get them."

The look on her face told me we had a problem.

"Uh, Mom, about those shoes . . . I kinda left them at home."

We ended up having to go to a Family Dollar store to get her a pair of shoes for the trip.

Now as we neared the hospital for the test, Hope announced that she had forgotten her shoes . . . again. I didn't worry about it because a pair of flip flops is usually stashed somewhere in the car. Experience had taught me to leave some in there for this very reason. At this point, she had every color flip flop Old Navy sold.

But not this time, of course.

So Hope went barefooted to the bone scan. A man in the waiting room saw her and apparently noticed her lack of shoes. After the nurses called us back for the test, he went up to Wendy and asked, "Does that little girl need money to buy some shoes?"

Wendy explained that this was just Hope being a typical 'tweenager. Or shall we say, Hope just being herself.

5

"I Am Afraid the News Is Not Good."

One indication that the biopsy on Friday morning, June 27, might not be favorable went right over my head, but not Shelby's. She picked up on it right away. After we left Hope downstairs in pre-op, a volunteer took us to the main waiting room on the fifth floor of Carolinas Medical Center. As we walked into the room, the volunteer stopped and told us, "We have a private waiting room reserved for you down the hall. You have such a big family, we wanted you to be comfortable."

How nice, I thought. And this made sense to me, because we certainly were a large group. There was Shelby, Austin, and me; Dean and Bud Shull, Shelby's mother and father; Kenny, Stan, and Jeff Shull, her brothers; and our pastor, Ken Lyon. Nine of us.

It did not enter my mind that these medical folks knew exactly what they were dealing with and wanted to give us some privacy.

Hope and I had made plans to see *Pirates of the Caribbean* that very afternoon after she got home from the biopsy. We were that sure the news would be good. After all, this was just a little biopsy to check for an infection. We would be on our way in about four hours.

Nothing to worry about.

An hour later, after the biopsy, Dr. Jeffrey Kneisl, a cancer surgeon with an impeccable reputation, walked into the room. In the seconds before he spoke, my mind raced. What kind of news would this man give us? Was the spot on the X-ray an infection, as had earlier been suggested? Or was it worse? For a whole week, as Holly and I had been in Tennessee on the mission trip, Hope had reassured us each night on the phone that she was fine. And why would she not be okay? She was the picture of health, a girl who had sprouted up four inches in one year. She couldn't possibly have anything wrong with her.

Dr. Kneisl leaned back against a desk next to the door, took a deep breath, and spoke the words that forever changed our lives.

"Well, I am afraid the news is not good. As we suspected, the results of the biopsy and tests have concluded that Hope has osteosarcoma, a form of bone cancer. Unfortunately, it is a rather aggressive form that has spread to her other leg, her hip, her back, and some small places in her lungs."

His words hung in the air like a stale, acrid smell. Then silence filled the room. The sounds of the hospital drummed away in the background as all of us sat there in stunned disbelief, taking in this unthinkable news. At first, we were unable to react. But ever so slowly, the news began to register for each one of us and in very different ways.

I began to have trouble breathing. Cancer? Did he just say Hope had cancer? And did he say the cancer was in her *other* leg, in her back, and in her lungs? In her lungs? This simply could not be happening, not to Hope. She had just finished playing a whole season of basketball, performing well enough to make the all-star team. She had decided to become a cheerleader, and despite everyone telling her that she was too tall, she had made the team. Two weeks earlier, Hope had been tubing behind a boat on a lake, bouncing along at break-neck speed and loving every minute of it.

Cancer? In Hope Stout? No way!

After a few seconds, Dr. Kneisl continued. "I realize that this news is devastating, but we do have a plan for treating Hope. For right now, however, it is important for you to take some time to get your heads around this as best you can. You will be meeting with Dr. Daniel McMahon, a pediatric oncologist. He is excellent. But that can take place later today.

"Now I think it is best for you to spend some time together as a family. You can see Hope in about thirty minutes, and it is important that you be there when she wakes up. I am very sorry to have to tell you this. I wish it were better news."

As quickly as he had come in, Dr. Kneisl left. He did not give us a chance to ask any questions. The man delivered the news and left and really, why not just leave? What else could you say to people whose world you just nuked?

In less time than it took to order lunch or make a deposit at a bank, cancer had invaded our lives. Dr. Kneisl's words began to play over and over in my mind. "I am afraid the news is not good . . . *as we suspected.*"

As who suspected? We didn't suspect this. What we suspected was that Hope would be fine, that this was something small, like an infection. That we would be going to see *Pirates of the Caribbean* this afternoon.

We all experience them. Those nightmares that terrify you, the kind that wake you up in the middle of the night, scaring you out of your sleep, leaving you sweaty. Those infernal nightmares where someone has died or you felt yourself falling.

Or that a loved one gets diagnosed with cancer.

At first light the nightmare goes away; the tears that you shed in the nightmare are blinked away with the realization: *It was only a dream.* You breathe a sigh of relief, wipe your brow.

It was just a bad dream.

Except that this time, for our family, it wasn't a dream. This nightmare was very real. As I blinked away the tears in my eyes, the nightmare didn't end.

It was only beginning.

Shelby sat in stunned disbelief, her face blank and almost expressionless, unable to comprehend what this doctor had just said. All week long, Shelby had been buoyed by Hope's insistence that she was fine. Shelby let herself think, even if it *is* cancer, this is Hope.

She is young and strong and can beat whatever comes her way. All of those wished-for results, all of the positive comments uttered all week ("this is probably nothing serious") were now shattered upon the rocks of reality. It was not an infection. It was cancer. And it had spread, ridiculously fast, or so it seemed.

As the realization of the moment finally began to register with her, Shelby began to sob. And she was not alone.

Dean Shull, my mother-in-law, is as strong a Christian woman as there is. She seems to take every crisis in stride. She has had three open-heart surgeries, and her faith in God is beyond question. But this news knocked her to her knees, where she began praying loudly, desperately.

Bud Shull, Shelby's father, sat in stony silence, until finally like his daughter, he began to weep softly. Shelby's brothers, Kenny, Stan, and Jeff, all had tears in their eyes but remained very quiet, not believing what they had just heard.

Austin buried her head into my chest, sobbing loudly. Despite the sibling rivalry and the inevitable issues that existed between the two sisters who were six years apart, this news ripped at her. She had just graduated from high school and was looking forward to college in the fall. This summer was supposed to be a special time of great fun and anticipation. College, with all of its freedom and challenges, beckoned for her.

Suddenly that didn't matter anymore.

Her baby sister had cancer.

Pastor Ken Lyon bore the look of a man who felt completely helpless, despite having experienced moments like this many times before with other members of his congregation. For this tall, bearded, soft-spoken man, hearing someone receive a life-threatening diagnosis was always difficult to make sense of. But this was happening to a child, and to Hope of all people. Ken later told me that as he grappled with the news that day, memories of when he had first come to Matthews United Methodist Church some nine years earlier washed over him.

The church had held a picnic lunch to welcome the new pastor and his family. After the meal, Ken had gathered all the children around him and told them a story about Daniel and the lions' den. The story was designed to help the children remember his name—Lyon—and this was not lost on three-year-old Hope Stout. She immediately forged a bond with the new preacher.

Every Sunday morning, Pastor Ken would have the Children's Moment. He would sit down on the steps at the front of the sanctuary and the kids would gather around him for the message. From day one, Hope had insisted on sitting right beside him. It was her spot. This arrangement worked out fine, until one Sunday morning when another little girl beat Hope to that special place. Hope surveyed the situation and discovered that the other spot beside Ken was also taken—by a boy, no less.

Undeterred by the circumstances, Hope sprang into action. She began to root between Pastor Ken and the other little girl, who happened to be another head-strong type. However, the other girl was not giving an inch, and Ken soon had a ruckus on his hands, much to the amusement of the congregation. He tried to make peace with both of them, but neither was giving up. The struggle continued unabated while the whole church roared in laughter.

Seeing that Hope was not giving up, I rose from my seat and managed to corral a very upset little redhead. After some prodding on my part, she finally sat down with me *in front* of Pastor Ken, all the while glaring at the little girl sitting in her spot.

After that incident, Ken learned his lesson. Before beginning the Children's Moment each Sunday, he would survey the congregation, looking for his little friend with the red hair. If Hope was there, he saved her a seat and, in doing so, avoided any other confrontations.

Pastor Ken Lyon now had to square up this news about Hope with those memories and it was shaking him to the core.

As our family continued to comfort each other, there was a small knock at the door and the mustached face of Tom Johnson appeared. Lucia, Tom's wife, works with Shelby. Our friend is a big, quiet guy who always has a smile on his face, as he did that day. Upon seeing our faces, his smile quickly faded.

Tom stammered out a few words, which further indicated how uncomfortable this was for him. I got up and walked with him into the hall, followed by Pastor Ken.

"Tom," I began slowly, "the doctor just told us Hope has bone cancer, and it has spread to her other leg, back, and lungs. She has it so bad that it seems . . ." And then my tears took over. I could not finish my thought. I didn't want to.

Immediately tears filled Tom's eyes, and he reached over and grabbed me in a warm embrace. He would be the first of many people to do so in the coming months. During this journey, we learned a lot about the language of hugs.

When someone is diagnosed with cancer, words just don't seem to cut it. You want to say something profound, but cannot. All you can do is hug them. And over the next six months, Shelby and I would get plenty of hugs.

The three of us talked a few more minutes, Pastor Ken said a prayer, and then Tom left, badly shaken.

Ken and I watched him walk away, and as we were about to go back into the waiting room, our eyes met. For a few seconds, nothing was said. We just looked at each other, not as a pastor to his parishioner but as two men who felt enormous pain, accompanied by an overwhelming feeling of helplessness.

Then very slowly, Pastor Ken Lyon, a man of God who can move congregations with his powerful messages of faith, said four words I will never forget.

"Sometimes . . . life just stinks."

Reflections of a Mother

I knew we needed a medical plan to deal with Hope's cancer. But I also knew that what we needed more than anything else was prayer. I got on the phone and made five calls—to my friends Danette Rutherford, Nina Wheeling, Margot Smith, and Wendy. And, of course, to Matthews United Methodist Church, and that got the ball rolling.

My vision was to make a prayer chain that reached all the way to heaven. I envisioned people stretching upward until we were so numerous that we could touch the garment of Christ, like the woman in Luke 8:44 who had been bleeding for twelve years and was healed the instant she touched His robe.

Thank goodness for computers and the Internet. The effort to get the prayer chain activated certainly worked. Before long we were getting e-mails from all over, including one from my cousins who were African missionaries. People all over the United States and the world were praying for us. Seeing this outpouring of support in such a short period of time convinced me that Hope would be healed.

Looking back now, I don't regret asking for prayers or getting the support those prayers evoked. We needed this kind of hope to continue on.

And our prayers were answered in a way we could never have anticipated.

6

The Journey Begins

When Shelby and I got to the recovery room, Hope was still asleep and would remain so for a while, according to the attending nurse who brought over two chairs so that we could sit near Hope in the recovery area. As Shelby and I watched our daughter sleeping, we both started to cry again. About that time, a familiar face appeared.

Phyllis Nussman, a nurse at CMC and a friend of ours from church where she and her husband, Howard, are youth counselors with me, came over and gave us both a hug.

"I saw the name Hope Stout on the list today, and I immediately took over her case. It says here she had knee surgery. What did she do, tear up her knee playing ball?" Phyllis asked cheerfully.

My words from the night before I left for REACH Camp came shooting back, haunting me yet again.

"Phyllis, Hope was just diagnosed with bone cancer," Shelby

said quietly while watching Hope very carefully. "We just found out about an hour ago and we are still reeling."

With tears in her eyes Phyllis hugged us both again. She asked which doctors were involved and who Hope's oncologist was going to be. Amazingly, we remembered Dr. McMahon's name and she very quickly responded.

"He is outstanding. You could not be in better hands," she said excitedly. "Hope will love him." Phyllis continued to talk as she checked Hope's chart and her vital signs.

Then she looked over at us, her nursing instincts taking over. "Hope will be waking up in a few minutes, and after she is fully awake we will transport her to a room upstairs. But she is doing fine now. Don't worry . . . I will take care of her." Then she left to see her other patients.

Shelby asked me to go check on her mom and dad, who were not going to leave until Hope was moved to her room. I didn't really want to leave, because I wanted to be there when Hope woke up. On the other hand, I didn't really want to stay either. Breaking this kind of news to Hope would be very hard.

I left the recovery area and found Shelby's parents. They were still shaken but had gotten some coffee and were in the waiting room. I sat with them for a few minutes and then took about four phone calls from friends and business associates. The word was spreading fast about Hope's illness. Very quickly, I headed to the recovery area and to Hope's bed.

Shelby quickly brought me up to date. "Hope woke up for just a few minutes while you were gone and asked why she was still here. I wanted to wait until you got here, but I went ahead and told her anyway."

"What did she say?"

"She just rolled her eyes and went back to sleep. She didn't cry or anything. It was almost like she knew."

For the next hour or so, Hope began to come out of the fog of anesthesia. When she woke up the second time, I hugged her, gave her nose a tweak, and told her not to worry about this. She managed a weak smile and then fell back to sleep again. Finally, about two hours after her surgery, she was awake enough to be transported upstairs.

On the way up, I stopped by the water fountain and grabbed a quick drink. Shelby went on with Hope and the orderlies to the room. As I was walking down the corridor, I saw my cousin, Wendy Reeder, striding purposely toward the Pediatric Oncology hall.

"Wendy!" I yelled at her just as she was turning the corner.

She quickly turned around and walked briskly toward me. We fell into each others' arms and I began crying much as I had nearly four hours earlier when we had gotten the horrible news. Wendy is four years older than I am and as close as a sister. She had been with Shelby and Hope during all the tests the previous week. As I began to regain my composure, she took me by the arm and dragged me into an unused waiting room, one very similar to the one we had been in that morning.

She grabbed my face and began speaking. "Cuz, I want you to listen to me, okay? Do you hear me? Today is bad, but it *will* get better. This is the worst day. Okay? We have taken this blow and now we start fighting.

"But remember this. Today is the worst day . . . There will be hard days but nothing like this one. So there. Now I have said it and now we start fighting! Cancer will not beat this kid. She is too tough."

Her words were very soothing and helped me immensely. One of the remarkable things about our family was that up to this point we had never experienced a real crisis. Naturally we had gone through deaths in the family, but it was always someone who was advanced in age. None of us had faced anything like this. Over the next six months, we got to see how tough and supportive our family is. Starting that day, we were never alone. They never left our side.

Wendy and I only stayed a minute more in the waiting room

and then we left to find Hope's room. We soon found the cancer wing of the Children's Hospital at Carolinas Medical Center. It would be a place we would get to know all too well over the next six months, but on that Friday evening, all we cared about was finding Hope.

She had been moved into a private room and after a brief visit from Shelby's parents, we were alone with her, along with Austin. Hope was in and out of sleep and over the next hour several close friends stopped by. They wanted to do something, anything for us. They tried to feed us, but, of course, food was the last thing on our minds.

Late in the afternoon we met Courtney Plaisted, the nurse who was on call when Hope came upstairs from recovery. Although Hope would have many nurses over the next six months, Courtney would quickly become her favorite. After checking Hope's vital signs, she asked Shelby and me to come out into the hall. Austin and Wendy remained in the room with Hope.

Courtney began: "I know this is very tough for both of you right now. You probably have a million questions, but let me say a few things that may help. First off, Dr. McMahon is simply the best. He is very gifted, and he will do everything to heal Hope, that I can promise you. Secondly, there is one thing you need to do . . . It is good that she is sleeping now, because I don't want her to hear this. You need to always tell Hope the truth, no matter what. If you aren't truthful with Hope, and she finds out the truth from someone else, she will not trust you and that would be bad.

"Naturally, she will be very scared when she wakes up and finds out what is going on. Be truthful with her. Don't hold anything back . . . You will want to, but don't do it. Parents want to protect their child, but keeping the truth from her will do more harm than good."

Shelby and I looked at each other. Had Courtney not explained this to us, it is likely we would have done that very thing. In our minds, telling Hope just how serious this was didn't make sense. But Courtney was telling us to do just that.

"She has to trust her parents. If she loses that, she really will be scared. By leveling with her, you are treating her like an adult, even though she is only twelve.

"Yes, it will be hard for her to accept, but you will be right there with her to help her understand, and that is critical," Courtney said and then paused to allow us to absorb the significance of her words. "We will help you, but our most difficult cases are the ones where the parents hide the truth from their children. And, despite their young ages, somehow most of them know anyway. I have only spoken to Hope briefly, but she seems very intelligent."

Courtney ended on a positive note. "She has the most beautiful blue eyes I have ever seen—and that red hair is gorgeous!"

After our conversation with Courtney ended, we went back into the room with Hope. We had not been there long when there was a knock at the door. Dr. Daniel McMahon came in and introduced himself to Shelby and me. Kim Barker, a social worker assigned to Hope's case, was with him.

I will never forget my first impression of Dr. McMahon. He has brown hair and wears glasses that do little to hide the compassion in his eyes. He has a very calm demeanor and bears a slight resemblance to Clint Eastwood. We would also learn that he has a very dry sense of humor.

Dr. McMahon asked if we could speak privately down the hall. Courtney came in and assured us Hope was fine and to go ahead. We walked back down the hall with the doctor and the social worker into a waiting room—ironically, the one Wendy and I were in a few hours earlier.

Dr. McMahon began: "First off, I want to say how sorry I am. Hope's diagnosis is a bad one, but we do have a plan for treating her. Hope's disease is called osteosarcoma. Bone cancer is its most common name. It is very rare, to be honest with you, but does occasionally strike children, most often when they are going through puberty. I understand Hope has grown four inches in the past year. Naturally her bones are changing rapidly. Did she have significant pain in her legs recently?"

Shelby then told Dr. McMahon about Hope's knee pain and the doctor visit in May. Upon hearing about Hope's physical activity during the past months, he was surprised.

"I am amazed she didn't have significant pain, based on the level of disease she has. Does she complain much?"

"She has had stitches twice: once at age four and then last year, and she didn't cry either time. She has a pretty high pain threshold," Shelby replied.

"Bone cancer usually manifests itself with pain. A person has a nagging ache that doesn't go away. In Hope's case, it should have been pretty severe. Unfortunately her high pain threshold actually worked against her."

Dr. McMahon pulled out his chart and continued. "Unfortunately as Dr. Kneisl said, Hope's case is rather advanced. She has tumors in her legs, her hip and back, and in a few small places in her lungs."

Hearing that again took the wind out of me. Lung cancer almost always was a death sentence, wasn't it?

"Dr. McMahon, I don't understand this," I said. "How could this disease be so advanced? We went to her pediatrician less than a month ago. He did an exam and felt nothing. What happened?"

Dr. McMahon fingered his glasses, cleared his throat, and began. "Normally, bone cancer doesn't spread fast. That is why a person with persistent pain usually gets it checked. It is hard to tell, but I would guess that your pediatrician didn't feel anything because a month ago, there was probably nothing to feel. Remember, bone cancer is very rare. A sprained or bruised knee or an injury to the ACL or MCL is much more likely than this. In fact, my guess is the disease would not have been traceable a month ago."

We sat there for a minute, absorbing this news as best

After a few more moments, Dr. McMahon spoke again. Typically, with this type of cancer, we use traditional chemotherapeutic
agents. However, in Hope's case . . ." His voice trailed off.

Immediately Shelby asked, "What about Hope's case?"

The oncologist again cleared his throat. "Well, with the level of
Hope's disease, some parents would opt to do nothing. They would
not subject their child to chemotherapy, given the level of the disease. They would let nature take its course. I am not saying to do
that, but that is one option."

Those words tore through Shelby and me like a lightning bolt.
We both reacted immediately. Shelby, her eyes hot with tears and
her voice rising, said, "Well, we are not giving up. You just tell us
what you are recommending, and we will do it. We are not just letting nature take its course. Hope will beat this thing . . . I know it."

"Okay. I agree. The bad news here is that Hope has a significant
amount of disease. The good news is the chemotherapy agents that
we use on this type of tumor typically work very well. Again, I am
very sorry to have to bring you this news, but for what it is worth,
I agree with you. I think we should give the chemotherapy a
chance. I have seen some incredible results with these type of
tumors," Dr. McMahon said.

Then Kim Barker, the social worker, spoke up. "My job here is to
help you with the psychological part of this. Cancer has struck your
family, not just Hope. You all have it. I want to be a part of helping
you cope with the mental part as best I can. That will include talking
to both of you, Hope's sisters, and Hope herself. Having a good
mental outlook on this is very important to the healing process."

Dr. McMahon then handed me a folder of papers. "This is the
treatment plan and the types of chemo we will be using. Look this
over and we can discuss them tomorrow. If it is okay, I will come
by around ten o'clock. I want to meet Hope and tell her about her
disease and what the treatment will be."

We said that would be fine and then Dr. McMahon and Kim left. For a minute Shelby and I sat in the room without speaking. Then my wife looked at me, tears streaming down her face.

"He thinks this is terminal. He didn't say that word but you can tell. I cannot believe this is happening to our baby."

I didn't know how to respond. I could think of no words that would matter, so I just held my wife and cried right along with her.

The rest of the evening is a bit of a blur to both Shelby and me. Elizabeth and Tom Reeder, Wendy's daughter and husband, stopped by, but Hope continued to be very groggy so they left with Wendy after a few minutes. Tom had been on the way to West Virginia for a meeting that morning when Wendy called him with the news of Hope's diagnosis. He had immediately turned around and come back to Charlotte. As we stood in the hall telling them good-bye, I encouraged them to go on to the beach for their vacation, which was starting tomorrow, but they wouldn't hear of it. Their life was deeply affected by this as well. The beach week suddenly didn't matter anymore.

Finally, at around nine o'clock, it became very quiet. Austin stayed with us a while and got to see Hope again for one of the few times she was awake long enough. Soon it was just Hope, Shelby, and me in the room. The television was not on; the pediatric oncology hall was eerily still. Courtney had said that, surprisingly, there were not many kids in the hospital on this night. Hope woke up briefly several times but soon fell back to sleep; we could not have a conversation of any kind with her.

Not that we really wanted to have *that* conversation with Hope anyway.

Finally, at around eleven o'clock, Courtney came in and said there was a bed in the room next door. She told one of us to sleep there. Shelby was in the recliner next to Hope's bed and insisted on staying there. I reluctantly went into the empty room and crawled into bed. Despite being mentally and physically exhausted, I could not get to sleep for quite a while. The frightening path of the journey ahead seemed ominous and dark, just like the stormy weather outside. The thunder rolled and the lightning flashed; the whipping rain against the window seemed to fit the mood perfectly. After a long time staring out the window at the storm, I drifted into a fitful sleep.

Early the next morning, I awoke with a start. At first, I couldn't recall where I was, and then the previous day's events came flooding back to me. No, yesterday was not a dream; we were in the hospital, Hope was next door in a bed . . . and she had cancer. The sickening feeling returned. It was like a large, cold stone just sitting in my stomach. No matter how big a breath I took, I felt as if I was suffocating.

The door opened slightly and Shelby walked in. She slipped into bed beside me and buried her head into my chest.

"Did yesterday really happen? Are we really here at the hospital? Does Hopie really have cancer? Please tell me this is some kind of dream we will wake up from," she said, beginning to cry softly.

"Honey, I wish it was a bad dream. But we are here," I said as my own tears started to fall. "Do you remember what I said last week about Hope maybe needing surgery and that it would screw up our vacation plans? What I wouldn't give to have that now instead of this."

We stayed in bed holding each other for a few more minutes and then went into Hope's room. At about eight o'clock, she woke up. The anesthesia had worn off and soon she was wide awake so Shelby, Courtney, and I began to explain the diagnosis to Hope who was very quiet throughout our explanation, which was not surprising. Courtney was very helpful and asked Hope if she had any questions. She did not cry but did not ask Courtney anything.

At around ten o'clock, Dr. McMahon came in. "Hope, I am Dr. McMahon. I am going to get you better. Do you have any questions for me?"

Hope sat on the bed, her head down. She said nothing. Shelby and I soon began talking to Dr. McMahon about the treatment. Suddenly, Hope spoke up.

"Will I lose my hair?" she asked in a very strong, demanding voice, her blue eyes piercing into his.

"Hope, yes, usually, most chemo patients do lose their hair . . . A few don't, but most do. But don't worry, it will grow back. It is just a side effect of the chemo."

At that moment, we heard Hope's primary worry. Having good hair and wearing makeup were beginning to be very important to her and her friends. The thought of losing her hair was simply out of the question.

"Is there anything I can do to keep my hair from falling out?" she asked.

"Well, there are some shampoos that help, but ultimately it will likely fall out. I'm so sorry," Dr. McMahon said. About that time, Austin came into the room. She and Hope began to talk, so Dr. McMahon asked to speak to Shelby and me next door. We left and went into the room where I had slept the night before. He pulled up a chair and laid out several forms on the bed. We took a seat and for the next forty-five minutes new words and terms entered our vocabulary.

Cisplatin, methotrexate, Herceptin, VP-16. They all sounded so foreign, but we would get to know all about each of them.

Dr. McMahon took us through Hope's course of treatment: We would start with cisplatin, follow that up with four treatments of methotrexate, and then another round of cisplatin. That would take about eight weeks. At that time we would do another round of tests to see how the chemotherapy was going.

"What about a bone marrow transplant?" I ventured. "Is that a possibility?" This seemed like a logical solution to Hope's disease.

"Unfortunately, no." Dr. McMahon went on to say that Hope's disease would not be affected by a bone marrow transplant. The same was true for radiation treatments, at least right now. If Hope's tumor was in one place, radiation would be an option. But her disease had spread, so a more global approach was warranted.

"As I said yesterday, the good news is that these chemo agents usually work very well against fast-growing cancer cells. While the cisplatin phase of the treatment kills all active cells—white blood cells, hair cells, etc.—the methotrexate phase will act more like a rifle shot, targeting only active cancer cells.

"We also want to test Hope's biopsy for a new drug that is very encouraging called Herceptin. If Hope's cells contain the markers needed for Herceptin to work, we can start her on that along with the chemo.

"Herceptin has had remarkable results in breast cancer patients. It targets the protein that forms in cancer cells and interferes with this process. The theory is that the cancer cell cannot form without protein and will die. The drug also has very few side affects."

Dr. McMahon then said something that twenty-four hours earlier had seemed unthinkable.

"Hope is ready to leave as soon as her discharge papers come down. What are you doing next week? Do you have any plans for the Fourth of July?"

Shelby and I just stared at each other. When I had broken the news yesterday to my sister, Beth, I had asked her to cancel the cottage rental. Did he just say it was okay to go?

"Yeah, we usually go to the beach the week of July Fourth," Shelby said. "In fact, we had a cottage rented."

"By all means go. It will take us about a week to get things squared away here. We need to schedule the surgery for Hope's port, and generally we do that and then start chemo the next day.

"Just leave me a phone number to reach you. But absolutely, take a week and have some fun. We can start the treatment a week from now."

It is funny how over the next six months, little things like this

would suddenly become so precious. The last thing we were thinking was that we would be able to go to the beach. Yet, here was Dr.
Daniel McMahon, the man Shelby and I were entrusting to save
our daughter, telling us we could go to the beach. Have fun and forget cancer, he seemed to be saying.

What a gift!

We went into Hope's room and told her the good news.

The smile on her face was priceless. "Then let's get out of
here!" she said.

Thirty minutes later we were wheeling Hope out to the car. She
had to ride in a wheelchair although she had insisted on walking.
"Hospital rules," the nurse said, and when she turned her back
Hope made a face at her, bringing a smile to Shelby and me. Phone
calls were made, first to my sister to un-cancel the reservation and
then to the Reeders to tell them we were coming after all. Everyone was thrilled.

As we were waiting to load Hope into the car, a summer thunderstorm was about to hit. The attendant at the front of the hospital asked Hope what was wrong with her knee.

"You got a basketball injury? You look like you are a player."

Before Hope could answer, Shelby said, "No, we have bone
cancer."

The attendant said he was sorry and helped us get our belong-
ings loaded in the car. Once inside, we took off and I asked Hope
what she wanted to eat.

"How about Krispy Kreme doughnuts or Wendy's #7? Anything you want. I'm buying."

No response from the backseat.

Shelby turned around to find a fuming Hope Stout, her arms
crossed, glaring at her mother.

"Mom, why did you tell that man I have cancer? I don't want
anybody to know. They will treat me different, and I don't want
that," she hissed.

"Because Hope, you do have cancer. Listen to me. We are not going to start lying to people. You are going to have to face up to it, because it is the truth. People will treat you differently only if you let them. You have cancer, but you are still Hope Stout." With that, Shelby turned back around.

There was no sound, other than the slapping of the wipers clearing the windshield of the pouring rain. Again, the weather fit the mood perfectly.

As a father of three girls, I have been witness to many a battle. With a house full of females, there are constant squabbles: sister versus sister, mom versus daughter, and even sometimes mom versus dad over what the sisters have done. I admit it. My daughters typically get away with murder from me. But not Shelby. My lovely wife is a sweetheart, but she is the tough one in the family. Usually with an exchange like that, the fight was on. I waited for Hope's retort and the rumble to start. But none came. Then something very telling happened.

From my vantage point, looking through the rearview mirror, I could see Hope continuing to glare at her mom, but she did not offer any argument. I could see my daughter processing this information. As hard as it was for Hope to hear her mom say that, it was even more difficult on Shelby.

But Courtney was right. We had to be honest with her about her condition. From that moment on, even though Hope would continue to tell people that she was fine—that it was just a knee injury—she realized that she was different. She did have cancer. Right in front of my eyes on that stormy Saturday morning, my little girl grew up.

7

The God Pump

Upon arriving home, we discovered that our house had been invaded: Wendy and Liz Reeder, Hope's best friend Emily Rutherford, and her mom, Danette, were there to greet us along with Austin. Shelby and I were concerned about how Emily would react to seeing Hope, knowing that her best friend had cancer. We helped Hope into the den (she was using crutches because of the incision in her leg) and to the sofa, which had been turned into Hope's personal comfort zone. Drinks and snacks were sitting on the coffee table, and the TV remote was within reach on the table beside the sofa. Several pillows and a blanket finished the décor.

Emily sat down with Hope on the sofa, and everyone else took a seat around the room. For the next hour or so, it was very lighthearted, and Hope was back to normal; the anesthesia was finally out of her system.

The next big task for Shelby and me was going to pick up Holly, who was returning from the REACH trip at the church later that afternoon. We had made Holly aware that Hope did have cancer as we had feared, but she had not been told how bad it was. That was going to be the hard part.

Shelby stayed on the phone almost all afternoon as our friends began to get the word about Hope's diagnosis. I stayed in the den with Hope and Emily watching TV. The word *cancer* was never mentioned. Instead, we soon returned to our normal battle over what we were going to watch. Hope had commandeered the remote and began to torture me. I love to watch golf and when the telecast came on, she switched to the golf tournament, just enough to whet my appetite—and then flipped it back to her show. She always did this to aggravate me, but today it didn't bother me a bit. Hope soon had Emily cackling at her jokes, and everything seemed just as it always had, except for that bandage on Hope's leg.

At around four o'clock we got a call from the church telling us that the youth group was about a half hour away. Shelby and I headed to Matthews United Methodist Church, about seven miles from our home.

As I watched the church vans come into the parking lot, I could not help but think about how much our life had changed in just six short days.

The excitement and promise that had begun with the trip the previous Sunday had now been replaced with uncertainty and a fear I had never experienced.

Just nine months earlier, after twenty-two years of working in the corporate world, I had taken my first real risk in life by starting my own business. That endeavor created some fear certainly, but nothing approaching this. The kind of fear I was experiencing now was ten times deeper. And both Shelby and I dreaded having to tell Holly about Hope's condition.

The first van came to a stop and several members of my "C" group came piling out. Because our youth group is so large (an aver-

age of three hundred or so attend each Sunday evening), "C" groups
had been formed at the first of the year. The idea is to develop a
"caring" group of eight to ten youth so a leader can get to know the
kids on a more personal level. My "C" group for that year, which
was nicknamed "The Fish," was a special group of guys. They were
all Holly's age, and we got very close over the course of the year.
The events surrounding Hope's situation brought us even closer.

Upon seeing Shelby and me, the guys immediately made a bee-
line for us. While it was heartwarming to have these guys comfort
us, our main concern was finding Holly. We did not want her to
hear the news from anyone but us.

Several of my fellow counselors at REACH also came to hug us,
most of them with tears in their eyes. It was easy to see why. The
worst possible scenario for a parent is having a child get diagnosed
with cancer. You could see the emotion registered on each one of
their faces. I could also see what they were thinking but couldn't
verbalize it in front of Shelby and me: *Thank God this didn't happen
to my child.*

After about ten minutes, we finally located Holly. She came
running toward us along with several of her close friends. As she
hugged first her mother and then me, Holly started to cry.

It would only get worse.

Seeing that there was obviously no way for any privacy, it was
clear to Shelby and me that we would have to wait for a while to
tell Holly about how bad the diagnosis was.

She was too upset anyway. So we gathered up her bags and just
hung around the parking lot. It seemed like almost everyone
wanted to come by and tell us how sorry they were. The outpouring of emotion from these special people was very powerful. Some
were very upbeat and others were very sad, saying how unfair it
was. But everyone was clearly shaken by the news.

After about thirty minutes, only a handful of people were left,
including Holly's friends, who did not seem to want to leave her.

It is strange how you remember things. I am not sure how or why we ended up on the far end of the parking lot under the breezeway adjacent to the education building, but that is where we were.

Shelby and I sat down with Holly on the curb of the breezeway. Several of her friends sat down on either side of Holly with their arms around her. As I watched this, it struck me that these girls were not going to let Holly face this news alone; they *had* to be there with her.

Shelby took both of Holly's hands into hers, looking straight into her eyes. "Holly," Shelby began, "you know that Hope does have cancer, but we did not tell you how bad it is. We did not want to tell you this and upset you while you were at REACH, but you need to know." Then she went on to tell her about the spread of the cancer.

"The doctors think the treatments will be really effective, but it is still a bad situation. Hope knows this too, but we wanted you to hear it from us. It has been tough for us to understand, but this is what we are facing." As she finished, Shelby squeezed Holly's hands. The *buts* in her explanation were as obvious to Holly as they were to us. Shelby had tried to be as positive as possible—and still be truthful. She did a good job, but this kind of news just isn't easy to convey to someone.

My middle daughter's face crumbled into tears as the news began to register. It was the same reaction Austin had the day before. Holly began sobbing and her friends, also in tears, moved in to comfort her. During the next few minutes, an event occurred that would repeat itself time and again over the next six months of this journey with Hope.

At this difficult moment, God showed up.

I have always had a hard time watching my children cry, especially when they have been hurt emotionally. Getting a knee scraped from a bike wreck or softball slide was different. I would help dust them off, clean up the scrapes, and tell them they were okay and to be tough. That's what dads are for. But when they were hurt emotionally, like when a pet died, it always ripped me up.

As I stood there watching Holly fall apart with the realization of how bad Hope's cancer was, so did I.

It was certainly not what I had planned: fathers are supposed to be strong in times like these, to be emotional rocks. Instead, I was sobbing like a baby, wanting to control my tears, but completely incapable of doing so.

I felt like a wimp.

As I began wiping away my tears, I looked into my wife's face, expecting to see her crying also. What I saw stunned me.

Shelby had the look of someone who was in total control. She exhibited love and courage as she began comforting our daughter. Here I was, falling completely apart, and a few feet away my wife was the Rock of Gibraltar. Shelby's calm demeanor had a soothing effect on me. I immediately began to regain control as I listened to her tell Holly that God was in charge and that we were going to pray and fight this with all our strength. As she continued to re-assure Holly, I soon felt God strengthen me. I didn't ask for it specif-ically; it just happened. It occurred to me that God *was* in control and to trust Him.

Soon, I was the one who found strength. I was the one hugging and comforting Holly and her friends.

And then Shelby began to lose control of her emotions.

And that was how it would go over the next six months. When one of us was at the end of our emotional rope, the other was the tower of strength. God would always show up and strengthen either Shelby or me.

We sat under the breezeway a few more minutes and then loaded up Holly's bags and headed home. Upon entering our den, Holly jokingly commented on the amenities that had been pro-vided. "I've never seen so many snacks," she commented. Then she hugged Hope and told her she loved her, whereupon Hope assured her she was fine and not to worry. Hope then asked about REACH week.

Seeing that Hope was acting normal, Holly began to excitedly tell her about all the fun she had and the people she had met. Holly even told Hope and Emily about how she fell off the stage during a skit on Talent Night. Although it was a completely unintentional act, the rest of the camp thought the clumsiness was a planned pratfall.

Hope loved hearing the story, and soon all three girls were yakking away, stopping only to comment about something on TV, which was playing in the background. They were just normal kids enjoying each others' company. The next day was the start of the best week of the year. The beach trip: sun, fun, and great food with all their cousins.

Cancer truly seemed far, far away.

Reflections of a Mother

Hope had a way of saying some of the funniest things and being so serious when saying them. I think you call that sarcasm. Her lying in the bed with cancer, however, was not funny. Here I was, watching a perfectly normal child whose health had been wonderful, except for the occasional cold and stitches, lie in the bed with a morphine pump, which had been given to her to ease the pain from the surgery. Dr. Kneisl had taken a large chunk of the tumor to facilitate getting the tissue to as many cancer research facilities as possible.

Hope could give herself a "pump" whenever the pain got to be too much for her. The medication goes directly into the system each time for immediate effect. Hope could hit the button and get quick relief from the pain.

I was grateful for that, but what could parents like Stuart and me do to ease the unbearable pain of watching our daughter lying there hurting? The only thing we would do was pray, and as we prayed we would feel an overwhelming peace overcome our feelings of despair.

This God-sent relief happened simultaneously to us. Stuart and I would both be in tears, feeling as if we were drowning in the storm. Then *wham!* Calm and relief would overwhelm us. This happened so many times that the relief became known as our "God Pump." When things began to close in on us, Stuart or I would reach up with our thumb and press down in mid-air.

The God Pump gave us the needed relief.

God knew when to calm us from the storm, to let us know that He was in control and not to worry.

> "Peace I leave with you; my peace I give you.
> I do not give to you as the world gives. Do not let your
> hearts be troubled and do not be afraid." —John 14:27

There is a song by Scott Tribane about calming personal storms. It says God sometimes calms the storms and other times He calms His child.

This is what we were feeling at those exact moments, and to this day He still calms His child.

8

Coming Out of the Closet

O n the morning of Sunday, June 29, I got up early and went to my office. Having been out the week before, and with our family leaving to go to the beach later that day, I wanted to get some work done. I had planned to do this before Hope's illness, but now I had a much different purpose. Before leaving REACH camp, one of the traditions is to exchange e-mail addresses so members of the work crews can communicate with each other. I felt that it was important to let my crew know what had happened. More pressing to me, however, was to enlist this special group of people to pray for Hope and our family as we began her treatments.

As I was driving to my office, I listened to a song on the local Christian music station. It is hard for me to remember which one, but I do remember the lyrics talked about rejoicing in the face of adversity, the very theme for REACH camp that year: "Consider it pure joy, my brothers, whenever you face trials of many kinds,

because you know that the testing of your faith develops perseverance. Perseverance must finish its work so that you may be mature
and complete, not lacking anything."[1] At the beginning of REACH
camp on June 22, I did not know how important this verse would
become to me.

It was very hard to make that drive to work and to write that e-
mail. As I was typing the letter, all I could think about was my precious daughter having cancer—and what she would now have to go
through. Fear began to engulf me as I thought back on a visit I had
made to a church member of ours early that February.

Bubba Smitha was a tall, strong, outgoing guy who was the picture of health. He had developed flu-like symptoms that were eventually diagnosed as multiple myloma. During his last hospital stay,
I visited Bubba at Presbyterian Hospital.

As I walked into his room, I saw Bubba, still a big, impressive
guy, lying in the bed. When he saw me, his face broke into the same
smile that had lit up Matthews United Methodist Church for years.
But the smile could not hide his physical appearance. He looked
twenty years older than his age, which was about forty-eight, but
what struck me was how pale he was.

His coarse red hair had not completely surrendered to the
chemotherapy but it was much thinner.

I walked over and embraced him as I had done many times at
church. He was very frail, and that not only shocked me but scared
me to death. How could a guy this strong get beat down so bad physically? I wondered. If chemo had done this to Bubba, what kind of
impact would the treatments have on our twelve-year-old daughter?

As we talked, Bubba soon began coughing and hacking. He had
lots of congestion, and after he had gotten most of it up and
regained control, he apologized. I, of course, told him no problem,
but truthfully his being so sick really bothered me.

Now the thought of Hope's chemotherapy nearly overwhelmed me. I was alone for the first time since the diagnosis,

and all the emotion just boiled up and came out. Strangely what got to me the most was the thought of Hope losing her beautiful red hair. At age twelve, the hair being "just right" was so important to her.

After finishing the e-mail to my REACH crew, I sent out a few more e-mails to some of my clients and headed back home. It was only mid-morning and I came home to a family that was still asleep. Quietly I went upstairs toward my bedroom and stuck my head into Hope's room to check on her.

My precious daughter was sleeping soundly. She looked so peaceful and for a few minutes I just sat beside her bed and watched her sleep. Again, I felt myself starting to cry, and, not wanting to wake her, I left the room.

One by one my family began to wake up. Shelby came downstairs first and we had a good cry together after which we both began to pick each other up. We did have Beach Week ahead of us; and nothing, not even cancer, could take that away from us.

I fixed Shelby a cup of coffee, and we sat down together at the kitchen table, looking out over our back yard. I looked out at the girls' swing set that they had grown up on and was getting misty-eyed again when I heard my wife say in a very strong voice, "You know, we are going to beat this thing and this week is the start of it. We are just going to go down there and get our heads right for this fight. We are gonna have fun, but we are going to get ready . . .

"This is going to be like Boot Camp."

And so that is what it became.

The rest of the afternoon was spent getting ready to head to the beach. As I was coming in from putting some luggage into the car, I heard the phone ringing in the house. It was Margot Smith, one of the friends Shelby had enlisted to pray for Hope on that prayer chain to heaven. She and I talked for a few minutes and then she asked to speak to Shelby. I went upstairs with the cordless phone and looked all over for my wife. Strangely, she was nowhere to be found. I told Margot to hang on and set the phone down on the bed.

After a few minutes of searching, I found Shelby lying in our closet, curled up into a ball, sobbing quietly. I had never seen her like this before, and it shocked me so badly, I did not know what to do next. Very carefully, I knelt down and told her Margot was on the phone, and it became obvious that she was in no shape to talk to her friend.

I hugged her and left her in the closet. Picking up the phone again, I told Margot that Shelby was pretty upset, and I felt sure she would be able to call her back after a while. Margot and I continued to talk and pretty soon, I heard Shelby call out from the closet that she was okay and to tell Margot to hold on. After washing her face, she got on the phone and talked to her friend for over an hour.

The closet episode was another example of God giving us strength when we least expected it. Shelby was so distraught yet as she told me later, all of a sudden God gave her an emotional lift, so much so that she and Margot ended up having a great conversation. We finally got packed up and around 5:00 p.m. headed down to our favorite place in the world, Holden Beach.

Boot Camp was about to begin.

Reflections of a Mother

That closet was a nurturing place for me. The three girls and I had watched our cat give birth to three precious kittens in this closet. In fact, we lived in the closet with them for a month—feeding them, playing with them, and holding them. The mother cat was named Baby (a compromise name because the girls could not agree on one), and she did not seem to mind: the cat let the girls play with her kittens and even allowed Daisy, our dachshund, to see her babies. Consequently, the kittens became very accustomed to having people around them.

Baby was from a litter born in my brother Stan's apartment in Iron Station, North Carolina, which was also where my mom and dad lived. Cracker, the mommy cat, had given birth to what we jokingly called "crack babies."

All we had to say to our girls was, "Some kittens have been born down at Maw Maws," and a trip to Iron Station was soon planned. Of course, once Austin, Holly, and Hope saw the kittens, they immediately started begging us to bring one home.

At the time I knew Stuart didn't want a third cat at our house; we already had Buffy and another cat, Abby, who was Hope's favorite cat before the kittens were born.

So I said, "Fine. If your dad says okay, we will take one home."

When they called their father, he surprisingly said yes. I couldn't believe he had given into those girls again, but that's what daddies do best, I guess.

Baby had given birth to three precious Hope cats—Tuffy, Pudge, and Peanut—in this very closet.

The girls promised to find homes for all three babies, since we now had five cats in the house. But after a while they started to back out of that promise. However, we did find a home for Tuffy, before Hope used the "cancer card" and got to keep Pudge and Peanut.

These kittens became a source of comfort for Hope. She forgot the cancer for a while when she played and cuddled them.

Before the kittens came along, we had the opportunity to meet a sweet, lonely man whom I delivered meals to: Mr. Sam. Stuart and I tried to teach our girls at a young age to help others in need whenever possible, and they always wanted to go with me to deliver meals to "Mr. Sam." We always spent time with him so the girls watched as he shared his meal with his cat that got to lick the plate clean. Like a lot of elderly folks, his cat didn't really have a name.

"I just call for the cat and he comes running," Mr. Sam explained to me one day. "It works out fine. I never have named him."

Just before Mr. Sam died, he asked the girls to take care of his cat when he was gone. Actually he asked Stuart if it would be alright for the girls to have his cat. Despite the fact that we already had two cats at the time and didn't need another one, Stuart could not say no to Mr. Sam. So we weren't really surprised when Mr. Sam's cat was officially willed to the Stouts.

And so we became the proud owners of his cat, which the girls quickly, and not surprisingly, named "Mr. Sam."

9

Boot Camp

When we arrived at our cottage late Sunday night, we were happily surprised to find the beds made and the refrigerator stocked by my sister, Beth, and my mother, Betty Stout. Hope was helped up the stairs, although by this time she was beginning to become more and more independent of the crutches by hopping on her good left leg. Even though it was around ten o'clock, her friend Gina Wheeling, who was staying just two doors down at her grandparents' house, came over. The two girls, along with Austin and Holly, started to watch TV and eat junk food. We got unpacked, and Shelby and I went to bed.

It had only been two days since the diagnosis, and neither one of us was sleeping very well. Shelby, in particular, had cried herself to sleep every night. This one was no exception. As the girls laughed and talked in the next room, Shelby and I lay in the bed and cried. Finally, sleep came.

At around three o'clock in the morning, Shelby shook me and asked if I was awake. After assuring her that I was *now*, she switched the light on.

"What's going on? Are you okay? Is something wrong with Hope?" I asked.

"No, I am fine. The girls are okay," Shelby said. "I just want to tell you about my dream."

"What dream? What are you talking about?" This seemed very strange to me, and I began to wonder if she was still asleep.

"I just had this very vivid dream. I know what we are supposed to do. We are supposed to write a book about how you get through something like this. Hope is also going to write one for kids. She is going to beat this cancer, and we are going to write about it," Shelby said very convincingly.

And with that, she switched the light off, snuggled back down under the covers, and very quickly went back to sleep, leaving me, literally and figuratively, in the dark.

It struck me how sure she was about this. As the many months have passed, we have talked about this dream many times and in the process of writing this book, we keep this in mind. God truly did want us to write this story. Starting the next day, Shelby began keeping a journal of her thoughts, which has served as the basis of this book.

The next morning I walked down the stairs of the cottage to bring up some luggage. The place we had rented for the week was in one of the most beautiful and unique areas of Holden Beach. From the large screened-in front porch (complete with seven rocking chairs) there was an almost unlimited view up and down the Intracoastal Waterway.

The backside of the cottage was on a deep-water canal, and the property had a floating dock where we tied up our jet skis. The serenity of the back porch contrasted to the constant activity of the Intracoastal Waterway out front. I paused just a minute to take in a motorboat screaming down the waterway, its twin outboard motors overwhelming all other sounds for a few seconds and then fading away as quickly as it appeared. The faint aroma of gasoline exhaust and salt air wafted over and hit me; it is one of my favorite smells. I was lost in the moment until I heard Curtis, the next-door neighbor, say hello.

Curtis and I chatted for a few minutes about how the fishing was going that summer. He owns a forty-two-foot Luhrs boat that was docked out behind the house. He had heard about Hope's diagnosis from Gina's grandfather, Don Glander. Although we did not know each other well, he made an offer that we will never forget.

"Listen, I want to take Hope and all you guys out for a boat cruise one afternoon. Just let me know when you want to go, and once it is high tide, we will get out for a couple of hours."

"Hope will love that, Curtis, I really appreciate it. I will tell her when I go upstairs."

"Great, it will be my pleasure." We talked fishing for a few more minutes and I went upstairs to give the girls the good news.

"Yo, Hope, you see that little boat out there?" I pointed out of the back window to the large boat that dominated the landscape. The Luhrs boat was white with blue trimming and looked as if it was going about thirty-five knots even though it was moored to the dock. It had the look of a serious fishing boat, complete with outriggers for trolling.

"Yeah, I see it. What did you do, buy it?"

"I could not afford the gas that goes into this boat, but I did arrange for you to go for a cruise on it this week. How would you like to go out on it?"

Despite the bandage on her leg, which was designed to keep her leg straight, Hope jumped up from the couch and hopped over to the window.

"You mean, that huge thing!? Are you kiddin' me?" She paused to look in my face and decided that I was serious. "When can we go?"

"I just talked to the owner, Curtis. He lives next door and said anytime you want to go, we can go—as long as it is high tide. A boat that big needs deep water to be able to get out of the channel. We just need to tell him when we can go."

"Now would be fine!"

"Uh, let's wait for a day or two. You just had surgery and need to take it easy," Shelby said, her motherly instincts taking over.

"Mom, chill. I am fine."

"Well, Hope, we have all week," I said, quickly to try to stop an ensuing argument. "Why don't you and Gina relax today, and we can see how you do . . . Mom is right."

And to divert attention I added: "Hope, who are you going to take on the cruise with you? Curtis said you can take anyone you want."

"Dad, as much as you love boats, if I don't take you, I will be dis-owned. Gina for sure and probably Aus and Hol," Hope said with a grin. "That is probably all."

"Hey, what about me?" Shelby protested.

"Mom, there is no way. I can see you now on that boat. You would be telling him how to drive it, what to do. He would end up throwing you overboard. You better stay here . . . It's for your own good."

Shelby looked hurt so Hope added, "And I will make Dad stay here with you."

"No, you will not, Hope. I am definitely going. I am the one who negotiated this deal. I have to go—end of discussion!"

The next day was Tuesday and as is our custom during Beach Week, Tom Reeder, my cousin Nathan Ritter, and his son Jonathan and I left early to play golf. My best friend in the world, Jerry Gregory, drove down from Fayetteville, North Carolina, to join us. Normally, this is one of the best times of the week: carefree golf early in the morning on a beautiful Carolina summer day.

Today was much different. I rode in the golf cart with Jerry and we talked about the battle we had ahead of us. My friend was very reassuring but was also worried about me as the primary breadwinner in the family. Jerry had been a huge help in getting me started in my health insurance business since he was also an insurance consultant in Fayetteville.

We talked about money and insurance issues and what Hope was facing. Both of us were more than aware of the costs involved with cancer treatment, some of which would not be covered by insurance. It was good that Jerry was there. As overwhelming as the upcoming treatments were, it had just begun to dawn on me that I still had to earn a living. My income largely depended on my ability to produce. How would that work, knowing we were facing a lot of time in the hospital over the next year?

On the thirteenth hole, my cell phone buzzed. It was Shelby and she was crying, but in a different, happy sort of way. She told me that while we were down here on vacation, our friends in Charlotte were mobilizing a prayer army. Shelby had received a phone call from Danette, one of the women on that prayer chain to heaven, who informed her that the next morning Weddington United Methodist Church was having a prayer service for Hope.

While this might not seem significant, remember we do not attend this church, but a lot of our friends do. Danette had gone on to say that literally hundreds of people had heard about Hope's diagnosis and wanted to help. Shelby immediately offered to come back home to attend the service, but Danette cut her off.

"No way! You guys stay there and enjoy your vacation. We will take care of this. I just wanted you and Stuart to know about the service. God is going to heal Hope. I just know it."

This was truly overwhelming to both of us. As hard as this journey was going to be, we began to realize again that we were not alone; hundreds of friends and neighbors were willing to do anything to help.

When we finished our round of golf, I headed back to the cottage where Hope and Gina were watching TV. Since Hope was unable to go to the beach because of her knee surgery, she had to spend most of her time watching TV and Gina volunteered to stay with her. Normally our whole family spends the afternoon on the beach, but during this week, we did not go at all.

That afternoon, Austin and Holly decided to take out the jet skis. Shelby would not let them go until I was able to watch them from the screened-in porch on the front of the house. I made a sandwich and sat down to keep an eye on them as they jetted back and forth in front of the house.

After about twenty minutes, I saw Austin and Holly returning back into the canal. They had only been out on the water about twenty minutes. Normally they stayed out there until I waved a broom from the porch, which was their signal to return. As I watched them heading in, I figured that something was wrong with one of the skis (a common occurrence, as most boat owners know). I walked down the stairs and around to the back of the house and met them at the dock.

"Is something wrong?" I asked as the girls pulled up to the dock.

"No," Austin said as she climbed off the ski. "We just don't feel like riding since Hope can't."

"It just isn't the same without her," Holly echoed. "We don't want her to feel bad because she can't ride. It isn't fair, so we will wait until she can ride the skis with us."

I watched as the girls tied the skis up and took their life jackets off. Normally they would be very excited, talking about the waves they jumped over and the boats and the boys they had seen. Not much was said as they hosed down the jackets to rinse off the salt water. Then they went upstairs to get a shower.

Right after that I pulled the two jet skis out of the water.

The next morning, Shelby and I got up, made some coffee, and went out on the front porch. It was about eight o'clock and we wanted to be alone together. About two hundred miles away in Weddington, North Carolina, hundreds of people were beginning to gather at Weddington United Methodist Church for the prayer service for Hope and our family. Shelby and I wanted to be present, at least in spirit.

We had looked up some passages about healing and faith in the Bible. Because of its impact on me at the REACH trip the previous week, I had taken James 1:2–3 as my personal favorite verse in the Bible. The challenge to be filled with joy in that bit of Scripture alone is compelling.

How could I consider this challenge to be joyful in these circumstances? For the first time in our lives, a real challenge was in front of Shelby and me. Was our faith up to the test?

At exactly 8:30 Shelby and I held hands and began to pray. When we started to pray, I felt awkward and stressed. Shelby did as well, but we just kept talking to God; first Shelby would pray and then I would. We were pouring our hearts out, begging God to heal our daughter completely and to give us the strength to get through this. I am not really sure how long we prayed, but as we got to the end, Shelby asked God for something.

"Lord, we know You are with us, but we need a sign. We are weak people, so we need You to let us know that Hope is going to be okay. We are so scared, but we know that You have all of this under control."

Again we were caught in a quandary of *buts.*

A few minutes later, when we ended our prayer and blinked away the tears, God gave us our sign . . . again.

Right outside the screened-in porch we saw two very unusual birds on the rail, not four feet away from where we were sitting. The birds were grayish-brown in color and were about the size of a cardinal. One was a little brighter than the other, but both had a shock of red feathers that stuck out from the top of their heads— the exact color of Hope's beautiful red hair.

The birds landed much closer than they should have. For a moment, we thought they did not see us. Shelby and I looked at each other and started to grin.

Shelby said, "Well, hello, little guys." Both birds looked in and cocked their heads, as if they understood her. Clearly they knew we were sitting there, but did not fly away.

"Uh, darlin', I believe this is our sign. I have never seen this kind of bird before, have you?"

"Never. I have no idea what they are. I guess they are 'Hope Birds'!"

We sat there for a few minutes, talking to those little birds. They continued to look in, cock their heads, and chirp, but they did not fly away.

Had any of the neighbors seen us, the police or medics would have been summoned. I can imagine the conversation.

"The folks next door have flipped. They are out there talking to birds or something. You better come quick!"

After entertaining (and comforting) us, the two little red-headed Hope Birds flew away.

"I cannot believe that just happened," Shelby said. "Did you feel anything when those birds flew down onto the rail? When I saw their red heads, I calmed down completely. I have never seen a bird land that close before and not get scared."

"I guess it is because they were under orders. God told 'em to stick around to help us."

To this day, we have never seen that species of bird at Holden Beach, and we have looked for them. Shelby and I firmly believe that God sent those little guys just for us. It is something we will never forget.

Reflections of a Mother

The morning after we arrived at Holden Beach my friend Nina who never visits empty-handed came over to see me. She handed me a wrapped box as she said, "This is not for Hope this time; this is for you."

Inside I saw a silver-plated box, embossed with an open Bible on three sides and praying hands on the fourth.

"This is a prayer box to put your prayers in. You give them to God and allow Him to answer them in His own time," Nina said as she handed me tiny strips of paper, about ½ by 2 inches, to write those prayers on.

During the next six months one small piece of paper held an enormous prayer request: for the cancer in all parts of Hope's body to go away. Complete healing in God's name. It was simple and to the point.

Hope also owned a prayer box that was meaningful to her. When she was about three, we decorated a white jewelry box (the type you get when you purchase a piece of jewelry at a department store) as part of a Sunday school project.

Inside this box Hope placed a felt heart, a rock to signify God's creation, two green plastic roosters, a button for clothes, and some money. Each night she would take out each item and pray a short prayer.

"Thank You for Your love," she would say as she got the heart out of the box. "Thank You for our cats and please take care of homeless animals," she said as she held the roosters. The money— a dime and a penny—was Hope's own addition to the box; the rest of the items had been provided by the church. She said, "We need to ask God for money to live on."

Then she would close the box and drift off to sleep, confident that her prayers would be answered. Simple prayers seemed natural to her.

As she grew older, however, she felt that she didn't know how to pray. She sensed that her prayers needed to sound like Pastor Ken's.

"Not so," I explained to her. "Praying is talking to your heavenly Father. Just talk to God like you talk to Daddy."

In the final months of her illness, prayer became an important part of each day for all of us.

10

"Ta-ta, Loyal Subjects!"

The doctors had encouraged Hope to walk without crutches as soon as she could, but to keep her right knee dry. By Wednesday, she had removed the large ace bandage and now only had a small one around the incision. She got around just fine and was in the middle of every activity.

That afternoon, the tide was favorable, and Curtis said that the best time to go for a ride on his boat was around four o'clock. Hope had decided that her cruising partners were going to be me and Gina and her dad, Mike. Shelby, who continued to pretend to pout because she could not go, and Nina, Gina's mom, along with her grandparents, joined us at the dock as we got underway.

Some of the pictures taken that day are among our most cherished. In every one of them, Hope is beaming. How in the world could she smile like that, knowing what must have been going through her mind? But the pictures only show a very happy kid with one of her best friends, getting ready to go on a boat ride.

"See ya, Mom," Hope teased. "Enjoy the dock while we are gone. Be back tomorrow."

"Oh, be quiet, Hope," Shelby teased back and couldn't help but add, "and be careful."

As Mike and I threw off the ropes, Hope and Gina began to do their "queen wave."

"Bye, ta-ta, loyal subjects. You will have dinner prepared when we return to port. A royal feast will be nice," Hope said in her thick British accent that we had come to hear constantly over the past two years when she and Gina were together. For some reason nobody can remember, Hope, Gina, and Emily had begun using the English accents when they talked to each other, and most importantly, to their parents. Hope, in particular, did it just to make the other two laugh. As Hope told the people on the dock goodbye, Gina cackled at her friend's antics.

With that, Curtis fired up the motors and the forty-two-foot boat began to slowly leave the dock. As we made our way out of the canal into the Intracoastal Waterway, Mike and I climbed up the ladder to the bridge with Curtis. The view was spectacular: the sun was beginning to fade, closing the chapter on another sun-splashed day at the beach.

The bridge where Curtis, Mike, and I were standing was the tallest part of the boat. We could look down and see the whole deck in front of us. There were two portholes down close to the bow of the boat. As we began to gain speed, all of a sudden one of those portholes on the lower deck popped open and a redhead appeared. Soon another head popped out. For a second, it startled both Mike and me, but it didn't take long for both of us to spring into action.

"What are you guys doing?" we yelled at about the same time. We were concerned that the girls might break something on the boat. How they had gotten down there was a mystery. It seemed like they had just disappeared below deck a minute before.

Unfortunately, they hadn't heard our question over the roar of the motors. They just waved and laughed at us, clearly enjoying the look of shock on both of our faces.

"They are fine," Curtis said with a laugh. "There isn't a thing on this boat they can hurt, especially down there. Let 'em have fun exploring. They do look like a couple of gophers, don't they?"

And that is how it went. The girls explored every nook and cranny of the boat and did not come topside until about an hour later.

"Dad," Hope said as she shimmied up the ladder as if nothing was wrong, "this boat is way too cool. There is a wide-screen TV down there, a bed, and a shower and a kitchen. You could live on this boat!"

"We have cable and HBO too," Curtis added.

"Make that totally cool," Hope said. "Hey, I want to drive."

Without saying a word, Curtis jumped out of the captain's chair. For a brief moment, no one was at the wheel.

"Well, Hope, it is all yours. You better grab the wheel or we are going to be on the beach." The boat continued right straight down the waterway, but Hope leaped up into the chair and grabbed the wheel.

"Everybody overboard! Hopeless is drivin'!" Mike screamed and pretended to head down the ladder. "Curtis, where are the life-jackets?"

Hope shot Mike a sneer and Gina, of course, was laughing at her friend as she normally did. Hope was the one always pushing the envelope, and her friends Gina and Emily would follow, laughing all the way at what Hope was going to do next. The more they laughed, the more Hope did.

Curtis picked up my camera and asked if he could take a picture. I stood behind Hope and he snapped a photo of us that I cherish to this day. It is a picture of a dad and his daughter, riding on a boat on a beautiful summer day. You would never guess that there was anything wrong. Hope's smile is from ear to ear.

We cruised for about an hour and then turned around to head

back home. From our perch high in the cockpit, we could see the beautiful marshes and how the tide had crafted intricate patterns in the sand. We watched as the sea birds fished in the shallows, and we took in the beauty of the homes, from the small shanties that had been built decades before to the newer, bigger homes that had just popped up in recent years. We steamed by the inlet that took boaters out to the Atlantic Ocean. It was a calm day and the water was dotted with white sails as the boats navigated the waves. The sun was beginning to fade in the west, and dark shadows had begun to creep along the water.

Hope and Gina had asked to go down and sit on the bow of the boat, which they did. As we cruised back to port (to the royal feast, we presumed), Mike and Curtis very carefully began asking about Hope's condition. I told them about the diagnosis and how difficult a struggle we had in front of us, and I could see the emotion on both men's faces, despite their sunglasses.

"That ain't possible!" Curtis said. "That kid seems healthy as a horse. She is jumping all around this boat. I don't see anyway she won't beat this. She is too strong."

Almost on cue, the girls began doing the "queen wave" to passing boaters. The reaction they were getting from the others on the water was fun to watch. Each boater returned the greeting enthusiastically with the same royal wave.

Just as the sun was beginning to set we returned to the dock. We had been out on the water for about two hours, but it seemed a lot longer than that. The same crowd was waiting on the dock for us, and the sight of the big boat coming down the canal got a lot of people's attention, which Hope and Gina took advantage of. The boat ride was special to me then, but is even more special to me now. Unfortunately, this would be the last time Hope would be able to get on a boat. The pictures and the memories from that day will last me until the day I die.

On Friday, the family gathered for the highlight of the week: the

Fourth of July cookout. It was the last night here for us, and it was now tinged with sadness for reasons beside the end of our vacation.

After eating, we walked over to Rob and Jean Kreisher's house to watch the fireworks going off up and down the Intracoastal Waterway. As everyone enjoyed the colorful lights, I got into a conversation with Buddy Page.

Buddy's middle-aged son, Sam, had been diagnosed with cancer at about the same time as Hope, and his diagnosis was also not very promising.

Buddy was retired and living mostly at the beach, four hours away from his son in Charlotte, and he was facing the same anguish we were. Although his son was in his forties, the pain was still the same.

"I am afraid he needs a miracle," Buddy said to me that night. "The doctors don't give him much chance."

"So do we. The doctors say we need a home run with this first chemo treatment. Not a double or a triple, but a homer. They say that if we get 85 to 90 percent reduction in her existing tumors, we have a chance to get her into remission." We paused for a moment to look out on the scene. Our families were watching the fireworks, which were now in full force.

"Buddy, Shelby and I are putting this 100 percent in God's hands. We want Hope's complete healing and that is what we are praying for. Miracles happen all the time, and we are counting on one here. And the same goes for Sam. We will be praying hard for his recovery too."

Buddy and I went back to be with the rest of our families to enjoy the fireworks. Now as we write this book, it should be noted that Sam is still alive and, so far, has beaten all the odds.

Miracles do happen.

We stayed down at the Kreishers' house for another hour or so and then headed back to our cottage. Shelby and I began to get packed up because we had to check out by noon the next day. As we did so, the dread of what next week would bring became more and more intense. We normally waited until the last minute to leave Holden Beach, often staying until late Sunday to head back. This time, however, we needed to be home for a day to prepare for the coming hospital visit that would last about four to five days.

The next day, we rose early and got the cars packed up for the trip back home. After checking out of the cottage, we went by to see my sister and my mom. When we pulled up to their house, Austin and Holly asked Hope to go to Provisions for lunch. They had been invited to go there by some friends who were also vacationing at Holden Beach.

Provisions is one of our favorites, since the restaurant has a nice big deck that overlooks the Intracoastal Waterway. It is a great place to sit and watch the boats go by while eating your meal.

Normally, Hope would have jumped at the chance. But today, she didn't. Instead, she said no, and Shelby and I became aware that she was scared, very scared. Despite repeated efforts by her sisters to get Hope to come with them, it didn't work. She became very upset, and although Shelby did her best to comfort her, Hope refused to even get out of the car when we got to my mother's home, despite the heat.

We finally got her to come upstairs into Mom's house. Reluctantly, Austin and Holly went on to lunch, and Hope sat down on the couch, silently watching TV.

This was the first time all week that Hope had showed the slightest sign of being worried. But now, with the ride back to Charlotte just ahead of us, she naturally began to think about the coming chemotherapy.

As Shelby, Beth, and my mom, Betty, tried to comfort Hope, I went outside.

I slumped down into a rocker and stared out at the view from my mom's front porch. I watched as a couple and their two young children walked down to the ocean. The children were laughing excitedly, ready for the beach. All around me, everybody's world was just fine, with "no worries" as Crocodile Dundee had made famous a few years earlier. I continued to watch as the young family disappeared over the dunes, a family a lot like mine when the girls were smaller. When they were out of sight, I went back in the house to check on Hope.

At this moment, I felt as helpless as I ever had in my life. Looking back on it now, that day still sticks out because it was day one. Boot Camp was over, and the battle was about to begin.

Reflections of a Mother

Even though I didn't go on the boat trip, I did get to spend some time with Hope during Boot Camp. On Friday afternoon, I took Gina, Holly, Austin, Liz, and Hope on a shopping trip to the mall in Wilmington, North Carolina. Before we left, Hope made it clear that no one would be told about her cancer. "If I have to get a wheelchair to get around, Gina is going to get one too."

Once we arrived at the mall, Hope took off the immobilizer, the large splint that had been wrapped around her leg after the surgery, and gave it to Gina who strapped it onto her leg.

Then the fun began. Talk about drawing attention!

One older couple was particularly interested in what had happened to the two girls.

"We kinda had a jet ski accident," Hope explained to the couple. (This was not exactly a lie, as you know, just bending the outcome of the scooter accident from a year earlier.)

"We ran into each other, and I got stitches in my knee."

It took all the control Gina had to keep from laughing.

Try getting two wheelchairs through small spaces in department stores, especially around all those tightly packed clothing racks.

At one time Gina got so interested in the designer jeans on one rack that she got out of her chair and walked over to the rack before she realized what she was doing. Then she quickly limped back to her wheelchair and resumed the charade.

Late in the afternoon the girls started getting hungry for the taste of Chick-Fil-A, so Austin, Holly, and I parked them at a table. When we came back we heard a "chair-cheer."

These two teenagers had just made the cheerleading squad at Weddington Middle School and now they were turning the two wheelchairs—first to the right, then to the left, back and forth, over and over again, and shouting cheers to go along with the motions.

I noticed that they also kept their eyes on any cute guys walking the mall. Hope would see a couple and start her wheelchair toward them. Her plan was to run into the boys with her wheelchair, apologize, and then introduce them to Holly, Liz, and Austin.

Leave it to Hope to use the wheelchair to gain a flirting advantage!

11

"Do Not Stop in Charlotte!"

The drive back to Charlotte was horrible. Even under normal circumstances, going back home after Beach Week was depressing; the return to the drudgery of work was always hard after the bliss of lying in the sun all week. But the circumstances that were present this year made all the other years pale in comparison. All week we had our spirits buoyed by the outpouring of emotion and support. However, the mid-week prayer service and the signs we had gotten became more and more distant the closer we got to Charlotte.

Hope was very quiet, undoubtedly feeling the fear of what lay ahead of her. Soon, however, she fell asleep.

After glancing into the seat behind her, Shelby looked at me and, with tears clouding her beautiful green eyes, began speaking.

"Stuart, just keep driving. Don't stop in Charlotte. I don't think I can do this. What does she have ahead of her?" Shelby buried her head in the blanket she kept in the front seat when we traveled. Normally the blanket was there because I like to keep the car cool when we are traveling. Today, it served another purpose.

I also began to feel the dread. I imagined doing what my wife suggested. "Do not stop in Charlotte at Carolinas Medical Center. Just keep driving until the money runs out. Leave cancer behind."

The three-and-one-half-hour trip seemed to take days.

Upon arriving home, my family slowly began to unpack the car. It was mid-afternoon on Saturday, and soon Hope had made a call to Emily and before long the girls were lounging on the couch watching TV. As had been the case the previous Saturday, the phone soon began ringing. We must have had a dozen phone calls from people asking about how the beach had been or telling Shelby and me how wonderful the Wednesday service had been, or offering prayers and support. The rest of the evening was spent taking it easy—and getting Hope packed up for the chemotherapy that would begin the next day.

On Sunday, we uncharacteristically stayed home from church. We wanted Hope to have as much time at home as possible before heading to CMC later that evening. But before then, our church was going to hold a healing service that began at seven o'clock. When we told Hope about it, at first she was very reluctant to go.

"I am fine. I don't want to be the center of attention there . . . Just what do you do at a healing service anyway?"

Shelby explained to her that the service was for anyone who needed healing, both physically and emotionally. At first, Hope did not believe her mom, but she soon agreed to go. Later that afternoon, on Sunday, July 6, 2003, we packed up our car and headed to the healing service at Matthews United Methodist Church.

We arrived early and only our family, Pastor Ken Lyon, and the Reeders were there. Hope was able to get around without her crutches so she walked to the front pew of the church. We visited together for a few minutes and soon folks began arriving.

Among the first were all of Hope's friends and their families. Her gang ran down to the front row and surrounded her. Most of the girls had not seen Hope since the diagnosis. There were no tears, only the normal giggling that comes from a group of teenage girls. Promptly at seven o'clock the service began.

A service such as this one is intended to call upon God to provide healing to anyone who wants it. While Hope was without question the focal point of the service, there were other people who were also suffering. As I looked around the sanctuary, it struck me how many of our church members had been battling cancer. I had been aware of some of them, but hadn't realized how many of our members had cancer, which shows how shallow and self-absorbed I had been.

One of the women who came that day was battling breast cancer. She had endured several surgeries, many rounds of chemotherapy, and radiation. The disease would go into remission and then come back. She was in a revolving door of treatments, a seemingly never-ending cycle to stay alive.

Now that Hope had this awful disease, why did I all of a sudden notice this woman who had been going to our church for years?

The service was very uplifting. Pastor Ken prayed for the complete spiritual and physical healing of everyone who needed it. At the end of the service, he asked everyone to gather in the center aisle of the church and lay hands on the ones who needed prayer. As the crowd gathered around Hope and the others, all of a sudden this seemed very uncomfortable to me and for good reason.

About six months earlier, there had been a similar healing service for Bubba Smitha who had died soon after my hospital visit in February. As I put my hand on Hope's head, I wondered if that would be her fate too. The thought terrorized me, but at the same time Hope dying from this seemed impossible.

Pastor Ken finished up the very emotional service, and we hung around as long as possible. In fact, our family would have preferred to spend the night there, rather than go to the hospital. Finally, the only ones left were us and the Reeders. Wendy came over and hugged all of us and said she would be at CMC first thing tomorrow morning.

As we left the church, Hope suddenly announced she was hungry. "Since I am going to be getting this chemo put in me and it will make me sick, I might as well get a big ol' burger before we get there."

It was vintage Hope. She had that gleam in her eye, that spitfire look that was so appealing about her. It also told us she was way too strong for this cancer. Her mood immediately lifted all of our spirits, and we quickly let her make the restaurant choice.

"Let's go to Chili's. That way Mom can get her fajitas and I can get some chicken fingers," Hope decided. "And of course, a brownie sundae for dessert."

"Done," I said, and we took off to Chili's where our whole family had a great meal together. Cancer was not discussed, nor was what was going to happen tomorrow.

12

"Jerry, Jerry, Jerry!"

The next morning, Holly and I arrived at the hospital bright and early to be with Hope and Shelby, who had spent the night there. Austin stayed home due to her work schedule. The first thing to happen was for Hope to have a Hickman catheter inserted into her chest. This catheter is tunneled under the skin and placed in one of the veins, just under the collarbone. The catheter is long enough to reach the large vein that enters the heart. The purpose of tunneling the catheter under the skin is to help prevent infection.

A small cuff is located around the catheter about one inch inside the place where the tube enters the child's skin. Skin grows into this cuff and keeps the catheter in place. The cuff also acts as a barrier to infection. Hope had been very concerned about the needle thing. She did not want to get stuck. Dr. McMahon came by first thing that morning and assured her there would be very little of that to worry about.

"Almost all of the medicine you take will go into the port. The most important thing is to keep it clean. Your mom and dad will be taught how to do that."

"Make that Mom, not Dad. Unless it can be fixed with a hammer, he is probably not the one to do that," Hope replied.

I gave her my very hurt look, which had no effect. After all, she was right.

Dr. McMahon continued. "The surgery will take about an hour. Once the Hickman is implanted, we will start your treatments right away. I will check by later today to see how you are doing."

At about 9:00 a.m., the orderlies came to get Hope and for the second time in ten days, our daughter headed to surgery.

Despite being told that implanting a Hickman was routine, it was a very nervous time for all of us until we were told Hope was out of surgery and doing okay. She stayed in recovery about an hour or so and then was transported to her room where she would be for the remainder of the hospital stay.

Unlike the previous surgery for the biopsy, Hope bounced back much quicker. Fortunately, we had a fairly large room, big enough for the recliner that Shelby slept in and a couple of chairs. Holly handed the remote to Hope, and the two sisters began to scroll through the channels to see what the hospital had to offer in the way of TV.

What happened next was perhaps the funniest event that occurred throughout this ordeal. In fact, even today it brings a smile to everyone's face when it is retold. The girls' channel surfing took them to America's classiest TV program: the infamous *Jerry Springer Show*. None of the adults in the room—particularly my cousin Wendy who had arrived along with her daughter Liz—had ever watched this show and its daily plunge into the depths of bad taste. And on this Monday morning, it was at the lowest point possible.

The images on the TV screen revealed two multi-tattooed women who were screaming obscenities at each other. Each woman was very large. At the center of their unbridled hatred of each other was an equally obese man who was also well tattooed. This fine specimen of manhood was apparently the object of their affection, which was troubling to say the least. The two women began to scream even louder, prompting both Holly and Liz to pump their fists and yell, "Jerry, Jerry, Jerry" along with the TV audience. This seemed to enrage the women even more until one finally decided to go after the other one, and a fight broke out in classic Jerry Springer fashion. The ruckus completely unnerved my cousin.

"Oh, my word! . . . Look at that! What are those women doing?" Her genuine shock was so profound that everyone in the room began to laugh, especially Hope. Holly and Liz got even louder with their chants, and Wendy looked at the two girls in stunned disbelief.

"Liz, stop that! Don't tell me you watch this show? Holly, I am disappointed in you too. You are both grounded," Wendy said and then glanced back up at the TV.

"This is unbelievable! How do they get away with this? It is the middle of the morning. Children could be watching." Despite her disgust, Wendy kept watching until the inevitable happened: one of the combatants began tearing the other one's clothes off.

When that happened, the laughter in the room was so loud a nurse came in to see what all the fuss was about.

Upon seeing the TV, she said, "Oh, Jerry Springer. I shoulda known," and with a slight smile, exited as quickly as she had come in.

For several days after that, every time Liz and Holly were around Wendy, they would torment her with the chant: "Jerry, Jerry, Jerry."

In the midst of beginning our battle against Hope's cancer, a memory was created that will last the rest of our lives. And that is how it would go for the next six months.

Just when events seemed to be intolerable, God would allow us some comic relief.

And Hope usually provided it.

Reflections of a Mother

Stuart and I have always picked our battles with the girls: that's what people of authority tell you to do in child rearing. But the influence of television shows on our children's beliefs had always been important to us. We had never even let the girls watch *The Simpsons*, much less *The Jerry Springer Show.*

Still, laughter can be the medicine you need when times are tough and you are frightened. You just need to pick your battles wisely.

Jerry! Jerry! Jerry!

Indeed!

13

Chemo Sucks, Part One

The rest of Monday, July 7, was spent getting ready for the chemotherapy that was scheduled to begin the next day. Shelby and Hope had several visitors during the day, and they spent most of the time watching TV and playing video games. Since I had not been at work in over two weeks, I left and went to my office. All of my co-workers were very anxious to find out what was going on, although I had been in touch with my partner, Chris Spivey, several times during the previous week. After bringing everyone up-to-date on what was happening, I spent the afternoon returning e-mails and phone calls and catching up on paperwork. Finally around six o'clock I left the office and on the way stopped by and picked up a Wendy's #7, Hope's favorite fast-food meal.

The three of us ate dinner together, and then a nurse came into the room with an IV pole, which held a yellow bag of fluid. She made some small talk with Hope as she hooked up the IV bag to Hope's port.

"What is that exactly?" Hope asked.

"Well, this is called cisplatin. It is the first of your treatments," the nurse replied.

We were very surprised by this. "I thought this was supposed to start tomorrow," Shelby commented.

"Well, we generally start the treatment as soon as we can. That shortens the hospital stay."

We watched as the nurse finished hooking up the IV. She told Hope it looked fine and she would check back later. With that, she turned and left.

There was an eerie silence. All three of us watched as the yellow fluid began to run down the IV tube into Hope's port.

Then I walked over and inspected the IV bag of fluid that was dripping into my daughter. *Go and kill cancer. Kill all of it. Make her better*, I said silently to the drugs in the bag.

"Well, I guess your chemo has started. Do you feel any different?" I asked Hope.

"Nope. I don't feel anything . . . Am I supposed to?" she asked, looking at her mother inquisitively.

"Apparently not," Shelby replied.

And just like that, the treatment to kill Hope's cancer had begun.

It is funny how things like this go. We expected the chemo to start with some fanfare, like, "Here it comes, get ready!" But it didn't happen like that at all. A nurse came in, hooked up the IV, and off we went killing cancer cells. I tried to get Shelby to go home and let me stay with Hope overnight, but she would have none of it.

"I will bring you a Chick-Fil-A biscuit tomorrow morning on the way over. Is that cool wid you, Cuz?" I asked my daughter.

Most fathers have nicknames they give their kids, and for some reason, I used "Cuz" with Hope from early on. It is short for cousin which makes, well, no sense at all, since she was my daughter. But a lot of nicknames don't make sense. Austin was "Austine-O" or "Aussie" and Holly was always "Holly-bird." For the life of me, I don't know where "Cuz" came from, but I also use it when I am talking to Wendy Reeder. She has always been "Cuz" too, which does make sense.

"Whatever." Hope shrugged. "I hope I sleep better tonight than last night . . . Why do those nurses come in and wake you up to ask how you are doing? Duh, I am sleeping, how do you think I'm doing?" Hope complained, barely looking up from the Game Boy she was playing.

"You better not let them hear that or they may find a needle for you." I gave her our Eskimo-style nose kiss, which had become our daddy/daughter thing, gave Shelby a kiss, and headed home.

Early the next morning I was awakened by a phone call from Shelby at around six thirty. Immediately I became concerned and asked what was going on.

"I think the Chick-Fil-A biscuit will have to wait. She got sick very early this morning like they said she would. She has been vomiting pretty regularly since. She is one sick pup!"

"I am on the way. Do you need anything?" I said, scrambling out of bed.

"No. Just get up here."

And for the next two days, that is how it went. The first chemotherapy treatment, this vile drug called cisplatin, was now making my daughter very sick. Cisplatin, as the name implies, has one job: to "splat" the immune system and kill all cells, both healthy and cancerous. Her treatment lasted two more days and after that she began to take anti-nausea drugs. They wanted to get her nausea under control before she was allowed to go home. All the while, she remained very nauseous and ate nothing.

Dr. McMahon said that the cisplatin would take about two to three days to get out of her system, and when it did, the nausea

would subside and her appetite would return. He then encouraged
her to eat—anything she wanted as long as it was a lot of it.

The oncologist did have good news. Back on June 27, he indicated that Hope would be tested for the markers to allow
Herceptin to be used. The blood work indicated that the protein
markers were present, and that Hope would be a good candidate
for Herceptin.

"I am going to use Herceptin right along with cisplatin. It is a
drug that has very little, if any, side effects. And hopefully it will
give us some good results."

Dr. McMahon also said that it would be very likely that her hair
would start to fall out over the next two weeks. He told her this was
even more likely because of her red hair color, since light-colored
hair tends to be finer. "But your hair will grow back," the doctor
assured her. "And in a lot of cases even thicker and curlier."

As we sat in the hospital over the next few days, Hope, in
between bouts of nausea, fretted more and more over the impending hair loss. Shelby, too, was worried about this because she knew
how important looks are to young teenage girls.

I decided to become the heavy. "Hope, you are gonna lose your
hair. Big deal. It is just hair and it will grow back. Don't worry
about it."

Hope glared at me and snarled that I didn't understand. Shelby
also piled on, saying that I didn't get how important hair was to her.

"Sure I do. But what can we do about it? I hope she doesn't lose
it either, but Dr. McMahon says she will. Tell you what, if it happens I will shave my dome too. We can be twins."

"Stop! I am already nauseous enough as it is," Hope said and
right on cue, got sick again.

For girls age twelve-going-on-sixteen, there is no question that
appearance is a big deal and hair is a big part of that. Hope was five
feet, six inches and obviously very tall for her age, so she had tried
hard not to stand out. But with crystal-blue eyes and flaming red

hair, blending in was impossible. Only in recent months had Hope embraced being who she was. Her hair was a big part of that. The thought of losing it was devastating.

The cisplatin treatment only lasted two days but its effect was immediate. Soon, controlling Hope's nausea became the biggest challenge. As would so often happen during her illness, Hope reacted differently to what was anticipated. Her nausea was so severe that the nurses had to resort to drugs not normally used.

Finally, on Friday, the nausea subsided to the point where she could travel home. Hope could not wait to be out of the hospital: cabin fever had set in, even with the nausea present. She was ready to get home to her bed and the kittens she missed desperately.

On Friday around 10:30 a.m., we loaded up the car. Hope rode down in a wheelchair, her "puke pail" close by. She did pretty well, only getting sick a few times during the thirty-minute ride. We got her upstairs and figured that once she was home, the sickness would go away.

It didn't. In fact, it got worse, much worse.

All of Friday night, Hope continued to have waves of nausea. She could not keep anything down, not even a soda cracker. Sometime after midnight, Shelby, fearing that our daughter was becoming dehydrated, called the number for Kid's Path, the nursing service that provides home health visits for pediatric oncology patients.

A male nurse named Jacques answered the phone and said he was on his way over to check on Hope and to bring some stronger anti-nausea medicine.

Outside, one of the most violent thunderstorms we have ever experienced was just beginning. The lightning and the thunder seemed to be right over our house. Hope was so sick, and yet there was nothing we could do for her but keep a cold compress on her head. At around 1:00 a.m. we saw lights coming down the driveway, and I went downstairs to let the nurse in through the garage.

As the garage door opened, Jacques came scampering in, as much to avoid the lightning that was flashing as the rain, which was reaching Ecclesiastical proportions. Water was gushing down our long, steep driveway in small waves before crashing into the drain, which was not coming close to keeping up with the volume of water.

Thunder cracked loudly as Jacques stepped into the garage and pulled off his hooded jacket, revealing Rastafarian locks that would have made Bob Marley blush. The locks fell way down below his beltline. Seeing this guy and knowing what he was here for put me on edge. To put it mildly, he did not impress me.

Who was this dude? This guy was going to take care of my daughter? I became very uneasy as we walked into the house and up the stairs.

Two hours later, he was one of my favorite people on the planet.

Part of this journey with Hope's disease revealed a lot about our character, in particular mine. My preconceived notions to the contrary, this man was an angel of mercy in every sense of the word. After introducing himself to Hope and Shelby, he immediately sat down beside Hope and asked her very specific questions about her nausea.

He spoke to her as an adult, yet was very tender with her. Jacques didn't sugarcoat anything, like "How often are you getting sick?" Instead he asked her how many times she had thrown up. Despite her unrelenting nausea, Hope began to respond to him. Soon, she was giving him the feedback he would need to determine which medicine to give her.

And once again, humor showed up.

Since returning home from the hospital, Hope had been surrounded by her kittens, Peanut and Pudge. The kittens, all of four months old, were at that cute stage. Both were extremely curious, having been treated like humans since birth. (It should be noted here that around the Stout house, animals are treated like deities.

This menagerie includes six cats and our dog, Daisy. All of the animals, but in particular these two kittens, were Hope's refuge.)

Jacques was digging into his medical bag to give Hope some additional nausea medicine when Peanut appeared from her hiding place under the couch. She circled around Jacques, looked into the bag, rubbed on his legs, and jumped up on Hope's bed. Soon, the mother cat, Baby, appeared and did the same thing followed by Pudge, Hope's favorite. All of the cats ended up on the bed with Hope, watching Jacques curiously.

"How many of these guys do you have, anyway?" he asked.

"Oh, there are a few more outside. If you don't like cats, you are in the wrong house," Shelby said. This actually brought a bit of a smile to Hope.

"I love cats. I have two at home also, but they skedaddle when someone comes over."

"Shelby actually helped birth these kittens," I said as Jacques prepared to give Hope the added nausea medicine. "They were born in our closet and have been around people all their lives. Plus, the dog thinks she is a cat! She has been around them since she was a pup and acts just like them."

Jacques administered the medicine as he continued his explanation. "Hope, this is going to do the trick. You are giving us a challenge, but I am about 100 percent sure this will stop your nausea. I know this really sucks, but the good news is that nausea tells us the cancer is dying. Also, we know now what to expect next time you take cisplatin. We can better prepare for it so you will not be so sick during your next treatment.

"You guys better have some food ready. When her appetite returns, it will return with a vengeance! I have seen it a million times."

"Don't mention food just yet," Hope warned weakly.

We talked with Jacques for about an hour or so, and then I realized it was in the wee hours of the morning. Hope's bouts of nausea had begun to decrease. Upon seeing Hope feeling better, Shelby told Jacques that he could leave anytime he wanted.

"Just a few more minutes. I want to be sure she is out of the woods," he said. And for another forty-five minutes, we sat there talking while Hope fell back to sleep. Somewhere around three o'clock in the morning, he left our house. When he arrived, my daughter was deathly nauseous. When he left, she was sleeping peacefully.

As I said, one of my favorite people on the planet!

Reflections of a Mother

Hope was so depressed that she was missing Rainbow Express, a camp for special-needs kids that our church puts together every summer. This week was a time when the mothers and fathers and families of special-needs children can have a break from the 24/7 care they give their kids. Laurie Little, our youth director, started this camp because of her own son, Will; she knows firsthand what it is like to be a caregiver to one of these children as you try to keep your other kids and family intact. She made a team of one youth, one special-needs child, and one regular camper buddy.

Rainbow Express was one of the highlights of all three of our girls' summer. They loved this camp and the children and learned so much about life from them each year. They hated that these children were looked at differently. They are normal kids, just a little hyper, the girls explained to me, with a few more obstacles to overcome. But people looked at them differently or, worse yet, didn't look at them at all. That bothered the girls greatly, Hope in particular, who had been a camper buddy since age seven.

That week Rainbow Express created a Hope room where all the campers made gifts for her. The most touching items were three giant, yellow smiley faces that were finger-painted by the Down syndrome, autistic, and cystic fibrosis children. There were lots of smudges on these smiley faces, which had been painted with so much love. We also heard that Will Little, Laurie's son, had said a special prayer that day for Hope. How could God not hear and answer prayers from this special boy?

This year's theme was Superheroes. So before turning in their costumes, three of the youth group members came to the hospital to visit Hope and bring her the gifts the children had made for her. The look on her face was of complete disgust. Batman and Spider-Man and Superman, heroes for kids nine and below, were in her hospital room. She looked at her friends and said sternly, "Get out of my room—now! Go visit the children down the hall. You are making me sicker."

It was a laughable moment, in between bouts of nausea.

14

Refried Beans

After getting virtually no sleep Friday night, we spent most of
Saturday resting. Hope continued to sleep for the most part; she
had some slight nausea but nothing like the prior two days. Food
was mentioned a few times to Hope, and the suggestion was received
with a nasty look or comment. Shelby and I desperately wanted to
get some nourishment into this kid. The nurses had told us that
when the chemo was out of Hope's system, she would get very hungry, very quickly. The poor child hadn't eaten much in two days, and
both of us could not wait to go out and get her a Wendy's #7.

When she had started getting sick from the chemo, Hope had
become very particular about who she wanted to see. Wendy was
basically the only one she would let come into her hospital room
other than her sisters. Around mid-afternoon on Saturday, my
cousin Wendy (no kin of course to the hamburger chain) came
over just to see if we needed a break.

When Wendy came in, Shelby and I visited for a few minutes with her in the downstairs kitchen but soon I left the women and went upstairs to sit with Hope. She had insisted on staying in the upstairs playroom rather than her bedroom so that she could watch TV.

As soon as I saw her face, I could see a dramatic change. She had that sparkle back, the kind you get when a fever finally breaks.

"Well, hello there, sunshine! How ya feelin'?" I greeted her with our Eskimo nose kiss.

"Dad, I am starving. What do we have down there to eat?"

"Hope, you can have anything. Want me to run to Wendy's? I will get you seven #7s if you want it. Just name it. We have been waiting for this so I will have to fight Mom to see who gets to go get the food."

"That would be great, but I need food *now*. I will eat Wendy's later, but right now I gotta have something," Hope said, color returning to her face almost before my eyes.

"Mom is down there with Wendy. They will fix you steak and lobster if you want that. What do you feel like eating?"

"Well, this is gonna sound crazy, but what I really want, I am sure Mom doesn't have."

"Try me."

"Okay, but don't say I didn't warn you. What I really am craving is refried beans and corn chips."

She might as well have said steak and lobster.

"You gotta be kiddin'? I have never seen you eat refried beans in your life. And it isn't like we run a Mexican restaurant around here. Are you sure?"

"Yep, that's what I want—and hurry! I'm about to eat this blanket."

"Done. I am on it!" With that, I ran down the stairs. Wendy and Shelby were standing in the kitchen talking. They stopped yakking when I bounded into the room.

"Well, we have a request from the queen bee upstairs. She needs food *now!*"

Both of the women nearly ran me over on their way to the stairs.

"Hold up, you two. She told me what she wants, but this isn't going to be easy. Refried beans and corn chips, and based on what I saw, I think we better hurry. She said something about being hungry enough to eat her blanket."

"Refried beans? Oh my word!" Wendy said with a laugh.

"What are we going to do? I don't think we have any refried beans," Shelby said as she began looking through the pantry.

"Well, the good news is we do have the corn chips," I said, pointing to the kitchen table.

Since returning home from the hospital, we had been inundated with junk food and candy. Someone had brought over a family-sized pack of Fritos corn chips. They had been sitting on the table for two days, unopened by anyone.

Wendy and I grabbed for them at the same time like two thirsty school children trying to get to the water fountain before anyone else.

"Gimme them. I was here first," my cousin said sternly, and since she used to baby-sit me many years ago, I minded her. She was serious.

"Oh, I don't believe this!"

Wendy and I both turned around to find Shelby standing in front of the pantry doors—holding a can of refried beans!

"Unbelievable!" I said, and then added, "Uh, dear, how long do you think those beans have been in that pantry?"

"Probably since we moved in here in 1994," Shelby replied, examining the can for a purchase date. "Wait, here is the date. I remember now. I bought this can of beans about two weeks ago when Austin had some of her girlfriends over. They were going to make nachos. I guess they didn't use these. Thank God for that."

"You better get them heated up quick. But I am taking them upstairs to her. We will have some fun with this."

In less than five minutes, piping hot refried beans were spooned into a bowl that was accompanied by a plate piled high with corn chips. Hope, now close to being back at full speed, had yelled down to "add lots of cheese too." I loaded the food onto a TV tray and the three of us headed upstairs.

"'Bout time. A kid could starve around here," Hope sniffed as we sat the TV tray down. She was about to dig in when I stopped her.

"Now, Cuz. I just want to say this before you start snarfin' down those beans and chips. You have been tossing up your cookies for two days. Are you sure you don't want something a little gentler on your tummy? What about some grits or eggs or something? That way, if you get sick, your mom won't have as big a mess to clean up."

"I am not cleaning it up," Shelby said. "Hope, please let me fix you something else."

Hope then gave us that infamous *watch this* look we have seen a million times—and quickly proceeded to dip several of the chips into the bowl and scoop up a huge mound of the beans and cheese. She hesitated, making sure she had our full attention, and shoveled the entire glop into her mouth. Strings of cheese were dangling out of her mouth. She chewed very fast and swallowed, scooped up another big mound, and tossed it into her mouth.

Within five minutes the whole bowl was gone. She asked for another bowl and soon it was gone. Finally, she slowed down and we all sat there and looked at her.

"What? You guys are making me nervous. I am fine. Go away or watch TV with me or something but quit staring. I am not going to explode or anything." With that she fluffed up her pillow, re-arranged the ever-present Pudge who had been napping on her bed, and picked up the remote.

Seeing that the food seemed to be staying down, Shelby, Wendy, and I retreated downstairs with the TV tray.

"Lord help us if that stuff comes up," I said. "We will have to replace the carpet."

Fortunately for us (and the carpet) it stayed down. The rest of the evening Hope asked for more and more food. She even called Emily and the two friends sat upstairs and watched TV together and ate junk food.

Wendy stayed for a while longer, getting all the details about Monday and Tuesday. Austin had to go to North Carolina State University for college orientation, and I was going with her. Wendy had offered to help out by coming by each day to let Shelby go to a church workshop that she was scheduled to attend. At first, she was going to cancel going to the workshop, but Hope had insisted that she would be fine with Wendy being there. Around seven o'clock or so, Wendy returned home. The rest of the weekend was spent in a rather normal fashion. Hope was up and around and as each hour passed, she became more and more of her old self.

And on Sunday for lunch, I went and got her a Wendy's #7, just as promised.

Reflections of a Mother

When we were at home after Hope's first chemo treatment, we received a phone call from Emily and her mom, Danette.

"Some of the girls want to come by your house to see Hope. Would that be okay?"

When I asked Hope, her immediate answer was no. She could be herself around Emily and Gina, but she didn't know how her other friends would react to her having cancer.

I told her, "You have to get over this and see the friends who care for you and want to see you."

It took a while, but Hope grudgingly agreed.

We expected seven girls, all members of The Core Club, a Bible study of which Hope was a member.

Instead thirty girls and boys appeared carrying balloons and streamers that said "We Love You, Hope!" and a special blanket.

For the past week or so the kids had met at Danette's house to make a blanket of love that Hope could carry with her to and from the hospital when her friends could not be with her. Each young person had painted his or her hand on the silk side of the furry pink blanket and signed his or her name. The kids had even gone so far as to break into our house when we were all at the hospital to steal the kittens and Daisy the dog who added their paw prints with much hesitation and encouragement. All except Pudge, that is, who wouldn't stay still for the autographing and moved to create a wavy blob so his signature read "Pudge's smudge."

The corner of the beautiful pink blanket said "God loves you, Hope, and so do we."

When these boys and girls rounded the corner of our house, and several of Hope's closest friends burst onto the porch (even though her blood counts were still low and visitors were to be limited), something in her changed. She realized how much her friends cared for her.

"Friendship is a gift to the soul." —Anonymous

What a gift this was for Hope! Now, instead of feeling alone and excluded, Hope felt loved.

As the group began leaving, Hope asked Emily to stick around. Soon Hope got hungry, which was good to see.

John and Martha Fisichello are neighbors of ours who own Mario's Pizza, a restaurant nearby. After hearing about Hope's diagnosis, they had given their employees strict orders: "Whenever Hope Stout orders something, there is no charge."

Hope took that to heart.

She called Mario's and ordered a large pizza and some of their famous garlic knots for herself and Emily—all without me knowing, until the delivery man showed up at our door.

As the girls began eating the feast, I overheard Hope tell her friend: "Emily, stick with me, and you will want for nothing!"

15

"Flexoblood"

The good news for the following week was that it was the middle of the summer and all of Hope's friends were out of school on summer break, so she had plenty of company now that the chemotherapy treatment had fully worn off, and she was happy to have visitors. The bad news was we began to watch for any sign of red hair falling out.

When her chemo treatments had begun, I started to have really bad dreams of waking up to find my daughter completely bald. I have no idea why that scared me so much, but each morning when I went in to check on Hope, I half expected to see all her hair in a big pile on the pillow beside her.

Hope had a visit scheduled with Dr. McMahon early in the week to get her blood checked. We had planned to take a trip to the beach when her white blood count returned to a normal level. She was sitting on the examination table when he walked in.

Shelby, because of her medical background, had begun to take very good notes about every medicine taken, what to expect of it, and any changes she saw in Hope. Dr. McMahon announced that Hope's white blood count was about normal. He proceeded to give her clearance to go to the mall, the movies, or whatever she wanted. That was certainly good news.

"How is she doing?" he asked Shelby. "Any changes in things? Is she throwing up flecks of blood?"

Shelby intently kept writing. "Flexoblood? Is that something I don't know about? Is that a new medicine?"

We all just stared at Shelby, not sure if she was kidding or what. With the silence, she looked up and it was obvious that she was serious.

Dr. McMahon and I both started laughing. Hope gazed at her mother with that teenage "I am so embarrassed" look. "Mom, you are such a dork!"

Shelby looked at us and still didn't get it. She was so into making sure about everything the doctor said that what he just asked her flew right over her head. "What is so funny? I just asked how you spell flexoblood. Why are ya'll laughing?"

"Honey, I think what Dr. McMahon asked was have you seen any *flecks of blood*, not flexoblood."

"Yeah, Mom . . . Duh."

"Oh, be quiet, Hope. I just misunderstood what Dr. McMahon was asking. Stop laughing. It isn't funny."

We continued to have a good chuckle about the "flexoblood" until Dr. McMahon turned his attention to Hope.

"How is the hair holding up?" He walked over to Hope and began to look at her hair closely. Then he reached up and gently tugged on a few strands.

Hope's red hair came out easily, way too easily.

The good doctor seemed a little embarrassed by what had happened. He stood there in front of Hope, holding a small clump of *her* hair. Hope had a look on her face that was a combination of rage and curiosity. I half expected her to take a swing at Dr. McMahon, but then I noticed the impish grin that was never far from her lips. It was trying to get out, despite her best efforts to keep it hidden.

"Oh, I am sorry, Hope. Didn't mean to do that. Here." And he handed the clump of hair back to her!

Not too many times did I see Hope Stout stumped, but this was one of them. She stared at the clump of red hair *in the doctor's hands.*

"Gee thanks. What exactly do you want me to do with this now?" she said, her voice loud and indignant. Despite her effort to try and act mean, it didn't have much effect on Dr. McMahon.

"Just tryin' to help . . . Have fun at the beach." He then turned around and left.

From that moment on, her fear of losing her hair wasn't as bad, although we all continued to pray that somehow her hair would stay put. With that small tug of the hair, Dr. Daniel McMahon had proved to her that it was just hair.

No big deal, really.

Before Hope's chemo treatments had begun, Shelby and Wendy had taken Hope to Wendy's hairdresser who specialized in making wigs for women who were chemo patients. At first Hope protested: "I am not going to lose my hair." Shelby got her to go by telling her, "If your hair doesn't fall out, we will give the wig to Pudge to play with."

The hairdresser matched Hope's hair perfectly. Hope even fooled me by wearing the wig one night when I came home from work.

We talked for a few minutes before Hope finally asked if anything looked different about her. It was only then that I noticed the wig, and only because the hairstyle was a little different.

"You see," I said, "even your dad cannot tell the difference. If you lose your hair, nobody will notice."

"You are a typical guy," Hope replied. "You would not notice it unless it was on ESPN or the Golf Channel and Tiger Woods was wearing it."

During this week our family had another milestone that was lost in the background of Hope's illness. Austin, our oldest daughter, was scheduled to go to her college orientation at NC State University. She and I made the three-hour drive to Raleigh, North Carolina, for the two-day program. Normally, wild horses could not have kept Shelby from attending this with her oldest child, but the circumstances with Hope's illness dictated otherwise.

During the second day of the orientation, the school officials placed all the parents into two groups: one group for parents of kids attending college for the first time and the other group for veterans of the process.

There were eight people sitting at my table. We each took a turn, voicing our concerns and fears about sending our children away to college for the first time. It just so happened that I was the last one to speak.

I started out slowly, not really sure what to say. This was supposed to be a happy time and I did not want to depress everyone, but what else could I say?

"Well, our family is dealing with a slightly different circumstance besides just sending our child to college for the first time." I then went on to tell them about Hope and what we were facing. Naturally, there was a strong and sympathetic reaction from the members of my group. About the time I finished with my story, our guide gave us a break for some refreshments.

During this time a man in my group came up and introduced himself to me. I don't remember his name, but I do remember what he said.

"Mr. Stout, about seven years ago my daughter was diagnosed with acute leukemia. She was only six at the time, and we went through three bone marrow transplants. The first two didn't take, but the last one did and she beat it. She is now almost fourteen and is very healthy."

This sounds good, I thought. But what he said next made me want to hit him.

"We are very thankful that she beat this disease, but it was not without its sacrifices. I lost my job, and my wife and I got a divorce. In fact, you will probably hate me for this, but I can almost guarantee you that your marriage will not survive this. The stress a child's cancer puts on a marriage is so hard, it usually destroys the relationship. I don't tell you this to depress you, but only to warn you, one father to another. I wish somebody would have warned me. Perhaps it would have changed the outcome," he said without the least hint of emotion.

I don't remember very much more of the conversation and looking back on it now, despite my first reaction, I really do thank him. He was right about the stress part: what took place during the next four months and beyond did put enormous stress on our marriage.

But it did not break it.

Later that night after Austin and I had returned from Raleigh, I sat down with Shelby to tell her about the orientation and how excited Austin was about going to North Carolina State University. It felt good to talk about something positive for a change.

And then I told her about my conversation with this man.

It scared Shelby as well, but at that moment, we both agreed to work very hard to keep our marriage intact throughout this journey. Both of us have Type A personalities; we both have to be in charge. However, this situation was already largely out of our control. We were dependent on a host of medical professionals, half of whom we did not know. That night, Shelby and I resolved that our marriage would not become a statistic.

We just didn't gauge how hard it would be.

During the next ten days, Hope continued to rebound, and she

began to do things with her friends. She wanted to be treated the
same as she always was, despite the fact that she had cancer.

"I have cancer, not the plague," she told her friends.

> **"Cancer patients are just the same as other people, except
> they have a disease that can't be cured with Tylenol." —
> Hope**

She also spent a lot of time IM'ing (Instant Messaging, for those
who do not have teenagers) her friends. She even showed me one
from a classmate of hers who asked her a point-blank question, as
kids often do.

"Hope, are you going to die?"

When I read the question, it made me very angry. What kind of
kid would ask that? I held my emotions in check and turned to face
Hope who did not seem the least bit upset. To the contrary, she had
that impish smile on her face.

"Well, what did you say back to him?" I asked my daughter.

"I told him, 'Yes, I am going to die . . . someday. And so are you.
I also told him, 'I will outlive you by a mile.'"

She handled that pretty well, I thought.

16

The Battle of the Crutches

Each morning the hair watch continued. When I got up to go to work, I checked the pillow. Each day, there was no hair there, other than a few strands of cat fur. And since we don't have any red-headed cats, I figured it wasn't Hope's. Shelby bought Hope this special shampoo that chemo patients use, which is supposed to strengthen the hair roots.

Prior to this experience, I often wondered why cancer patients lost their hair from chemo. I really didn't understand until Dr. McMahon told me.

"The kind of chemo Hope is taking kills all cells, particularly the most active ones. Those would be cancer cells and the cells in our hair, which are constantly growing—well in most people's cases anyway. Consequently, the chemo has a dramatic effect on them. The same holds true for cancer cells. They are the most active and the chemo seeks them out and kills them."

Chemo lesson 101: Why hair falls out.

Because there was a three-week break in her chemo treatments, and since she was feeling so well, the much-anticipated beach trip was planned for the weekend of July 25. Austin had been invited to visit some friends in Ohio and had flown up there a couple of days earlier. Wendy and Tom gave us their beach house to stay at for a few days, and Holly invited Griffin Kenemer, a friend of hers from the youth group at our church. Griff, as he is called by about everyone who knows him, is one of those kids who is always making people laugh. He has mischievous eyes and is usually up to something most of the time.

Holly and he are pretty much opposites, both in looks (his hair is as dark as hers is blonde) and personalities (Griff openly challenges the status quo and Holly is much more likely to stay in line). However, Griff and Hope were very much alike in the personality department. Both were constantly playing the clown. Griff didn't treat Hope any differently than he had before she got cancer, and you could tell she loved that about him.

Hope also invited Emily, and we took off to spend a few days at Holden Beach.

As we left the house that day, it did not occur to us that this would be the last time Hope Elizabeth Stout would get to come to the beach.

After getting settled in, Holly and Griff took the girls over to the shops at Holden Beach, and Shelby and I stayed at the house. Hope was told to be careful using her knee, which was full of disease. And the biopsy took a pretty good chunk out of it as well.

"It is okay to walk on it, Hope. Just do not overdo it," Dr. McMahon had cautioned. "I don't want you to break the bone. That would complicate your treatment. Use the crutches as much as you can, but if you feel like walking without them, that is also okay. However, if you feel pain, use the crutches."

The issue about how much to use the leg became one of the first battles for Shelby and me.

Hope had insisted on leaving her crutches at home when they went shopping and I had sided with her. Shelby, being the mother and the one with a medical background, felt differently, so an argument ensued between mother and daughter.

"Mom, I am fine . . . I hate those things. They make my arms hurt, and it is much easier to get around without them. I will take it easy, I promise," Hope had said pleadingly.

Shelby was not so sure. "Hope, Dr. McMahon said not to overdo it. Just take the crutches with you, and if you need them, at least they will be there."

"Dad, please tell her it is okay."

As both pairs of eyes looked to me for the final judgment on this issue, I knew this would not end well either way for me, no matter what I decided.

Unfortunately the decision I made was based on a healthy Hope, not the one with cancer. The coach in me came out: Always push hard. A little pain will make you stronger had been my motto.

These are good, solid coaching tactics, right? Unless, of course, you have cancer in your leg. Then it is just plain dumb.

Nevertheless, I told Hope what she wanted to hear. "As long as you don't overdo it, you can leave the crutches here. Dr. McMahon said it was okay to use your leg as much as you can. Just be careful and hurry back."

Holly and Griff both agreed to watch out for Hope and off they went, leaving me alone with Shelby. The second they left, the mortar fire started. And as I realized later, she was right.

"You do not know what you are talking about," Shelby hissed at me as soon as the kids were out the door. "This isn't some sports injury she has; it is cancer. What if she steps wrong and breaks that leg? What then? If that happens, I am never speaking to you again!"

I tried to assure her that Hope was old enough to know what she could and could not do, but it had little effect. Shelby did not speak to me or sit still until the kids returned an hour or so later.

We were both relieved, but Hope could not help but throw some more gas on the fire.

"Look, Mom. My leg is still attached. Nothing happened. Quit worrying about me," Miss Smart Aleck said, bringing the standard giggle from Emily.

And the death ray glare at me from Shelby.

Reflections of a Mother

You can see the differences between a dad's approach to illness and a mom's in this chapter. I was always overly cautious; Stuart was more likely to allow Hope extra leeway.

This tension is probably part of the conflict that leads to divorce, which the man had warned Stuart about. Certainly Stuart's and my relationship was tested during our child's terminal cancer.

We never expected such a tragedy when we met in 1980. We lived in the same apartment complex in Charlotte, North Carolina. The first day I saw him I had just returned home from my medical assisting job at Eastover OBGYN. His apartment was right above the mailboxes for our unit. As I was checking my mailbox I saw this grungy-looking guy who had been lifting weights on his patio. I saw him put the weights back on the bar and begin pouring out the charcoal for the fire he was preparing. As he did so, a briquette of charcoal bounced out of the small grill and fell off the patio, hitting me on the shoulder. I looked up as he was looking down. He apologized for the black streak on my white uniform, and as I looked at him, it never occurred to me that this was my prince, my future husband. Some start, huh?

We both come from close-knit families, and that is just one of the many things we loved about each other. Also, we both come from very strong Christian backgrounds, and that was how we wanted to start our marriage, with God at the center of everything.

A few years after we were married we dreamed of having kids and raising them together, and that came to fruition when our first child, a daughter, was born. Austin Dean Stout arrived on January 11, 1985. We loved our little girl so much and enjoyed being parents immensely. So much so that we wanted another child. And Holly Ann Stout was born October 30, 1987. We were now the parents of two blonde cuties!

A few years later, we decided to have our third child, and why not try for a boy this time? After all, we had begun to run out of names for girls, and naturally Stuart wanted a son. He had always wanted our first son to be named Andrew William.

However, we decided to pick another girl's name, just in case. I remember we were discussing this one day in our bedroom and frankly we were stumped. What Stuart liked, I didn't—and vice versa. I remember sitting on my hope chest, which had been a gift from Stuart before we got married. HOPE is carved in very large letters right on the front.

"Hey," I said, "how about Hope?"

I told Stuart that Hope would be a great name and this chest could be an heirloom for her to have later in life.

And he agreed.

So that was it. Hope would be her name, just in case it was another girl. As the day of our third child's birth approached, the jokester Stuart started replying, "I *hope* it is a boy" or "I *hope* this is the last one" or "I *hope* it comes on time," when we were asked about the third child's name.

Well, baby number three did arrive on time on March 4, 1991, and the tiny person was, of course, another girl.

From the very beginning Hope Elizabeth Stout was different from the other two girls. She was a redhead, and the nurse announced that the second she was born: "Well, hello there, little red!"

Three girls kept us very busy and we now wonder, where did the time go? It seemed like Austin went from diapers one day to a fast-pitch softball player and senior in high school the next; Holly was one day dressing up as a princess and all of a sudden she was a traveling competitive cheerleader; and Hope was toddling around in her Crazy Coupe one minute and the next a rising middle schooler who loved her friends, her electric scooter, her cats, basketball, and shopping.

Life is so precious. Life is so sweet. Life moves all too fast. All those years seem like they took place yesterday.

17

Hair Today, Gone Tomorrow

Early the next morning, I got up and read my devotional. Then, as now, God speaks to us in so many ways. This would be one of them. Coincidentally (or not so coincidententally), the devotion for that day was entitled "Hair Today, Gone Tomorrow." It was about a lady who owned a store that sold wigs.

"Okay, God, You now have my full attention."

The author was recounting an event that took place in her store when the owner was helping a lady wearing a bandana get fitted for a wig. The writer watched as the store owner meticulously worked until she found just the right wig for the cancer patient. The lady left the store, wearing the wig proudly, no longer having to worry about people staring at her bald head.

"I want to commend you on what you just did," the author told the store owner. "That woman left here a different person. You should be very proud of that."

"Well, I kinda know what she is going through," the store owner said, pulling the wig from her own bald head. "I am going through the same thing."

God was telling me that this was the day when Hope's red hair would finally come out.

Hope had already admitted that she was not brushing her hair much anymore. The impending loss of her hair, which was critical to her several weeks ago, wasn't as important now. Still, we held out hope that her hair would be the exception to the rule.

No such luck as it turned out. And once again, God provided some humor to ease the disappointment. It happened over breakfast.

When I am at the beach, I get up early and make breakfast for the family. On this day I fried bacon and sausage, made some coffee, and enjoyed the magnificent view of the Intracoastal Waterway from the Reeders' kitchen. The alluring aroma of the brewing coffee and sizzling bacon roused Shelby out of bed, followed soon by Griff and Holly. We were all enjoying a cup of coffee when Hope and Emily finally made it to the kitchen.

Everyone took their seats at the table as I was finishing up with the last batch of pancakes, which was the special request from Hope. I sat down beside her as she began to pour the syrup onto the steaming stack of hotcakes. She looked very hungry and was about to dive into the stack when I noticed it.

A *big* shock of red hair was hanging on to the side of her head. All that was keeping the hair from hitting the plate was static electricity.

At this split second, I realized the hair had finally given in to the chemo. This was the moment we had been dreading. There might soon be wailing and gnashing of teeth, but, thinking quickly, I decided to play the humor card. I prayed it would work; there wasn't much time to ponder what I would say because the hair clump was about to hit her plate.

"Yo, Cuz. You might want to get that ball of hair outta the way before it flops down into your pancakes," I said without missing a beat. I took a bite of sausage as the rest of the table took notice.

Hope reached up and pulled the clump of hair off her head. A whole range of emotions crossed over my youngest daughter's face—from rage, to fear, to embarrassment. For a split second, I thought my attempt at humor was going to humiliate her, which was exactly what I didn't want to happen.

And then I saw the corners of her mouth turn upward. The infamous impish grin was beginning to appear! She and I fell into a staring contest that seemed to go on for several minutes. She sat there looking at me, not saying a word, but I saw the grin fighting to overcome the frown. And then the grin won out and vintage Hope took over.

"Ha, ha, very funny, Dad. But you know, these pancakes would probably taste better with hair in them. Who cooked these anyway?"

And just like that, all the anxiety and worry over losing the hair was gone!

The whole table, particularly Griff, began to have fun with the hair loss. Less than a month after her chemo started and the Hair Watch began, the moment we had all been dreading was actually met with laughter. It truly was just hair.

"I do not want to look like one of Austin's old baby dolls or something, with half of the hair in and half out. I would rather have it all out!" Hope told her mother. After breakfast was over, Shelby called my sister to see if her hairdresser could get the rest of the hair out. The girls were planning to go straight to the salon.

But the trip never took place. Beth took one look at Hope's hair, began brushing, and in two minutes all of Hope's red hair was in small piles.

"Well, I guess we saved a trip to the hairdresser," Hope said. "I can now use the money to go shopping. Pay up please." She extended her hand to receive the expected compensation.

Instead Shelby picked up the hair and put it in a bag.

When Hope looked at her kind of funny, Shelby told Hope, "I want to keep this hair to compare to the new hair, which will be growing back once your chemo is over."

The hair Shelby saved would end up serving a much different, much more important purpose later on.

The next day we went down to the beach for some pictures. Hope and Shelby had purchased several bandanas, just in case the hair came out. Bandanas were "in" anyway, with lots of teenage girls wearing them (and a lot of guys too).

At first, Hope did not want to go to the beach. Despite having handled the hair loss fairly well, she now seemed a little hesitant to go. Holly and Griff began working on her. Finally Griff made it happen.

"If you will go, I will paint my nails," Griff said. This zany kid acted just like Hope's brother, doing all the things brothers do to torment their sisters.

"You paint your nails and I will go to the beach," Hope agreed. "But I get to pick the color."

"Done . . . What color? Pink works best for me," Griff said in a prissy voice. "Or blue."

"Nope, black is your color. Paint 'em black," Hope said.

Griffin immediately found some black nail polish the girls had. Within minutes he was proudly applying the polish to his nails.

They looked hideous, but that mattered not a whit to Griff.

After properly drying them, he buffed his nails to a shine and announced he was ready to go. We all trooped down to the beach together. This time the crutches went with us.

Since swimming was not an option for Hope, the weather had unexpectedly cooperated. Despite being the middle of July, it was an overcast day and slightly on the cool side. None of the kids expressed any interest in the water the whole time we were there, out of respect for Hope. She wore a pink bandana on that day, which would later become famous. All the kids posed for pictures in the dunes.

"Mom, we want to walk to the pier. Is that okay?" Holly asked.

"No way! That is a long way, Holly," Shelby said, and immediately Hope began to howl.

"It is only about a half mile . . . I can make that easily. And without the crutches."

Here would be argument number two about the crutches. Once again, Hope appealed to her dad to let her go. Once again, I was in the middle of the disagreement with no way to make everyone happy.

An argument ensued involving Shelby, Hope, and me. The "discussion" went back and forth for about fifteen minutes and Hope began to get very upset. In fact, she started crying.

"All I want to do is walk to the pier. I can't go swimming or much of anything else. I just want to do this," she wailed through her tears.

Seeing her daughter so upset and realizing her frustration, Shelby reluctantly gave in under one condition: when they got to the pier, we would come pick them up in the car. They agreed and took off—without the crutches.

Once again, Shelby and I got into it, big time. She lit into me again about Hope walking that far on the uneven sand even though she had agreed to it. We went back to the house and waited impatiently. In about thirty minutes Holly called, and we jumped in the car and drove to the pier. When we pulled into the parking lot, we saw Griff carrying Hope piggyback style. Both were laughing.

"See, Mom, I made it and no broken bones. Once again, I am right and you are wrong."

While it was a relief to see her okay, it was not until some months later that Holly told us that about halfway to the pier, Hope stopped everyone. She said her knee was really hurting, but did not want to call Mom.

"She will kill me and never let me do anything," Hope had said. Griffin then volunteered to carry Hope the rest of the way to the pier. After that incident, Hope didn't push us too much about the crutches. They stayed with her much of the rest of the time she was able to walk.

18

The Methotrexate Mombo

On Wednesday, July 30, we went back to the hospital for round two of Hope's chemotherapy treatments. The first round of cisplatin was designed as a shotgun blast of chemo to kill all active cells, cancer and otherwise. The next treatment was methotrexate, which is more of a rifle shot that specifically hits the cancer cells, rather than affecting the healthy ones.

This drug also had fewer side effects. Basically a near-fatal dosage of methotrexate is administered and then the nurses immediately begin to flush the drug out of the patient's system. Once the "meth" level is low enough, the patient can go home. There would be three treatments of methotrexate after which the doctors would do another round of tests to determine how well Hope's cancer had responded to the chemo.

We were given protocols on all the chemo drugs that would be administered to her along with the side effects. Methotrexate, for most patients, consisted of about a three to four-day hospital stay.

Hope's treatment began on Wednesday. Dr. McMahon came in after the methotrexate was administered and the flushing process had started. He took Hope's blood readings and was amazed at how much her levels had dropped in less than twelve hours.

"That is pretty good progress, Hope. You still have a long way to go, but you may be out of here by Saturday or Sunday." He paused as he saw her eyes light up, and then added. "But don't get your hopes up too high. There is usually a slower drop during the next twenty-four hours or so. Just get comfortable."

"I want outta here by Saturday. Be sure to make it happen!"

And with that, we began the wait.

Naturally, it did not go as planned. Hope had always done things differently during her life, so we should have expected that this would not go according to plan either.

Every morning the nurses would come and test Hope's blood to see if the meth level had dropped enough. After first dropping rapidly, over the next few days, her level stubbornly remained about the same.

There is only so much TV you can watch and so many video games you can play when you are hospitalized for a long period of time. Very shortly we went through all of the videos the hospital had. Boredom set in and for a kid as active as Hope, this was sheer torture.

That coupled with the fact that she knew her friends were out in the sunshine enjoying the summer while she was stuck in the hospital fighting cancer really brought her spirits down.

Also, her right leg was not moving as easily anymore. Getting around became more of an issue. Other than getting up to go to the bathroom, she had no interest in walking up and down the hall. In fact, I could not even get her to go downstairs in a wheelchair for some fresh air; she only did this about twice during all of her hospital stays.

It was mostly just sitting in the room and looking outside at the beautiful summer weather, which seemed to be mocking us.

After three straight days of this, Hope really became upset. She cried a lot and we became very concerned about her mental health. She refused to see any of her friends although they wanted to come by and see her.

Looking back on this now, I really did not realize how much this must have worn on Hope. She didn't really talk about it a lot, but I don't know how she handled it. Age twelve is that netherland between being a kid and becoming an adult. Hope had a whole new set of circumstances thrust on her that would be difficult for any adult.

Finally, after spending the weekend in the hospital, on Monday morning—six days later—the level had dropped to an acceptable level and we were allowed to come home. Within a day or two of being home, Hope had returned to her old self, but a new issue was now present.

Back in the early summer before Hope got sick, she had looked forward to going to school on the first day and being a part of her cheerleading squad. Now she could not do that.

The start of school also affected Shelby badly. A week earlier, she had gotten really upset that she was not out buying school supplies for Hope, like all the other mothers.

Just before school started, the cheerleading squad was to meet at the football stadium for their team picture.

Hope went with Shelby for the picture-taking session in her dark green cheerleading uniform with the word *Wildcats* emblazoned on the front. The uniform was trimmed in gold, and Hope was so proud of it.

It was a brutally hot day, and the pictures were taken in the full sunshine. Hope had her wig on, and she was melting in that heat as were several of the other girls. For the team picture, Hope was seated on the front row along with Gina. Despite the heat, she looked so happy and proud to be on that team!

Soon Hope began to dread the second methotrexate treatment

scheduled for August 13. The nurses told us to expect about the same hospital stay of about seven to ten days. When told that, Hope became more depressed as each day passed.

Another significant milestone was scheduled to take place right in the middle of Hope's scheduled treatment. Austin was scheduled to move in to her dorm at NC State on Saturday, August 16. It was decided that I would take Austin to school along with Holly. My sister, Beth, and my mom were also driving up to help with the move.

Shelby spent as much time as possible with Austin before she left, buying her all the essentials for her dorm room and needed school supplies. Austin and I also went out and bought a laptop computer she would need for her classes.

These preparations should have been a happy, exciting time to celebrate this major event in Austin's life. Instead, we had to focus on Hope and her treatment. While Austin understood this, it was still difficult for her. Likewise, Holly was a sophomore at Weddington High School where she had made the girls' golf team (much to my satisfaction). I tried to balance being at as many of her matches as possible with giving needed breaks to Shelby at the hospital.

Oh, and I still had to run my own insurance business and earn a living to support all of us.

Cancer didn't just strike Hope. It hit our entire family and impacted everything we did, just as Kim Barker, the social worker, had said when Hope was diagnosed.

While we were moving Austin in at North Carolina State, we had to get a piece of carpet for her dorm room and move all her stuff up four floors in the summer heat. The process took most of the day.

I dreaded having to leave her at school, but we were so busy from the moment we arrived, I forgot about it up until the time we were ready to leave.

At around four o'clock we were finally done and father and daughter stood outside her dorm. We just looked at each other. I was leaving my oldest child at school. Shelby and Hope should both be here. At that moment, I felt very cheated and despite my best efforts, began to cry.

"Dad, I will be okay, and so will Hope," Austin said, trying to comfort me. "Please don't worry about me. I am fine."

When Austin said that, I lost it. I hugged her in the parking lot of Tucker Dorm as hard as I ever had.

She responded by making a positive suggestion. "Maybe Hope can come up here next week when she gets out of the hospital. We don't start classes until next Wednesday." We got on the phone with Shelby and Hope who were at the hospital, and Austin told her little sister how much she wanted her to come to Raleigh to see her dorm room.

"If these prison guards will ever let me out of here, I will be there," Hope assured her older sister. "Of course, Mom will be with me and will rearrange your room."

Hope did get to break out of the hospital that Monday. She and her mom drove to Raleigh on Wednesday and got to see Austin's room. Hope felt good enough to look around the campus some, including the bookstore where she bought an NC State sweatshirt.

The good news was Hope's treatments appeared to be working. Her right knee had really swollen up and become very hard. At the same time, Hope's calf had become very small, due to her inactivity, and coupled with the largeness of her knee, this was quite noticeable.

At first we were concerned, but Dr. McMahon explained that as bone cancer dies, it typically calcifies and gets hard.

"The fact that her right knee is that hard tells me a lot of the cancer has died. We will know for sure in a couple of weeks when we do the tests to see how the chemo is doing."

Reflections of a Mother

On August 14, around mid-morning, Dr. McMahon came in and told me there were some new spots on the chest X-rays they had taken the day before, as they always did when Hope came in for treatments. He said they had scheduled a CAT scan for that afternoon. Dr. McMahon seemed very concerned and it scared me to death. Stuart was at lunch with some clients but was coming by afterward to send me home for some rest. I was exhausted, and as soon as he arrived, I snapped at him. Stuart could tell I was beat, and as I left the room to go home, thankfully my husband made a suggestion.

He said to stop by the hospital chapel on my way out.

I had visited the chapel at Carolinas Medical many times before, just stopping in for a moment here and there to send up a quick prayer for the day. Stuart was right: I needed to go there again.

I entered the chapel and thankfully discovered that I was all alone. As I knelt down, numb and scared, I prayed to God, *Why would You do this? We have prayer chains going all over the world, and we are not seeing any good results.*

Then I opened my eyes and for some reason looked to the right side of the chapel where there are three stained-glass windows I had not noticed in such detail before. In the window next to me was a girl about Hope's height who had injured legs and was on crutches. The girl had red hair, parted in the middle just like Hope's, and she was standing next to a man who was the "Beloved Physician." She was being healed by Him!

What took my breath away was the name of the window. It was called "The Hope Window." I kid you not! The word *hope* appears four times on this window. My eyes filled with tears as I looked at the beautiful colors of the stained glass.

That was my sign from God that He was going to heal my beautiful, fiery redhead. What a feeling it was for a mother who was in complete despair several minutes earlier.

As I drove Stuart's Cadillac home, I opened the sunroof to get some fresh air. Stuart loved this car, which was really the first one he had ever really wanted. Most of his life he had driven boring company cars.

His Cadillac, which he called "Pearl" because of the color, was a sleek, fast car that was very comfortable to travel in and had all the extras. He kept it so clean, you could eat off the floors. This car was his "baby," and when the family rode in it, we all knew to make sure not to spill anything.

I had driven it quite a bit and always enjoyed having the sunroof open, but I always forgot to close it when I got home. Many times he scolded me about that but I kept forgetting.

On the ride home, despite my time in the chapel, I quickly lost the faith I had gained as I remembered Dr. McMahon's statement that some spots on the X-ray were suspicious.

After arriving home, I went to bed and cried myself to sleep, but not before begging God to save my child. About three hours later, I was awakened by a phone call from Stuart.

"I have great news," he said. "The CAT scan they just did actually shows that the existing tumors in the lungs are shrinking. Whatever was there on the chest X-ray is not there now. Dr. M considers this significant progress."

Stuart was adamant about that, telling me that he had pinned down Dr. McMahon pretty hard on that point. I felt like God had understood my despair and His grace had come when I cried out. We were blessed that day, and after his phone call, I was so relieved that I went back to sleep.

I didn't even hear the violent thunderstorm that hit about twenty minutes later. Once I woke up from my nap, however, it suddenly hit me.

Did I remember to close the sunroof to Stuart's car?

Panicked, I ran outside and my heart fell as I saw the sunroof wide open. Although the rain had stopped, water was still pouring down the driveway, so I knew we had a gully washer as they say down here in the South. I peered into the car through the sunroof and saw large puddles of water about two inches deep covering the carpet!

Panicked by all that water, I called Rick Smith, our next-door neighbor who had fed our cats when we were at the hospital. He just laughed, told me not to worry, and then brought over his Wet-Vac. He sucked up nearly two inches of rainwater out of that car! By the time Rick was finished, the floors were completely dry. I told him he had saved me from an ugly divorce.

I debated whether to tell Stuart what had happened, but I figured he would find out sooner or later, so I told him anyway, figuring he was going to blow a gasket.

Instead, he just laughed. "Now maybe you will remember to close the sunroof" is all he said.

Prior to Hope's diagnosis, this would have been a huge deal and he would have fretted over whether the car was ruined or not. Now, he just shrugged it off.

It is amazing how much our perspective changed on June 27, 2003, when the word *cancer* was first uttered. Those material things that were important to us like cars, TV, and the latest clothes really didn't matter much anymore.

Hope's recovery was all that mattered.

19

Fore, Lord!

On Tuesday, August 26, Tom Reeder, Bruce Mullan, and a host of others scheduled a golf tournament to raise money to offset some of the expenses of Hope's treatment. Several weeks earlier, when Tom and Bruce had asked our permission to hold this tournament, Shelby and I had felt honored, and yet a little uncomfortable. While we were quite humbled that our friends would think enough of us to do this, the fact that we were the subjects of it felt strange.

One day at lunch, I made the mistake of telling these guys how we felt.

"Okay you, listen up!" Bruce said emphatically, the emotion evident in his eyes. "There are so many of your friends hurting for your family right now, we *want* to do this. We *have* to do something!"

"All you need to do is show up," Tom assured me. We are going to take care of the rest. We want your whole family there—in particular Miss Hope. Just don't worry about this. We've got it under control."

Frankly, the reality of our situation forced Shelby and me to allow the tournament to happen. My new consulting business had just been beginning to get off the ground before the morning of June 27, 2003. Like most people who start a business, it was my main focus. However, with those chilling words from Dr. Kneisl, chasing dollar bills became much less of a priority. Fortunately for me, I had good friends who realized this and took steps to make sure our family would have some financial resources to fall back on if needed.

A week before the event, I received a phone call from Bruce. He sounded really weird. I asked Bruce, who is normally very chatty on the phone, if he felt okay.

"Of course I am. I just want to be sure you guys are coming next Tuesday."

"Sure we are. Hope is also planning to be there, assuming she feels okay. So far, so good."

"Good. We are expecting a . . . uh . . . decent turnout."

From the odd tone in my friend's voice, I could tell something was up.

"Good. Did you fill out the foursomes?" I asked.

"Yeah, uh huh. We didn't have much problem doing that. Just plan on being there early, okay? We may want you and Shelby to say a few words to kick things off. If Hopester could be there when things start, that would be cool too. We are also having a dinner afterwards."

Normally Bruce wants to chit-chat and talk about golf or what is happening at work. Now he sounded as if he was preoccupied or something. I became concerned and my first thought was: they cannot get enough guys to play and are embarrassed to say so.

Several weeks before, when Tom and Bruce had begun planning this golf tournament, they had thought thirty-two to forty players would be a good turnout. Since they were both sales and marketing types, the guys had set a goal to raise about five to eight thousand dollars, which would have gone a long way to offset most of our medical expenses. Now I wondered if they were having problems.

"You sure everything is okay? Do I need to help out?"

Bruce cut me off immediately. "Everything is taken care of. You do not need to do anything but show up. . . . Is that clear? We do not need your help!"

I felt as if he had snapped my head off, which was not like him at all—and he wasn't kidding either.

"Easy, big fella . . . I get it. Don't stroke out. We will just show up."

"Good. See you next Tuesday. If I need anything from you, I will call. Otherwise, plan on being at Firethorne Country Club around noon. We are planning to start the tournament around one o'clock. We need you guys there to say a few words around twelve forty-five."

I got very little more information out of either Bruce or Tom. In fact, their silence began to bug me. Putting on a golf tournament, even a charity-type event like this one, is hard work. I figured that Tom and Bruce had their hands full but didn't want me to worry about it. Given what we were dealing with, I let it go.

Before leaving for the tournament that Tuesday morning, I checked on Hope. She was still sleeping, which was good. Unfortunately, she was getting more and more uncomfortable each passing day. Her right knee was very swollen, which made it difficult for her to get the knee into a position where it didn't hurt. She was using crutches because she was barely able to put any weight on her leg.

As I was walking out the door Shelby said, "Tell everybody that we will try to be there around twelve thirty, but if Hope doesn't feel up to it, we will probably wait until the afternoon. It is supposed to be very hot today . . . I know you want her and Emily to ride around the course on her golf cart, but we will have to wait and see. She cannot be out in this heat very long."

"No problem," I said. "Her golf cart is at the club. It will be sitting right there as you pull into the parking lot at Firethorne." The night before, Bryan Forbis had hauled Hope's personalized golf cart over to the course. His daughter Blair was one of Austin's oldest friends. Austin and Blair first met when they were in preschool at our church and had been buddies ever since.

When I left the house on August 26 for the golf tournament, I prayed that Hope would feel well enough to come out that day. It was nine thirty and already very hot. There was a heat advisory according to the local radio station that I listen to, WBT. On the way to the course, I prayed that God would enable me to soak in the day's events and not be uncomfortable that this tournament was being held for our family. But when I turned into the parking lot, it suddenly became clear to me why Tom and Bruce had been acting so weird the past few weeks.

Firethorne Country Club has a large parking lot. If there were forty players or so, it would not have been 25 percent full.

I could not find a parking space anywhere!

I drove to the street and parked my car. As I walked up toward the clubhouse, it became obvious that all these people were here for this event, which had been dubbed "The Hope Stout Miracle Golf Classic." The first two people I saw were Tom and Bruce. Both had smiles a mile wide.

"You have got to be kiddin' me. Are all these people playing in this?" I asked.

Tom came up and hugged me. With tears in his eyes, he said "Stu, when Bruce sent out the e-mail to the thirty-two guys we thought might play, this thing exploded. We started getting calls from everybody. We called Howard Nifong and asked if we could use Firethorne for the event. He donated the course for the whole day. We have 128 players coming and have had to turn away folks because we ran out of carts."

While I was standing there with tears running down my face,

he continued. "That's how much these people love you guys. We have friends of yours here from everywhere, from Tennessee and Jacksonville, Florida, and listen to this: Your cousin Roger heard about it and flew in from Japan. Nathan is bringing him over today. He got into Greensboro last night."

My cousin Roger Brown was in the marine corps, stationed in Okinawa. Returning to Japan following his discharge, he met a Japanese woman whom he fell in love with and married. The couple stayed in Japan, and Roger went back to school, graduating with a doctorate in Japanese history. Now he was teaching at a local university. Imagine, an American marine teaching Japanese history. Weird, huh?

At twelve forty-five, Tom and Bruce told the crowd to head to their carts so the tournament could get started. Tom called the group to order and welcomed everyone to the event.

The scene in front of me was a kaleidoscope of our life. There were people who were clients and competitors, friends from high school and college, people we had met eighteen years earlier from our two years living in Tampa, Florida, and many members of our church. There were also many people whom I did not know but who had heard about Hope's diagnosis and simply wanted to help out.

At no point in my life have I felt such a range of intense emotions.

It is critical to understand that before Hope was diagnosed, we were caught up in the race. (The term *rat race* comes to mind but that would be unfair to the rats; at least they have a purpose: to scavenge and survive.) We were focused *only* on what was happening in our lives. How much money could we make? Was our furniture out-of-date? Was the car in need of replacement? The Stouts wanted to keep up with the Joneses, or at least keep them in sight.

Additionally and more disappointingly was how we showed our faith. We wore our faith a lot like our clothes, adjusting it according to the climate of our lives. When it was warm and sunny, not much faith would come out of the closet. If rainy weather arrived, we put on a little more, but just enough to ward off the wetness. In cold and stormy weather, we dug a little deeper for something heavier, but always returned the heavy stuff back to the closet when the storm passed and the weather got better.

We then resumed our all-important pursuit of prosperity.

Simply put, we were "Convenient Christians."

June 27, 2003, had changed all that.

As I scanned all of those faces, my emotions again got the better of me. Tom asked me to say a few words and through my tears, I told them how much this meant to our family. I could see that many of these guys, despite getting ready to play a round of golf, were also fighting back tears.

Thankfully, Tom and Bruce came up to go over the rules, which rescued me from some serious crying. And the tournament began.

My cousin Roger rode in my cart so we could catch up; it had been several years since we had seen each other, and I really enjoyed that special time together.

When we were playing the twelfth hole, Shelby called to tell me that Hope was coming, despite not feeling all that great. However, because of the heat, she was not going to ride around in her cart and would instead just come to the dinner.

When the tournament was over, we arrived back at the pro shop, and I saw Shelby sitting in the car with Hope and Emily. Her mom had given her permission to get out of school early so she could go with Hope to the golf tournament.

It was brutally hot; you broke into a sweat just standing around. I jumped into the air-conditioned car with Hope.

"Dad, are all these people here for the tournament?" she asked, wide-eyed.

"Believe it or not, yes. There were 128 golfers and a bunch more wanted to play, but they ran out of room."

I watched my daughter's eyes as she took in the scene.

She was having the same reaction I had when I arrived that morning, and I could see it was overwhelming to her as well.

"Hope, can you believe this many people came out to support us? You know what they are calling this tournament, don't you? The Hope Stout Miracle Golf Classic. Kinda cool, huh? You got your own tournament!"

We continued to watch as the players were returning to the clubhouse after putting their clubs in their cars. Everyone was drenched in sweat.

"Can you make it in okay or do you need some help?"

"Me and Emily are coming in soon. We are waiting on Mom who is of course yakkin' away with somebody," Hope said, nodding toward her mother.

I looked over and saw that my wife was in conversation with Mike Schaefer and Bob Livingston. Mike, as I mentioned earlier, lives in Knoxville, Tennessee, and Bob in Jacksonville, Florida. Both of these guys started their insurance careers with me back before Shelby and I had gotten married. I could not believe they had come to Charlotte for this.

About forty-five minutes later, after dinner was finished, Bruce pulled me aside and asked if Hope could make an appearance during the awards ceremony, so I went to check on her. Hope had come into the clubhouse while dinner was being served but had begun to feel light-headed. She had been escorted to a small parlor down the hall, which has several chairs and a couch. Shelby, Emily, and Holly, who had just arrived from golf practice, were sitting with her. Some of the staff at Firethorne had taken food to the girls and they were eating.

I found Hope lying on the couch in this parlor.

"She just got too hot, but I think she is okay now," Shelby explained.

"Hope, if you can, they want you to come in for the ceremony. If not, that is cool. It is up to you," I told her.

"Uh, Dad, I don't know. I am not feeling that good right now. Maybe in a few minutes." She did look really pale and I became concerned, which she quickly noticed.

"I am fine. Go back in there with all those stinky men. I will see you in a few minutes," she snorted at me, bringing a giggle from Emily.

That was more like it!

As I walked back into the ballroom, the awards were underway. All the winners were getting their trophies when suddenly loud applause started from the back of the room. Everyone turned to look.

Hope Elizabeth Stout was walking across the floor with Emily in tow. She was using her crutches, but she was striding purposely up to the podium. Everyone was on their feet. And virtually everyone was in tears.

Two big stuffed chairs were brought in for the girls, and Hope took her seat, looking somewhat sheepish as the ovation continued.

Shelby and I stood at the back of the room with Holly, taking it all in. The three of us held on to each other, crying.

After the lengthy ovation ended, it was Tom's unfortunate duty to speak. He told Hope how much he loved her and how much everyone who was at the tournament thought of her and her family. She did not speak; she just sat there in that big chair. The mood lightened somewhat as the winners were announced and the door prizes, which were numerous, were handed out.

Despite the intense heat, the event was a huge success. Over thirty-five thousand dollars was raised, way more than enough for our medical expenses. After most of the crowd had left, I told Tom and Bruce that they were on to something. "This needs to be an annual event where we pick out a family and help them out, just as you helped us."

The following year that is exactly what we did. The Hope Stout Golf Classic is held every year and is now helping out a lot of families.

Reflections of a Mother

Hope's golf cart was a gift from my brother, Stan Shull. About three weeks earlier, Stan told me that he had a surprise for Hope. Before he gave it to her, he wanted to make sure it was okay with Stuart, because the surprise was pretty big, according to Stan.

"What is it?" Stuart asked Stan. "We do not need another dog. If it has four legs and fur, the answer is no."

Hope had been working on Stuart and me to let her get a dog. Not just any dog, mind you. Hope had insisted on rescuing one from the pound. And she wanted a big outdoor dog, like a lab or beagle. We were beginning to weaken, for obvious reasons, despite the fact that we already had a houseful of critters.

Stan assured Stuart it was not a dog or anything with four legs and fur, and so he agreed to let my brother bring Hope's gift.

Later that day, we heard a horn blow, and as we opened the garage door, Stan came down our driveway with a trailer carrying a personalized gas-powered golf cart with SpongeBob floor mats and a purple fuzzy steering wheel cover and fuzzy dice to match. Hope was ecstatic!

She was all smiles as Uncle Stan showed her how to operate the newly installed AM/FM/CD player and speakers. Hope didn't wait for any further instruction, and before we knew it, she asked me to jump in with her and we took off.

"How on earth did you come up with this idea?" I asked my brother.

"Last Christmas, after she had opened all her presents, Hope told me that another Christmas had passed and she didn't get what she wanted. I asked her what that was and she said, 'A golf cart.' I asked her if she was serious and she said yes. She told me she needed a golf cart to ride around the neighborhood. I think she was kiddin' around, sort of, but when she got cancer, I thought this might be a good way for her to get around and see her buddies.

"So I put up a sign at work telling about her cancer and my desire to get her a golf cart. I asked the guys to give up one cup of coffee per week and donate it to the Golf Cart Fund. Within two weeks I had more than enough for the cart, the stereo, and all the decals. In fact, money is still coming in. I will send it to Hope, and she can use it to buy gas for the cart or some CDs."

This golf cart became a Godsend for Hope. She could again get around the neighborhood, even better than before. Everyone knew when Hope and Emily were out and about. The stereo was blasting, and the queen wave greeted anyone who was walking through the neighborhood.

Hope named the cart Little Ricky, since Austin had named her car Lucy.

She was able to scoot back and forth to Emily's house up the street, and although we didn't know it then, Little Ricky would come in really handy in October.

20

Chemo Sucks, Part Two

The following Thursday I took Hope to Dr. McMahon's office for her final checkup before our planned Labor Day Weekend at Holden Beach. We had been looking forward to this trip for several weeks and had in fact planned Hope's last chemo treatment around it so that her white blood count would be normal enough to go. Because of the chemo treatments, infection was always a concern since her white blood count dropped so much.

After her visit to Dr. McMahon, at which point he said her white blood count was normal enough to proceed with our planned beach trip, I surprised Hope with a visit to The Cheesecake Factory, one of her favorite restaurants. She was starving and it was so nice to see her appetite return. Even though people were waiting in line, the hostess, seeing Hope's crutches, seated us immediately.

"Rats. I was ready to play the 'cancer card,' but that lady beat me to it," Hope said indignantly.

"I don't know what you mean. They seated us because I am a very important insurance executive. That hostess recognized me immediately and knew not to make me mad. And here we sit, ready to eat."

"Right, Dad. You go on dreamin'."

Hope's eyes were much bigger than her stomach, but that didn't matter to me. It was so nice to spend some time with her that wasn't hospital- or doctor-related. She seemed completely normal, except for the crutches leaning against the table. We had a great meal and brought enough food home for dinner as well.

The next morning, a nurse from Kid's Path was coming to our house to check Hope's white blood count. Before she arrived, Shelby told me that Hope's head felt warm. She was still asleep when we went in to check on her. Reaching down, I put my hand on my daughter's forehead, something I had done a thousand times before. Sure enough, her head felt warm to me also.

"Maybe it is because she is covered up. You know how she sleeps," I said, recalling the many nights Shelby and I had to unwrap Hope's favorite blanket from around her head. Every child has some strange sleeping habit, and Hope's was falling asleep with her blanket over her head. Oftentimes, the blanket made her head sweat to the point where her hair would be sopping wet.

Her bed was cluttered with all types of stuffed animals. In fact, there was barely enough room for Hope between the stuffed animals and the real ones—Pudge and Peanut, who both lay sleeping at the foot of the bed.

Truthfully though, I knew she had a fever. With her low white blood count, this was not good news.

As we stood over her bed, we took turns gently feeling Hope's head, hoping that we had imagined the fever or that it was miraculously going down now that we had moved the blanket.

"You know we are probably not going to the beach now," Shelby said to me very softly.

With that, Hope's eyes shot open; she had been playing possum.

"Yes, we are too! I am fine. I am just way down here under these covers. Let me get out from under them and you will see," she said very loudly.

Despite Hope's protests, Shelby got the thermometer and took her temperature. It was around 101. That high a fever would be a concern for anyone, but especially for a chemotherapy patient. Hope became very upset. She knew what was going on: she had a fever and that would keep her from going to the beach. She immediately began to beg us to let her go anyway.

"Look, even if this fever doesn't go away, which it will, I can just sit on the couch at Gran's and take it easy. If I have a fever here, I can have it there just as well," she pleaded.

Around nine o'clock the Kid's Path nurse arrived. She checked Hope over and then took her temperature.

There was no change.

"Try again," Hope said to the nurse. "I told my mom and dad I was all bundled up and had two cats lying on me. I don't feel hot at all. Wait a few minutes and try again." Seeing how badly Hope wanted this, the nurse agreed, waited for a few more minutes, and took it again.

The temperature was still 101.

"Hope, I know you are disappointed, but this is very serious. Your white blood count is very low, and you are susceptible to any germ that comes along. I am sure Dr. McMahon will want to see you today. I am going to call his office with these results. I am so sorry," the nurse said firmly but soothingly. She left the room, and we heard her talking to Michelle at Dr. McMahon's office.

Hope began to cry very hard. "This is so unfair . . . Why is this happening? I just want to go to the beach. Why won't God let me do that? Nothing seems to be working out for me."

Shelby and I tried to calm her down, but it did no good. She pushed us away and told us to leave her alone. She was right: it was unfair. All the kid wanted was to go to the beach with her family. Cancer, however, had other ideas. We had been looking forward to Labor Day weekend since right after the July Fourth trip. As the chemotherapy treatments had continued, Hope had made sure that Dr. McMahon scheduled them so she could go. As recently as yesterday, we thought we were home free.

When the nurse returned, she announced that Michelle wanted Hope to come to CMC as soon as possible. "Don't mess around with this fever. We need to get her on some antibiotics ASAP," she said. "And plan on staying at the hospital for a few days too."

That news sent Hope into another fit. It was bad enough to miss Labor Day weekend at the beach, but to have to spend it at the hospital? The crying turned to sobbing. There was little we could do but let her get it out.

Reflections of a Mother

Hope had hated the hospital from the very first day, but what kid likes it? The smells, the food, the medicine, the IVs, you name it. She disliked peeing into "hats" (her term for the device used to measure urine output) and putting her head into the puke pan. "Why can't they use a different color rather than this puke yellow color?" she complained. "How about pink or purple?"

The Decorating Bandits helped to make these stays more bearable. Composed of Wendy, Liz, Holly, and Austin—and later The Core Club and Hope's Confirmation Group, the Bandits created themed rooms.

The first was the popular cartoon character SpongeBob SquarePants. Stuffed SpongeBobs were in every corner of the room and even on the IV pole, which Hope had quickly named Lucifer, and on the bathroom door. SpongeBob balloons were even hanging from the ceiling.

The next visit to the hospital room produced a Jimmy Buffett theme, transforming her room into a tropical paradise, complete with palm trees, a big shining sun, and parrots. Hope loved both Cancun, which she had visited a year ago, and Jimmy Buffett music. While she was in Cancun she got to swim with the dolphins, snorkel for the first time, and enjoy dancing with her two sisters at Señor Frogs, the infamous restaurant and bar chain. The Cancun theme brought back many happy memories.

The Confirmation Group provided a F.R.O.G. (Fully Rely on God) theme for her third visit. Frogs of every shape and size cavorted around the room, along with encouraging messages and posters.

Hospital visit number four was done by the Core Club. They provided rainbow and butterfly decorations, giving Hope the promise she needed from God that He would always be there for her.

One constant decoration for all the visits was a picture of Paul Walker from *The Fast and Furious*, which hung on the wall in front of her bed so she could dream about him and not cancer. Hope's room decorations became famous around the hospital; nurses would stop by just to see what the Decorating Bandits had done, whether or not they were assigned to Hope.

The last visit prior to Labor Day was a beach theme for the upcoming trip to Holden Beach.

Unfortunately, this room would be the closest Hope Stout got to the beach once the low white blood count hit.

21
The Test

The next few days were pretty uneventful. Hope's fever stubbornly refused to go away and she continued to receive antibiotics. Mainly, she was just bored. I upgraded an old laptop PC and brought it to the hospital so that Hope could get on AOL and instant-message with her friends once they were out of school. Hope slept most of the time until about three o'clock in the afternoon when she stayed on the computer almost constantly until she fell asleep each night.

She also began to take time to update the CaringBridge Web site www.caringbridge.org/nc/hope, which we had created on August 10. (We continue to update this site frequently as many people still want to know how we are doing.)

At first, Hope had been reluctant to get on the site, but after reading how Shelby and I were updating the site on a daily basis, she had taken over. It still amazes us how many people hit the site, but when Hope wrote on it, we received the most return comments.

In fact, Hope had to decipher the code she was using for a lot of our friends, particularly the ones who didn't have kids that sent IMs.

Hope's writing was dotted with IM code and she let all the "old-timers" in on it. On September 5, she wrote the following:

> LoL- NOT lots of love, LAUGH OUT LOUD.
> :)-If u look sideways, its a smiley face.
> :P-Smiley face w/ tounge sticking out. (HINT) Look sideways.
> G2G-GOT 2 GO.
> TTYL-Talk 2 U Later
> Now I think and I HOPE that covers it all... if u have any other questions ask me and Ill translate. Ok Well I G2G (GOT 2 GOOO) TTYL (TALK 2 U LATER) $~*HoPe*~$

(For some reason, Hope always started and ended her name with dollar signs when she was online. She never explained why.)

We got more comments from that entry than almost any during Hope's illness. Several of my buddies felt honored to be educated in the ways of instant-messaging by a scholar of the art.

Finally, on Wednesday, September 3, the fever broke, and we planned to hightail it out of the Hospital Hilton, as we were calling it, before returning the next day for a series of tests to tell us how the chemo was working on Hope's tumors.

When Dr. McMahon came by on Wednesday morning, instead of giving us the okay to leave, he suggested we just stay put since the PET scan was scheduled for the next day.

Positron Emission Tomography, called PET imaging or a PET scan, is a diagnostic examination that reveals physiologic images based on the detection of radiation from the emission of "positrons."

Hope glowered at her oncologist and told him in no uncertain terms that she would come back, thank you very much, and to get out of her way. Dr. McMahon gave her a wry smile and said, "See you tomorrow."

We booked out of the hospital at light speed!

Reflections of a Mother

The hospital and its staff could not have been any nicer. Someone from the administrative office would come by to see if everything was going smoothly and usually gave us a couple free meal tickets for use in the cafeteria. After this happened a few times, Hope began to ask about the coupons.

"Are you doing this for all the patients in the hospital?" she asked a visiting administrator one day.

"No, Hope," the administrator replied. "These are only for very important patients." The woman might have said that to make Hope feel special, but Hope didn't see it that way.

"Well," she said defiantly, "my dad has money, so maybe you need to give them to someone who can't afford food."

I quickly tried to get Hope off her soap box so that the administrator would not be embarrassed; I expressed our gratitude for all the good care we were getting and walked her to the door. When I came back in the room, I started in on Hope and her attitude toward the adult staff members who were only doing their job.

I told her that the meal tickets and free parking really helped our family because her dad had recently started his own business. He had been forced to do this because of downsizing.

Hope remained defiant. She continued to say, "No one, no kid should have to eat hospital food all the time."

So we made a deal. I would collect meal cards as they were offered to us and would carry them in my pocket; if I saw someone who looked like they needed a good meal or some help, I would share the cards with them. This sounded like a good plan to Hope, but she still couldn't believe all people weren't treated the same.

Stuart and I tried to explain to her that some of the kids in the hospital didn't have insurance, but they were not being turned away because of that. They were being taken care of in different ways.

She still had a problem with it, but kept mum about her feelings *most* of the time.

Then Hope started hearing stories from the nurses as they came in to check on her. Sometimes they would show up late because another child demanded more help since his or her parents weren't there because they had to go back to work. Some children lived out of town and were left to face chemotherapy alone for the same reason. Hope couldn't understand how anyone could do that to a child. The nurses and I would try to explain that sometimes you don't have a choice. The parents had to keep working. "If you miss too many days at work, there goes the job and the insurance," I pointed out to her. "Or," I said, "the parents might have small children or babies to care for at home." She understood what I was saying, but this bothered Hope to no end.

"What do you mean these kids are here by themselves? Nurses don't listen to us. What if these kids have to go to the bathroom or need to throw up? What do they do then? You can buzz for a nurse, but that doesn't mean they come right away unless you have an 'adult voice.'"

One time, Hope tried to lower her voice to sound more like an adult when I had left to get a drink. Her machine started beeping, indicating that the medicine needed to be checked, and she knew a nurse would come sooner if an adult asked instead of a kid. Hope was beginning to realize firsthand what family love and support was all about, and how important it was to have her parents there whenever she needed something.

22

The Shocking PET Scan

B ecause Shelby had to work, I took Hope for her PET scan the next day. We checked into CMC (again), although this time on an outpatient basis. Hope was wheeled down to the lab area and without much waiting, the PET scan began.

Before the test, Hope was given a small injection of radioactive substance and positrons, which are tiny particles. They begin emitting a "footprint" that allows the doctors to track the disease's progress.

The PET scan involves lying very still for about forty-five minutes while the machine passes around you, much like taking an innertube and passing it over your head down to your feet.

It was very quiet in the room; only Hope and I and the PET technician, a very nice young lady who chatted easily with Hope, were present. The room darkened and the scan began.

To my surprise, and very shortly to my horror, the images from the test began to appear on a monitor easily visible by me *and* Hope. The tube started to slide over Hope's head first and shortly her noggin appeared on the screen.

Naturally I could not help but comment about how small her brain looked. "It is about the size of a mouse's—but it looks intact," I said to her jokingly.

Not being able to speak or move, she just glared at me. The scan continued.

Nothing much showed up. I could see her skull, then her jaw and neck on the monitor. Suddenly, the images began to change. When the scan reached her shoulder, the screen lit up in the area of her right clavicle. I was very careful not to immediately react, but it scared me to death.

Was that cancer? Hope did not seem to be affected by what she was seeing. Inside, I began to panic. Why on earth had they left this monitor on for her to see this?

The scan moved down past her spine and more white images appeared, although not as large as the ones in her shoulder. Over the next ten minutes, the scan exposed her hip where the screen again lit up, showing a lot of white areas.

Finally, the picture came to her legs, where we knew the tumors were largest. The right knee area was almost completely white and the left knee was almost the same. The white images also went almost continuously up her right leg into her hip.

For one of the few times in my life, I thought I was going to pass out. My head started to swim and the room, already darkened, turned a shade of gray. So as not to alarm Hope, I grabbed onto the chair beside the gurney and eased myself down. I was trying very hard not to let Hope see me. Fortunately, she didn't. I watched the rest of the scan from the chair, trying to regain my composure.

Those images horrified me as none I have ever seen. Back in June, when Hope was first diagnosed, Dr. McMahon had used the phrase "a picture reveals more than I can explain" as he showed Shelby and me the initial PET scan and MRI images.

The white images that were now appearing on the screen in front of me appeared worse—much worse.

We heard a loud beep and the nurse came out and announced that the scan was completed. "Hope, you did great! I know it is hard to stay still that long, but you did fine," she said, helping Hope off the table and back into her wheelchair. "You can go home now . . . Have a great day," she said cheerily and went back into the adjacent room.

As we left the hospital, I tried to get those awful images out of my head. It is funny how much rationalizing we were all doing these days. *Dummy, you ain't no doctor. Don't read into this,* I thought to myself on the drive home. Yet once Hope and I arrived there, the first thing I wanted to do was to call Dr. McMahon's office. Shelby was at work and that was fortunate; she would have seen my face and known that something was not right. After getting Hope in the house and feeding her lunch, I went upstairs to make the call to Dr. McMahon's office. I was put in touch with Michelle and I told her about the scan.

"Do not worry about that," she told me. "The PET scan is so sensitive it can pick up anything. We do know Hope has a lot of disease in her legs and all, but don't read into what you saw. Let Dr. McMahon review all the scans."

Although I continued to let those numerous white images replay in my mind for a while longer, Michelle's reassuring words eventually won out and I let it go.

It wasn't until September 24 when I realized that what I saw was, in fact, very real.

Reflections of a Mother

Hope's favorite time of year was here: fall and Halloween. Fall had always been Hope's favorite, as she mentioned in a fifth-grade project, *My Life after 11 Years*. She took great pride in picking just the right costume for Halloween. During previous Halloweens she had been a kitty (no surprise there), a Dalmatian, a ghost, a kitty again, the Statue of Liberty, and during her fifth-grade year, the best Pippy Longstocking anybody had ever seen. She was a natural with her red piggy tails, which I made stick out by braiding them around coat hangers. "Pippy" was a hoot at our neighborhood Halloween hot dog and trick-or-treat party.

That fifth-grade project had told us a lot about how Hope saw herself and her future. On one page in the book she listed her three wishes, complimented by illustrations: to be a movie star (illustrated by a picture of her hands on the Walk of Fame beside Brad Pitt's hands); to be the first female president (an illustration of the presidential emblem and a podium with "Hope Stout, President," on the front); to be the future Mrs. Brad Pitt (the words *just married*, a heart with "Brad and Hope" written on it, and a four-carat diamond ring).

23
Tests, Tests, and More Tests

O ver the next two weeks, Hope began to get into somewhat of a routine. Her school, Weddington Middle, had set up a schedule whereby her teachers came by with her assignments so that she could keep up with her classmates. Hope met this news as you might expect a normal teenager to do. We had always battled with Hope over her homework. Her mind tended to wander, so we had decided that rather than having her do her homework right when she got home from school, she needed some time to unwind.

When that didn't solve the problem, I bought her a desk so she could study in her room, but she spent more time playing with Milton, her hamster. Then we tried the den, but the TV was too much of a temptation. Finally, Shelby hit on the best approach: the kitchen. That way she could monitor Hope while dinner was being prepared.

Now her teachers were determined to keep her up with the rest of the seventh grade, and Hope had reluctantly complied with this during the first two weeks of September. Both Shelby and I constantly reminded her that she had to keep up so that she would not be behind her class when she got back into school. That seemed to work, and for once Hope did her homework without too much struggle.

Hope's next treatment wasn't until Monday, September 15. The weekend before that was a big one for her. First, Shelby's mom and dad celebrated their fiftieth wedding anniversary, and we attended the party that Saturday night. Hope looked great, and in looking back at the pictures from the event, you would never have guessed she was sick, except that she looked a little thinner than usual. But her smile! She was beaming in every picture. She even had a photograph taken with an earring clamped on her nose.

On Sunday, September 14, International Sports Center, the cheerleading school Holly had competed for, held a fund-raiser for our family and another family whose daughter was also facing some health issues. Several gymnastic and cheerleading exhibitions were held at a local high school.

It was a brutally hot day, and, because it was the weekend, school officials had turned the air-conditioning off. Holly and Shelby spoke briefly to the crowd at the gym, thanking them for supporting us. There was not an empty seat in the house. In fact, when we were parking, I had mentioned to Holly that there must be some other event that day at the high school, based on the number of cars in the lot.

"Uh, Dad, all of these cars are here for the exhibition. This place will be packed," Holly said to me.

Looking back on it now, the outpouring of support our family received during this trying time was amazing. Shelby and I often tell people that we would not wish this experience on anyone, except for the love we were shown by so many. Every human being should experience that.

The exhibition was a huge success, and both families received quite a contribution to help out with medical bills. But more importantly, we felt the love and prayers of all who attended. Several cancer survivors came up and talked to Hope and our family. These survivors encouraged us to keep fighting: God would be there for us and would heal Hope's body. It was very gratifying to talk to other families who had been down this path.

And, more importantly, who had beaten the disease.

After a full weekend, we checked back into Carolinas Medical Center on Tuesday, September 16, for another round of methotrexate, the treatment Hope hated.

We spent the rest of the week taking the remainder of the tests, which would evaluate her progress. She had three MRIs, a chest X-ray, an echocardiogram, an audiology test (to see if the chemo had affected her hearing, which it sometimes does), and a bone scan. Her chemo level was a 6.2 on Wednesday morning. It needed to be 0.1 in order for us to go home.

As noted before, the process involves giving Hope a near-lethal dose of the drug, after which the hospital staff immediately starts to flush the methotrexate out of her system. So after the tests were completed, all we did was flush out and test, flush out and test, flush out and test. And by flushing out, I mean literally flushing out. Hope went to the bathroom constantly and had to keep track of her urine output, which she hated.

One not-so-surprising thing happened during this ordeal. Before each treatment or test, they would tell us what to expect from it. For example, with methotrexate, normally a patient's blood levels return to normal within thirty-six to forty-eight hours. However, *normal* and Hope never collided in the same sentence.

By Thursday, her "meth" levels had dropped like a stone, much like the last time, a good sign that meant she might be going home the next day, if the level kept dropping. Unfortunately when Hope heard that, she chiseled it in stone.

After Friday morning's test, however, the level had not moved, which meant at least another twelve hours of flushing to get it lower. She was devastated. All day Friday we sat in the hospital room, not doing much but playing video games, watching TV and movies, and reading. Around three o'clock, Hope got on her computer and that helped her pass the time.

The nurses came in around six o'clock and took her blood again. The levels were still too high. Dr. McMahon came by and said another night in the hospital was needed.

"Go and get a water hose and flush it through me," Hope told her doctor. "I want out of here!"

Dr. McMahon smiled and told her she would probably be able to go home sometime tomorrow.

"I am whether you say it is okay or not!" Hope asserted.

Fortunately for the doctor, early the next morning the test showed her blood level where it needed to be, and we hightailed it out of there.

Although Hope did not have any nausea or loss of appetite from the methotrexate, whenever she was in the hospital, she basically didn't eat much—only an occasional Wendy's #7. When she got home, that was another story. She ate constantly.

That afternoon, she attended the seventh-grade football game, which was homecoming. The team honored Hope by putting an HES (Hope Elizabeth Stout) sticker on their helmets, and her cheerleading team started out each cheer with her name. They also bought her a corsage and insisted she sit down on the field with them. It was very hot, but Hope got to wear her cheerleading uniform and had a great time.

Early in the following week, Dr. McMahon and the other physicians handling her case were going to evaluate all the tests to determine where things stood and what the next treatments should be. If we were making significant progress, another round of cisplatin and methotrexate would follow. Our family and friends

knew we were in the waiting mode, and naturally we got asked
about it a lot. Hope began updating CaringBridge during this time
and nearly every day informed visitors to the site about the lack of
information.

Sunday, September 7, 2003 9:51 AM CDT

*Heyy everyone Its me again. Ok im sorry that I didnt write yester-
day, its just NOTHING HAPPENED yesterday! LoL I gotta take a
break once in a while. So if there is ever a day that I dont write.
Dont freak out! Im just taking a break. O ya I still havent heard
any results from my scan and when we get the results we will tell
u. Nothing really is happening today either. My dad and sis went
2 the Panther game and me and my mom are just going 2 relax.
Well thats about it for today Im gonna split. TTYL $~*HoPe*~$
:) :) :)*

*P.S. My mom thought it was a ggood idea 2 have a bible verse of
the day thing so 2 kick it off, here is the first one.*

*"Dear brothers and sisters, whenever trouble comes your way, let
it be an opportunity for joy. For when your faith is tested, your
endurance has a chance to grow." James 1:2–3 (NLT)*

Reflections of a Mother

For the first time since the ordeal began, Hope asked me the "why"
question. I got into bed with her to hold her and told her that I
would gladly switch places with her if I could. Then all of a sudden,
the tears stopped, and she said how special I was to her: how much
I already had done for her. Even if it was just holding the puke pan,
wheeling Lucifer, the IV pole, to the bathroom for her as she used
her crutches, or giving her washcloths for her face after getting
sick—I was simply *there* for her.

I didn't feel that I was doing very much for Hope, but in her eyes it was everything. Even if I was annoying to Hope (as she would sometimes tell me) she was glad I asked her if she wanted anything to eat or drink every *thirty minutes*.

"Mom," she said, "I would never *ever* let anyone take this journey for me, even as bad as it is."

What perspective and courage from a twelve-year-old! She told her dad the same thing one time when he said he would gladly take her place.

"Dad," she said, "you couldn't handle it!"

24

VP-16

On Wednesday, September 24, I went to work at my office. The weather had finally cooled off, and that afternoon several friends and I were going to enjoy the beautiful North Carolina fall weather with a round of golf. There are memories that are burned vividly in your mind as you travel through life. Obvious ones are your wedding day, the birth of your children, and the day you get awful news. That September morning I was having coffee with Chris Spivey in my office when my cell phone rang. Looking down at the caller ID, I saw it was Dr. McMahon's office. I walked to my office and answered the call.

"Mr. Stout, I wanted to talk to you about the test results on Hope. We have had some rather extraordinary changes."

Those words, as written, do sound encouraging. However, the somber tone of Dr. McMahon's voice was what got my attention.

"We have reviewed the test results, and even though there was some initial reduction in the tumors, the cancer grew back once the chemo stopped and has, in fact, spread to other areas. The spot on her shoulder, which I thought was just a hot spot due to puberty, is unfortunately a new area of cancer. There are other spots now on her lungs as well. The growth is, well, unlike anything I have ever seen. I am very sorry to have to tell you this."

The air went completely out of me. My knees buckled and I slumped into my chair, trying to get my mind around what he had just said. It took a few moments for me to summon any words. Finally I managed to ask him, "What happened, Dr. McMahon? I thought we were making some decent progress."

Before the oncologist could respond, I said something that I promised myself I would never say. "Doc, level with me . . . Is this a terminal situation?"

Without any hesitation, he said, "Yes, Mr. Stout, I believe it is. The level of her disease to start with was significant, but we have clear evidence now that, in spite of the treatment, the disease has grown. That is the reason I called. I want to meet with you and Mrs. Stout, without Hope being present, to discuss this further. As you know, Hope is supposed to come in tomorrow to begin another round of chemotherapy, and frankly, I am not sure it is worth putting her through it."

My mouth went dry. Did this man just tell me to give up?

The doctor continued. "As I said, these results are discouraging, but we do have some other options. There are more intense chemo treatments that have shown great results with other patients in this situation. But I want to be sure you and your wife understand where we are at."

After telling Dr. McMahon that we would be there later that afternoon, I struggled to my feet and walked into Chris's office. He was sitting behind his desk with tears in his eyes; he had overheard enough of the conversation. Still I spoke those dreaded words that could no longer be avoided.

"Chris, my little girl is gonna die!" Then I slumped to the floor, sobbing as I have never done before.

Chris did the best he could; he tried to help me to my feet, telling me that all was not lost and not to give up.

"No, you don't understand. He used the word *terminal*. He said the cancer was growing despite the chemo. After all she has been through, she is even sicker than when we first started. This is just not fair . . . What did she do to deserve this?!" I screamed, and the whole office came running to find out what was going on.

Everyone did the best they could to console me. After regaining some composure, I called Shelby's work and paged Barbara, the director of the preschool at our church. She assured me that she would get Shelby out of class and have her ready to go in fifteen minutes. Numbly, I went out to my car and headed for the church to meet my wife.

Shelby was waiting for me in the parking lot. As she opened the car door, I didn't know what to say. I really didn't have time to prepare her for this.

When she got in, she asked what was going on and why we were going to the hospital. I simply said, "I got a call from Dr. McMahon, and he wants to see us without Hope to discuss the test results."

"Why didn't he want Hope to be there?"

I gripped the steering wheel hard. Shelby and I are very honest with each other, and even though I knew how bad things were, at that point I could not tell my wife what I knew.

"He didn't go into a lot of detail, but my guess is this is not going to be good news. He did say the test results were rather remarkable, but his tone of voice was not good."

Tears began to form in my beautiful wife's eyes. She just looked at me for a second and then turned to gaze out the window. She didn't say another word on the drive to the hospital.

Upon arriving at the clinic, we went into an office with Dr.

McMahon and Kim Barker, the social worker. We all sat down and
Dr. McMahon began speaking.

"Hope's tests have revealed some rather major changes.
Unfortunately, the cancer has continued to grow through these
chemo treatments. Instead of telling you, let me show you." He
stood up, opened a file, and laid out several pictures on the desk.

I walked over to look at them, assuming my wife would be right
behind me.

Shelby did not move. "I don't need to see those," she said, the
tears beginning to flow.

Kim walked over, sat down with Shelby, and put her arms
around her. Dr. McMahon and I began looking at the scans. The
first picture I looked at was the PET scan. It looked just like the
images I had seen on the monitor the week before.

Dr. McMahon pointed to the other picture. "Here is the original PET scan from the week of June 22, and here is the one from
last week."

It did not take a degree in oncology to see the changes. Hope's
entire right leg from the knee up through her hip was covered with
white spots, and there was a significant mass in her left leg and
spots in her spine and lungs.

The place on her shoulder was about the size of a baseball.
Despite Dr. McMahon thinking this was just a spot due to puberty,
it had turned out to be cancer.

The images in front of me were horrifying. To eliminate all of
the tumors looked impossible.

Shelby was crying very softly now, and I sat down beside her and
held her close. "Okay, Dr. McMahon. What do you suggest?" I said.

He cleared his throat, adjusted his glasses, and began speaking.
"Frankly, a lot of people would do nothing at this point. With the
level of her disease being what it is, many people would let nature
takes its course, to use a term I am not comfortable with.

"There are other treatments, but they may jeopardize Hope's

health. We have a chemo treatment called VP-16. It is very severe, and I must tell you that it could cause her death in and of itself."

Suddenly my wife's head jerked up. "I can tell you one thing! We are *not* giving up. If there is a chance this can cure her, we are going to try."

She was saying exactly what I was thinking. "I agree with Shelby. If there is a chance, we are taking it. From what I see over there (nodding to the scans that were still on the desk), this is her only shot. If this VP stuff has a chance of working, let's do it."

25

A Cool Breeze from Heaven

The drive back from the hospital that day, Wednesday, September 24, 2003, was one of the worst times Shelby and I have ever spent together. Despite the beauty of the cloudless fall day around us, we both felt utterly helpless. As we drove south down Providence Road, the oncologist's words kept ringing in my ears: "Some parents would just give up at this point."

Suddenly many questions started to wander through my mind.

What kind of monster was living inside our daughter? Why hadn't any of these treatments, which had made her so sick and had taken her beautiful red hair, worked? What about all the prayers that were being said on Hope's behalf? Why weren't they working?

And where are You, God? Aren't You listening?

Then Shelby, who had been very quiet as we drove home, spoke up. "Go by the church. I need to see Pastor Ken. I need to talk to him before we tell Hopie," she said, softly dabbing at her green eyes with a tissue. She then picked up the phone and dialed Ken's number.

I didn't have the heart to tell my wife that I *did not* want to see Ken Lyon or even go to the church.

At that moment, God and I were not on speaking terms.

But I realized that now was not the time to express this thought to my wife. I turned left off Providence Road and headed toward Matthews United Methodist Church.

It was about four o'clock when we arrived. We went straight to Ken's study and were met there by one of the other pastors, Mike Swofford. He could see how upset we were, and we had just started to tell him the news when Ken walked in the room. He hugged both of us before taking a seat across from us, and then I repeated what we had just heard from Dr. McMahon. When I finished, I asked Ken the question that had been nagging at me all day.

"Ken, just where is God? Why is He not answering all these prayers? I just don't get it . . . What did Hope do to deserve this? Furthermore, all these people are praying for her healing and now this: the cancer is *even worse*. What is this news going to do for everyone's faith? I don't want to sound disrespectful and I do have faith, but . . ."

I couldn't finish the sentence because my tears took over. Despite having heard this news over two hours ago, the reality of the situation was just now beginning to seep into my conscious thought.

Dr. McMahon thinks our little girl is going to die.

It was the first time since June 27 that I had even allowed that thought to enter my mind. After her diagnosis, whenever I let myself begin to think about Hope's disease taking her life, I chased it away, much like you would when remembering a bad experience. I had built up my own defense mechanism by constantly telling myself: *She is going to beat this cancer. This is the strong, athletic Hope Elizabeth Stout. Dying is not an option!*

Until today, that is. Now the doctor we trusted the most had told us that the disease was probably terminal.

As the four of us sat in Ken's office, I could see that my pastor and friend really had no answer. He cleared his throat, his eyes heavy with tears, and began to speak.

"During Jesus' ministry, He did heal many people. But without question other people who had physical needs came in contact with Jesus and He did not heal them. The Bible doesn't record those moments, but they certainly happened.

"This is the mystery and the difficult part of our faith walk. We all believe and expect Hope to be healed, but unfortunately God's plans are not shared with us in most cases. We must continue to hold on to His promise that He is with us, no matter the circumstances, and sometimes that is the most difficult thing to do."

The pastor's words did not help, at least at that moment. But as I recalled them sometime later, they would make perfect sense.

After spending a few more minutes praying with Ken and Mike, Shelby and I left the church to come home. When we pulled down the driveway, I had this overwhelming sense of dread. How in the world were we going to explain this to Hope? She was going to be devastated.

No, not the kind of devastation she *should* be feeling at this age, like being dumped by her first boyfriend or not making a cheerleading squad or basketball team; those "devastations" are mere potholes along the road of adolescence.

This was not a pothole. This was far worse. No child should have to be told that the chemo she had suffered through was not working and the cancer was still growing inside her at an even faster rate.

And that she might die.

Shelby and I climbed the stairs to the playroom. Hope had been sleeping on the futon, which was low enough to allow her to get to and from the bathroom much more easily than getting down off her bed. As we came into the room, Hope was watching TV. Wendy, who had been staying with Hope while we were at the hospital, was sitting beside her in the chair at the computer stand.

Shelby knelt down near Hope. I took a seat at the end of the bed. Very slowly, with as much love, compassion, and kindness as I have ever experienced, Shelby began to tell Hope what Dr. McMahon had said. In keeping with what Courtney said to us way back in June, Shelby did not hold anything back from Hope. But she was unrelenting in telling Hope that we were not giving up, that God could heal her at any moment, and that we were going to keep on trying to kill the cancer. This again was a moment when God infused Shelby with unbelievable courage and strength—and it is a good thing because I had absolutely zero amount of either.

Hope was very quiet, but before long she began to cry softly. At that moment, as her father, I have never felt so inadequate. Someone getting this kind of news at age seventy is one thing: a good, long life has been lived, one can rationalize, and because of that, accepting death as inevitable is much easier. But this was a twelve-year-old girl with her entire life ahead of her. I could see her eventually asking the question I did not want to deal with:

Am I going to die?

Once Shelby finished telling Hope about the diagnosis, Wendy told us she was going to run home. She hugged each of us and gave Hope a kiss before heading down the stairs. As she did, she stole a look over her shoulder at me and our eyes met.

My cousin Wendy has the family trait, the red hair that was passed on to her by our Grandmother Brown. Wendy in turn passed along the red hair to two of her sons. Along with Hope, the three cousins were called "The Fireheads," and they had their picture taken together each year at the beach.

Wendy took charge on June 27 and had been our emotional anchor since then. Nothing fazes her.

But on this day, as she was heading home, Wendy Reeder looked totally devastated, and I could tell she was hanging on to her emotions by the slimmest of threads. With watery eyes she mouthed, "I love you" and left.

The minute Wendy was out of the room, Hope broke down. She screamed and cried, and we all just sat there on the futon together. A couple of times I reached over to try to hug her, but she pushed me away. Although that really hurt, I could see Hope's frustration and realized she needed to get it out.

At Dr. McMahon's office we had decided to go ahead with the hospital stay that day, which had been scheduled for another round of chemo, and substitute the VP-16 instead. After hearing this news, Hope flatly refused to go back to CMC.

While we wanted to give Hope some say-so about her treatments, as her parents, we had decided to try the VP-16. Now Hope wanted no part of it.

Not that I blamed her.

What was to follow over the next few minutes was to be one of the toughest, and yet most grace-filled, times we would experience during Hope's illness.

Holly had come home from golf practice right after Wendy left, and after hearing the news had also tried to soothe Hope. Shelby and I even left the two sisters alone for a while, and I found out later from Holly that Hope truly was scared, more so than Holly had ever seen.

After a few minutes with her sister, Hope got up and went to our bathroom. Even though she was getting around reasonably well on her crutches, I followed Hope at a safe distance. She was so upset that I didn't want to leave her, but I knew she needed some privacy. Thankfully she was not aware that I was watching her through the partially open door. I was about to turn away when I saw her sit down on the edge of the bathtub.

Hope put her head into her hands and began to cry again. As she did so, her crutches, which had been leaning against the sink, began to slide slowly toward her. She looked up just before they fell into her and with one giant push shoved the crutches hard, and they clattered against the bathroom wall.

Seeing Hope sling those crutches against that wall is a scene that is burned into my memory and will stay there forever. Recalling it now fills me with an utter sense of helplessness that I never want to experience again.

My first reaction was to run toward her, but something stopped me. As hard as it was, I realized Hope needed this moment to herself. Unless I could waltz into that bathroom and make this cancer disappear, she didn't want me to come in there. So I just stood and watched with tears streaming down my face.

When Shelby heard the crutches clatter to the floor, she came running up the stairs, but I stopped her from entering the bathroom.

"Leave her be. She is okay," I said to my wife, and then I told her what I had observed. We listened to Hope's sniffles and crying and then left the room to get her things together for the upcoming hospital stay.

After about twenty minutes, Shelby sent me to check on Hope. I looked everywhere: the bathroom, our closet, the playroom, Holly's room. Due to immobility, Hope was not trying to go downstairs by herself so I ruled that out. Soon Holly and Shelby joined in the search.

Where was she?

We called out for her but got no answer, and despite the realization that she had to be upstairs somewhere, we began to panic. Shelby, in particular, began yelling for Hope, the fright evident in her voice.

"I am in here."

We went toward the direction of Hope's voice and found her in the far corner of our bedroom behind the nightstand. Somehow, despite her immobility, she had managed to crawl back there and was hiding from us—and the world.

She looked up at us and pleaded, "I don't want to go to the hospital again . . . Please don't make me. What's the use anyway? Let me just stay here at home, please?" Hope then buried her face in her hands, crying harder.

And, as I will remind you time and again in this book, the presence of God and His incredible grace arrived at the exact time when Shelby and I were emotionally spent or physically out of steam. What took place next was a family moment that none of us will ever forget.

Holly, Shelby, and I sat down around Hope and tried to be there for her. We just listened to her sob. After a few minutes, Hope regained some of her composure.

And then, like an unexpected gust of a cool wind on a hot day, this wonderful calmness engulfed all of us.

Suddenly Shelby, Holly, and I found strength. We began to reassure Hope and we could see that it truly picked her up. She was still scared, but all of a sudden, our words comforted her. And, of course, as had been the case since she first came home from the hospital, Pudge and Peanut appeared, right on cue, and began to hover around her, each one vying for her attention. The mood lightened as the kittens jumped on her lap and then over her legs.

During Hope's illness, these kittens did uncanny things. As Hope's disease progressed, she could not stand anyone to touch her legs—except those cats. They literally took turns sitting on her legs, as if they knew where the disease was. Prior to Hope getting sick, the cats would sit on her lap, but never on her legs.

"Now this is my kind of CAT scan," Hope said suddenly.

The despair that had been present a few minutes ago was now gone.

We must have sat there for thirty minutes or so, playing with the cats and talking. Then Hope picked herself up and went to get ready for the trip to the hospital. It was late, about 9:30 p.m. or so, when we finally made it to Carolinas Medical Center. Later that evening when Holly and I left the hospital, Hope's spirits were much better; she even joked some with the nurses.

As we drove home that night Holly and I didn't say much; we were both exhausted from the day's events. Still, the silence was somewhat awkward between us, and I reached over to turn on the radio, just to hear something that would drown out the silence.

As I did, the clock changed to midnight. I was never so happy to see a day end in my life.

September 24, 2003. May you never pass this way again.

Reflections of a Mother

When we found out that the cancer was spreading, despite the chemotherapy, we knew prayer might be our only cure.

Danette came over that day, and Stuart told her that Hope was worried that she wasn't praying the right way.

The next day Danette returned with a prayer she wrote especially for Hope. "She can read it three times a day," Danette said.

When I showed it to Hope, she said, "Well, that just about says it all, doesn't it?"

And I agreed with her 100 percent.

In the next days and weeks and months, Hope prayed this prayer every day:

> Thank You, God, for another day . . .
> You have done so much for me.
> Thank You for being my heavenly Father.
> Forgive me for anything I have said or done
> that was not pleasing to You.
> Lord, You designed me and created me.
> Please keep my body strong and give me the
> power to fight my cancer.

Cause my body to accept this medicine.
Give my body the nourishment it needs
to shield infection and fever.
When my day is difficult, let me feel Your tender touch.
Clear my mind so that I may hear You.
I know that when I don't have the strength to pray,
You listen to my heart.
Lord, I love You and I need You.
Continue to use me as Your instrument
so that others may know Your Son.
Thank You for the promise that You will never leave me.
I patiently call upon You for my complete healing.
In Jesus' name,
Amen.

26

Operation Pudge

We began the VP-16 treatment on Thursday morning, September 25. Dr. McMahon informed us that VP-16 would take Hope's white blood count down to virtually nothing. The drug would completely break down the cell-making process, which unfortunately meant killing good cells as well as bad ones.

Then the oncologist warned us. "Hope will be much more susceptible to infections with this chemotherapy, particularly in her already weakened state from the previous treatments."

The VP-16 treatment was scheduled to last about five days, and we were hoping to have Hope home by early the following week. The good news about this treatment is that the pain medicines made her sleep virtually all the time. She would wake up for a few minutes and then drift back off again. We spent a lot of time reading and watching TV, and when Hope woke up, we would watch a movie or update the Web site on the computer.

During this hospital visit we managed to pull off "Operation Pudge" again.

On Friday night, Holly smuggled Hope's favorite cat into the hospital in a duffle bag! Pudgy did pretty well until they were in the hospital elevator, at which point he began yowling and poked his head out of the bag, much to the amusement of the other passengers. Holly finally got him to quiet down long enough to get past the nurse's station into Hope's room. The poor cat had been traumatized by being stuck in the bag on the trip over. Upon arriving in Hope's room, he immediately fell asleep on her bed and didn't move for nearly two hours.

When a nurse would come into the room, Shelby would quickly throw Hope's quilt, the one we nicknamed "A Blanket of Love," which the Core Club members had made for her, over the cat to hide him. Pudge never moved—until Hope got an unexpected visit from the hospital administrator.

On this night, there was a slight knock at the door, and before we could throw the Blanket of Love over Pudge, in walked Joe, the night administrator. He had been by several times before and had taken an obvious liking to Hope.

We all froze and Hope especially looked terrified. Joe, who is a friendly man in his early sixties, with a crop of thick, white hair, walked over to the bed and asked Hope how she was doing. Hope told him very meekly that she was fine but did not include any attempt to chit-chat.

And, of course, on this night Joe seemed intent on having a longer-than-usual conversation. He asked Hope how her studies were going and if she liked homeschooling, what TV shows she watched, and on and on. He then told her, "If there is anything you need, make sure you call me personally." Finally, Joe seemed to be ready to leave; we might just get away with having a cat in the room, after all. Pudge had not moved a muscle the whole time the administrator had been talking.

That is, until Joe finally noticed him.

"My, what a beautiful stuffed animal you have here . . . He looks so real!"

And then he reached over and stroked Pudge softly.

The cat, now awakened from his nap, rose, arched his back, stretched, yawned, and then resumed his place at the foot of Hope's bed.

We were busted!

For a few seconds, nobody said anything. I half expected the administrator to call for the nurse and throw us all out.

Then Shelby broke the ice. "Please don't tell on us. Hope just had to see her kitty."

"Don't worry. I didn't see anything," Joe said. He actually petted Pudge for a few minutes as Shelby and Hope told him about all the cats at the Stout house. Joe then told Hope to take care and left the room.

The second he was out of earshot, we all had a good laugh over the incident.

"I was hoping he would throw us out," Hope said. "I guess Pudge couldn't resist getting noticed by somebody important."

The next day, as Austin, Holly, and I entered Hope's room, I immediately noticed that she was hooked up to a breathing monitor. After getting the news on Wednesday that the cancer had spread in her lungs, seeing her hooked up to that machine hit me like a punch in the stomach.

"What is that?" I asked Shelby anxiously, noticing that Hope was asleep. "Why is she hooked up to oxygen?" I could tell by the look on their faces that Austin and Holly were also very concerned.

Shelby tearfully explained to us that it was mainly a precaution to see how much oxygenation Hope was getting. "One of her blood tests came back with a below-normal reading, and they want to check it out." Shelby went on to explain that Dr. McMahon said that this truly wasn't a big deal.

As she talked I could see that Shelby was totally exhausted after spending the previous night and all day with Hope while Austin, Holly, and I went to the NC State/North Carolina football game. So I sent Shelby home with the girls, and I spent the night with Hope.

I got a blanket and tried to get comfortable in the recliner beside Hope's bed. I cut the TV off and the room became eerily quiet. The only noise was the humming of the breathing machine. Although this sound was very slight, it added an unwelcomed sound to Hope's room. That is until I heard these words from the girl in the bed next to me.

"Okay, you, no snoring or you are outta here!"

Even hooked up to an oxygen machine, she gave me the needle.

On Sunday, Shelby arrived at the hospital around mid-morning. Hope had slept pretty well most of the night but early in the morning she had become very nauseous; I was up with her several times. We spent the rest of the morning getting her nausea under control.

The Carolina Panthers had a home game against the Atlanta Falcons that day, a four o'clock kickoff, which was a later-than-usual start. Our family had become huge Panthers fans ever since the inception of the team in 1995. When season tickets first went on sale, Shelby and I had immediately gotten four of them. Hope loved going to the games with me and had, in fact, gone to the very first game in the new stadium. And that was where another Hope moment had taken place.

It was in mid-August of 1996. My father, Bill Stout, had died earlier that month after a long bout with diabetes. My mother, Betty, had been Dad's caregiver for three years after his stroke in 1993 and, along with my sister, Beth, was visiting with us for a few days. The very first game at the new stadium was a pre-season game, and Mom, my sister, Hope, and I went to the game. We got there early, and we were walking around the new facility, checking it out, just like all the other enthusiastic fans.

One caveat of being an original season-ticket holder was the honor of having your name engraved on the base of one of the four large panthers, each statue a focal point on one of the four sides of the stadium. Hope was five years old and wanted to see our names, so we made our way to the huge panther that sat on top of the marble rectangle with our names inscribed on it. Once there, she began climbing around on the edge of the massive statue. Several TV crews were milling around the crowd, randomly filming people's reaction to the new stadium.

I was keeping an eye on Hope as she maneuvered around the edge, making sure she did not slip and fall off, when a reporter approached me and asked if he could interview my daughter.

"Go ahead, but there is no telling what she will say," I warned him.

He and his cameraman walked over to Hope who stopped her climbing when she saw the camera light come on. The reporter then asked what her name was.

"Hope," she replied, staring intently into the camera. I could see the cameraman turning the lens to get a close-up of Hope's face. She had gotten a small Panther logo spray-painted onto her cheek.

"Are you a Panthers fan, Hope?" the reporter asked.

"Yes," she said and then began to resume her crawl around the statue, not giving the reporter much attention.

"Well, aren't you afraid of this panther?" he asked.

"No," she replied curtly.

"Why not? It is pretty big and ferocious looking."

Hope Stout, age five, then stopped her climbing, jumped off the marble base, and stared right at him with those big blue eyes.

Then she responded in a loud voice. "Because . . . he's not real, silly!"

The camera crew and about twenty people watching the interview lost it! The reporter, who was from the Charleston, South Carolina, area, assured me that clip would make the local news that night. "It is priceless," he said.

Since Hope was such a huge Panthers fan, Shelby and I had

decided that we were going to have a tailgate party right there in her hospital room and watch the game together. Hope had given permission for Austin and Holly to bring some Kentucky Fried Chicken for us to eat before they went to the game, even though food usually made her nauseous when she was in the Hospital Hilton.

As the football game was about to start, I heard Hope sniffling and realized she was crying. Shelby and I got on either side of her bed, and then I did a stupid thing: I asked her what was wrong.

As soon as the words escaped my lips, I knew what a ridiculous question that was.

Well, dummy, for starters, she has cancer; the chemo she has had to suffer through isn't working all that well, and she is in the hospital for the umpteenth time since June 27. Her sisters just left for the game and despite telling them it was okay to go, Hope wanted to do that more than anything in the world, but could not because of this damn cancer.

That was a real good question to ask your daughter, you idiot. What could possibly be wrong?

Hope tried to control her tears but then broke down and began wailing. She grabbed the edges of the bed and began yelling. "I will tell you what is wrong, Dad. I want to be at the Panthers game . . . I want to cheer. I want to go to school and be normal, not to sit in this stupid hospital day after day," she said, her blue eyes wet with tears.

"I don't want to have cancer anymore! I want to go home and just be normal! That is what's wrong."

I have never felt so low in my life. As parents, we were trying to balance our other girls' lives with treating Hope's cancer. We didn't want to deprive Austin and Holly from going to football games and such; that would not be fair to them. Still, at that moment, Hope had every right to feel sorry for herself. Her sisters were going to the Panthers game; she was sitting in a hospital bed with an IV in her arm. It would have been hard for an adult to grapple with this.

Hope was only twelve.

Shelby got in the bed with Hope and held her as close as she could without hurting her. All I could do was hold her hand while she cried.

Some comfort I was. I was surprised she even let me touch her after what I'd said.

At that moment, the frustration of this whole situation started to build up in me again. I became very angry at God; I wanted to yell and scream at Him. Instead, I just held my daughter's hand, fuming silently at the cards God had dealt my daughter and my family.

The three of us sat there until the combination of the crying and the medicine took over, and Hope thankfully dozed off. It's not that I wanted her to sleep necessarily. I would have loved to talk to her, but because of her hatred for the hospital, I knew her sleepiness would make the time pass faster.

While Shelby continued lying with Hope, I went over to the window and looked out at the scenery. We were on the seventh floor of Carolinas Medical Center, which is set in one of the prettiest areas of Charlotte. Massive oaks and elms dominate the landscape. The sight of the changing colors of the leaves painted against the crystal blue sky was a sight you only see in autumn. And less than three miles away, seventy-two thousand people were gathering at Ericsson Stadium (renamed the Bank of America Stadium in 2004) to watch an NFL game. They had no worries.

I snapped the blinds shut, not wanting to see the beauty of the sun setting on this gorgeous fall day. Shelby had gotten out of Hope's bed and had curled up in the recliner and was crying softly. Before long, she too fell asleep.

So there in the semi-darkness, I glumly began watching the game on TV as my wife and daughter slept. Even though the Panthers won, I couldn't have cared less. I kept asking, *God, why don't You care?*

Reflections of a Mother

This was not Pudge's first trip to the hospital. Austin and Blair had smuggled Hope's favorite cat into the hospital during her first chemotherapy treatment because she was so homesick. The girls did not tell anyone they were bringing the cat; they just arrived at the room, out of breath and giggling, unzipped a duffle bag, and out popped a wide-eyed Pudge.

I couldn't believe Austin and Blair did this without asking my permission. So naturally, I started to panic. And so did Wendy, who was in the room with us. Immediately we began making plans on what to do if somebody came walking in unexpectedly. Wendy was assigned to guard the door. Blair would snatch up Pudge and take him into the bathroom. And the rest of us would try to look innocent.

When Pastor Mike from our church came to the door, Wendy assumed he was a doctor, since she had never met him. So she stopped him from entering.

"They are having a family moment and Hope is very upset," she explained, lying through her teeth to the "doctor." She told him to wait and she would check and see if everyone was okay. Wendy slipped in and I went to the door.

"Oh, that's just Pastor Mike. He isn't a doctor," I said and pulled him into the room.

He was sworn to secrecy about the cat-napping!

It's hard to ask a minister to lie for you, but in this case, Mike figured God would be okay with this little white lie.

I had started to sleep with Hope at night to try to keep the pillows under her leg comfortable. She was experiencing a lot of pain, and she would ask me to find something—anything—in the Bible to help her get through her pain.

I remember one night in particular. She could not get comfortable, so we started to read out of a book called *The Bible Promise*

Book, which had topics arranged in alphabetical order so you could find verses of comfort quickly. The introduction at the front of the book reads: "Whatever the need of the moment, the answer is to be found in Scripture, if we take time to search for it. Whatever we are feeling, whatever we are suffering, whatever we are hoping, the Bible has something to say to us."

We read one verse after another. Hope then told me she was worried that she was not praying with her heart.

That night she decided she was going to do so. She prayed for the pain to go away so she could get to sleep. And . . . she slept the rest of the night without pain.

However, I could not get any sleep, because I had hip and back pain all night long. Stuart got up the next morning and said he didn't get any sleep either; he had shooting pains in his legs. He told me that after seeing Hope so uncomfortable, he had asked God to take Hope's pain away and give it to him. I had prayed the same prayer. God let us have her pain that night so she could sleep.

27

The Official Hand Holder

Hope's hospitalization lasted two more days. Austin, who was home for a few days on fall break, and Holly got to spend all day Monday with her. Once after Hope fell asleep, Austin decided that she was going to donate blood. She went downstairs to the blood drive that was being held outside the hospital cafeteria. Holly went with her for moral support. Despite the fact that Austin had never given blood before, she did pretty well—right up until she looked down at the needle in her arm, noticed the size of it, and saw her blood running into the bag.

Upon seeing that, she nearly fainted. The nurses managed to get her through it okay, and afterward, she and Holly had a good time telling Hope all about it.

"Austin, you are such a wimp," Hope said to her big sister. "Fainting after giving blood? Give me a break!" The two girls kept on teasing each other over who was tougher. It was very refreshing to see Hope doing so much better emotionally after yesterday. It was then that Shelby suggested that I return to work.

"Yeah, Dad, go make some money, because when I get my strength back, I am going shopping. It will cost you big time!" Hope warned me. As she stared at me, I could see that wonderful sparkle in her blue eyes.

My day immediately got better.

I went to the office (which I desperately needed to do) and around five thirty called and found out that Hope had a little bit of an appetite. That meant one thing. I rushed to the hospital after stopping to get Wendy's meals for my family, including a #7 for Hope. She managed a few bites, not as much as we would have liked but she at least ate *something*. Getting food into that kid when she was in the hospital was all but impossible.

Around mid-morning on the following day, Tuesday, September 30, the nurse announced that Hope's white blood count was stable enough to allow her to go home. As we were being discharged, Dr. McMahon informed us to be extremely careful to limit her visitors during the first few days at home.

He told Hope, "Your white blood count is low now and will go lower over the next few days. Any kind of germ could be a problem. I am going to have you get a shot of Neupogen each day, which will help your body build up white blood cells faster."

The word *shot* immediately got Hope's attention.

"That shot goes in my port, right?" Hope asked. "No sticking me or anything?"

Dr. McMahon, a very smart man who got his degree in oncology at Duke University, moved away from the bed and did not make eye contact with Hope Elizabeth Stout as he answered her question.

"Uh, no. Unfortunately, the shot has to be administered the old-fashioned way—with a needle. You only get it once a day, and as soon as your white blood count is high enough, you don't have to take it anymore. It should only be for a few days at the most," he assured Hope. "Either your mom or dad can give you the shot; it is really pretty easy to do and the needle is very small."

Hope reacted immediately. In fact she nearly shot off the bed. "My dad *is not* going to give me a shot . . . Mom can do it, but there is no way Dad is going to stick a needle in me. I would rather stay in the hospital."

That hurt. Despite my offers to the contrary, Hope insisted that Mom, and only Mom, would give the shot. Hope really wasn't that afraid of the shot, just the thought of me giving it to her.

In fact, Shelby's medical assisting background had come in handy. The nurses said she had done a great job thus far, keeping Hope's Hickman catheter clean. A lot of chemo patients have infections around the catheter site, but Hope never had one because of Shelby's expertise.

I did get assigned a great job, though. After seeing how hurt I was, Hope designated me hand holder when Shelby gave her the shot.

I would rather have that job anyway.

Once the discharge papers were finished up, we headed home where Hope was immediately escorted into the den by her sisters. She spent the rest of the day with cats all around her as well as Daisy. We told Hope to take it easy for a few days so her white blood count would increase. We just wanted to avoid getting a fever, which was a sure sign of an infection and meant an immediate trip back to Hospital Hilton.

Two days later, on Thursday, Hope was noticeably weaker, which was not unexpected. Dr. McMahon had said she would be weaker as her white blood count dropped. Still, she looked very frail and we hated seeing that. Plus, she could have no visitors and all of us had to wash our hands constantly. The home healthcare nurse had been coming by daily to check Hope's blood work.

Shelby took Hope's temperature constantly. Hope hated seeing her mom coming at her with the thermometer and made a big deal about having her temp taken so much. But through Thursday, her temperature remained normal. We thought we were out of the woods.

On Friday morning that changed.

Immediately after waking up, Shelby went in and felt Hope's head. It was not warm but very hot, and the thermometer soon told the story. Her fever was 101. A call to Dr. McMahon's office was made, and Michelle told us to get to the hospital right away.

Hope became very upset when she heard this news. Michelle also told us to plan on being in the hospital for at least a few days, so we began to pack accordingly with Hope protesting the whole time.

Because of Hope's procrastination—she kept putting us off in getting ready to go—we took our sweet time getting her to the hospital.

And it nearly cost our daughter her life.

Nearly forty-five minutes later, as we were walking out the door, my cell phone rang. It was Michelle wondering where we were.

"We are on the way right now," I told her.

"Mr. Stout, you need to hurry up and get Hope here. With her blood count so low, she is very susceptible to anything and she is running a high fever. Make it quick! We are waiting on you. Come straight to Dr. McMahon's office."

The concern in her voice shook me, but since we were on the way to the hospital and Hope seemed fine, I forgot about her warning . . . until we arrived at the hospital, when I quickly realized how sick Hope really was. We went straight to Dr. McMahon's office on the sixth floor, and after a quick check of her vital signs, the look on his face told me something was wrong. Shelby and Wendy, who had met us there, were beside the examination table, watching Hope intently, when Dr. McMahon motioned for me to come into the hall with him.

"Her blood pressure is very low, and she has a very high fever.

We need to start an IV immediately. I am afraid she is dehydrated and shock is a very real possibility. Get her to her room, and I will make sure the nurse is waiting on you," Dr. McMahon said quietly to me and then headed off to make the arrangements.

I went back into the room and began to help Hope off the table and into the wheelchair. "Okay, Cuz, we need to get you to your room," I said, trying to keep it as light as possible.

Hope started to sit up to maneuver herself into the wheel-chair—but stopped suddenly.

"Dad, I don't feel very good. Let me lay back down. I need to rest." She began to lie back down on the exam table with her legs hanging off. The way she was lying looked very awkward, so I tried again.

"Hope, we need to get to the room right now. The nurses are waiting. In five minutes you will be in your bed and can get some sleep."

"No, I need to lay down now." And then I looked at her face, which was a pasty, pale color, even paler than before, as if she had no blood in her body at all.

I helped her get her legs back onto the table as Shelby went to get Dr. McMahon. He came into the room wheeling a blood pressure monitor. The room we were in was very small, so I went to the other side of the room and stepped into the doorway. Shelby and Wendy were beside the bed as Dr. McMahon slid the blood pressure cuff down onto her tiny arm. I watched as the monitor began to register the numbers.

Before this moment I had never thought much about blood pressure. As a heart beats, it contracts, sending a surge of pressure into the bloodstream. This surge period is called systolic, which is the first number in a blood pressure reading. After the surge period, the heart rests briefly and expands in preparation for another beat, which is called diastolic and provides the second number in a blood pressure reading. Thus, a blood pressure reading of 120 over 80 means you have a systolic pressure of 120 and a diastolic pressure of 80. That is considered normal, and Hope's BP had been at this normal range every other time it was taken.

Slightly higher readings—140 to 159 and 90 to 94—are considered mild high blood pressure (mild hypertension). Readings from 160 to 179 and 94 to 114 signal moderate hypertension. Anything above these limits is considered serious.

And numbers way under those ain't good either as I would soon find out.

The monitor hummed for a few seconds and then beeped. The blood pressure reading was finished.

The numbers read 85 over 28.

Thankfully, from their vantage point beside the table, Shelby and Wendy could not see the monitor. Before I could react, Dr. McMahon calmly, but forcefully, told Michelle, who had been standing in the doorway with me, to bring in an IV. In less than thirty seconds she returned with an IV pole containing a bag of clear liquid called bolus. As Michelle quickly hooked up the IV, Dr. McMahon led me into the hall.

"We are in a tough situation here. She is very dehydrated and close to being in shock. We may need to move her to the pediatric intensive care unit. I have paged the PIC-U doctor to see what he thinks."

No sooner had the words left his mouth than the PIC-U doctor appeared. I don't remember his name, but he had a pleasant smile on his face as he first spoke briefly with Dr. McMahon and then went in to see Hope.

"How are you feeling, young lady? Those are some gorgeous blue eyes you have."

"I feel really light-headed," Hope said weakly.

"That's okay. You just lay there and hold on to your mom so she doesn't get away. We will see how you feel in a few minutes."

With that he led Dr. McMahon and me back into the hall.

"I think she will be okay. Let's get a bag or two of bolus fluid in her and maintain a watch on her vitals. If they don't go up any in the next few minutes, let's get her into the PIC-U."

The two doctors and I then went back into the room. They made small talk with Shelby and Hope, but the concern was clear on their faces. As the bolus infusions dripped into Hope, Michelle took her vital signs every few minutes. Not much changed until about fifteen minutes later when Hope's blood pressure began to rise. It was still far from normal but it was enough for the PIC-U doctor.

"She should be fine now. That was a close one, but fortunately we got some IV fluid in her just in time."

My newest hero then shook my hand and headed off to save more lives.

For the next hour Dr. McMahon let two bolus infusions drip into Hope, and then she recovered enough to be moved upstairs. It was about two o'clock in the afternoon and Hope fell asleep immediately.

Shelby, Wendy, and I sat in the room, the three of us finally relaxing a little bit. It was then that we began to realize just how close a call that had been.

"Her blood pressure must have been nearly nothing," Shelby said to me as she leaned back into the recliner. "I couldn't see the monitor. What was it? Could you tell?"

For a second I debated whether or not to tell her but decided the crisis had passed. "Uh, I think it said 85 over 28 or something like that."

My wife's reaction stunned Wendy and me.

"What? You are kidding me? You cannot have a blood pressure that low and live. Are you sure?" Shelby Stout spoke so loudly it was a miracle that Hope did not wake up. I assured my wife that was the number and she got teary-eyed again. "Then we nearly lost her."

Hope did not wake up at all that evening, and the nurses told us that she would likely sleep right through the night. Because she was so dehydrated, it was critical to get the fever down and make sure her kidneys were functioning.

"Let me stay with her tonight. You go home," I told Shelby. And after some mild protesting, she agreed.

Later that evening, as I was catching up on some paperwork I heard a knock at the door, and Dr. McMahon came in the room, which surprised me. He was usually the first person we saw in the morning, but being here that late, especially on a Friday, seemed odd. I put down my work as he came in and was about to get up when he stopped me.

Dr. Daniel McMahon was usually all business when he made his rounds and rarely sat and visited. This time, he pulled up a chair, removed his glasses, rubbed his eyes, and then crossed his legs. I could see he was trying to get comfortable. As he put his glasses back on, I became alarmed. Did he have additional bad news? Had this incident done something to Hope? It seemed like hours until he finally spoke.

"That was a close call. For a few minutes there, I thought we were going to lose her."

Seeing him this way, very vulnerable and now very relieved, showed me how much compassion was hidden behind this man's calm demeanor. Clearly he cared a great deal about Hope.

We talked for a few more minutes, and he assured me that getting her fever under control would be easier here in the hospital because they could monitor her more closely. He then switched gears and asked me about my business and how it was going; we also talked some about our children. I found out that he had a son who was attending NC State.

"When he decided on NC State, I figured I could live with that. Had he chosen UNC that would have been tough to take since I attended Duke." (The rivalry between these two North Carolina universities is a healthy and longstanding one. Put simply, there isn't much love lost between the Tar Heels and the Blue Devils.)

He continued. "NC State I could live with . . . But UNC? That would have been hard," he said as he was leaving the room.

As the door closed behind him, I realized how lucky we were to have this wonderful man caring for Hope. In addition to being an oncologist, Dr. McMahon was also a parent who realized what Shelby and I were going through.

And one other thought occurred to me.

Those words were spoken like a true Dookie!

Reflections of a Mother

Hope had a habit of putting things off even before she got sick. As a small child at home, she usually waited until the last minute to come to the dinner table, get her bath, get ready for church (many times I lost my religion before I even got there), get ready for bed, turn off the TV, and start her homework. A year before her illness, she finally wrote fifteen responsibilities on the computer and printed them out to keep her on track. Two of these responsibilities were in caps: DON'T GOOF OFF WHEN THERE IS WORK TO BE DONE!!! And TELL EVERYONE IN MY FAMILY THAT I LOVE THEM!!

Now she was starting to stall the nurses for more time. When it came to taking medicine, eating lunch, or changing the dressing of her port, it was always, "Just give me five more minutes and I'll do it." And then it would be five more minutes, and then another five. Patience ran thin with her on many occasions.

One day when we were going through this last chemo treatment, she spent the entire day asking for more time. Finally two nurses came in to change her bed. At this point any movement of her leg was beginning to be very painful. We propped and cushioned her leg with at least three pillows stationed in various places.

The nurses were being very careful as they changed the sheets, but I could tell that Hope was getting anxious and moody. Then she started yelling at the nurses, "You are not being careful of my leg!!"

Before I realized what I was doing I stopped her. "They're trying to do the best they can. I know your leg hurts, but you are not going to disrespect these adults, no matter what—so cooperate!"

Hope started to cry as she said, "I'm so sorry, Mom." Then she apologized to the nurses for being so rude. After that she still procrastinated, but with a sweeter tone.

Hope had procrastinated that day when her fever soared. She started crying as I began packing her suitcase, and not knowing how serious this could get, she kept stalling for time.

However, after this scare, she made a new discovery: as much as she hated the hospital, she knew she was in good hands there.

28
Miracle Girl

Around seven o'clock on Saturday morning, October 4, I was awakened by these words:

"Dad, wake up! Look!"

My eyes began to focus in the early morning light streaming through the slight crack in the blinds, which I had closed the night before. I could make out Hope sitting up in the bed. It took a second for this fact to register.

She is sitting up! By herself! What is going on? This seemed very odd since we had come close to losing her the day before. Now she seemed almost ready to leap out of the bed.

Immediately my mind jerked into gear and so did my body. I jumped out of the recliner and over to the side of her bed. "Hey, you. What is going on? Hang on a minute and I will help you get to the bathroom."

"No, I don't need any help," she said confidently. "Just watch."

Hope Elizabeth Stout swung her legs over the side of the bed almost as if nothing was wrong. Yesterday she had been as weak as a kitten, barely able to move.

Now this.

She slid down off the bed and actually *put some weight* on her right leg without the use of her crutches. Not much weight, but some for sure.

I slumped back against the wall in utter astonishment as she grabbed one of her crutches, which was leaning against the wall next to the bathroom. She stuck the crutch under her arm and went into the bathroom, completely without help.

For a second, I had to make sure this wasn't a dream. Many thoughts danced through my mind, but one in particular stuck with me. We had been praying, as had so many others, for Hope's complete healing from this cancer.

Had this happened? Had God healed her?

It seemed like hours before she emerged from the bathroom. I could not wait to talk to her and see how she felt, but as she came out, I didn't need to.

She all but hopped out of the bathroom, set her crutch against the wall, and plopped herself onto the side of the bed. Normally Shelby or I would have to gently lift her legs onto the bed.

Not today!

"Watch this," she said excitedly and, without any help from me, pulled both of her legs up onto the bed! She didn't even put her hands under her bad leg; she just lifted it up and put it down on her own.

Now I had to find a chair. I pulled the recliner up close to my now-beaming daughter. Let me remind you that it was seven o'clock in the morning. Hope hardly ever woke up before ten o'clock, and even though she had been pretty much asleep since two o'clock yesterday afternoon, the fact that she was wide awake at seven o'clock was, well, nutso. Anyone with teenagers knows that getting them up before the crack of noon is all but impossible. Yet here we were: up and at 'em at seven o'clock . . . a.m.!

"Uh, Miss Hope, what is going on? I am a little shocked at this . . . How do you feel?" I ventured.

"I feel great. Watch!"

My daughter lifted her right leg—the one with cancer from the top of her knee all the way up through the hip—about two feet off the bed, held her leg in the air for a second or two, and then lowered it back down.

"That," I said, "is amazing! Do you have any pain when you do that?"

"A little. But only when I get up this high." She lifted her leg again to show me.

Seeing this miracle overwhelmed me, and I jumped out of the chair and gave her a big hug, a real one this time, not the gentle hugs of the past couple of months. And she hugged me back! What a gift!

Then she announced, "I am *hungry!*" Another miracle! Hope was in the hospital and wanted to eat? Any second I half expected Jesus Himself to come walking into the room! No sooner than Hope had said that, my cell phone vibrated. When Shelby did not spend the night with Hope, you could always count on a call early from the chief "Hovering Hen" to see what had happened.

"Well," I said, "things are somewhat different this morning."

And before I could finish, Hope asked me for the phone. "Mom, stop by the grocery store and bring us some food. We are starving!"

About twenty minutes later, Dr. McMahon came in. Hope was very eager to show him the newfound flexibility in her leg. To say that he was pleased would be an understatement.

He felt around her leg very gently, which was unusual, because Hope did not like anyone touching this leg because of the resulting pain. Yet Hope didn't wince once.

"This is truly a good sign. VP-16 tends to work that way. What apparently has happened is the chemo has killed a lot of the cancer cells, and that is allowing your leg to have more movement. We will take it."

Hope actually cut up some with Dr. McMahon. Usually she was either asleep when he came in or didn't say much. Today she was almost chatty.

Right after he left, Shelby showed up with two big bags of food, and Hope and I gave her a hard time about that. We enjoyed a rarity: a family meal in the hospital.

Over the next few days, the infection and fever stubbornly hung on, but finally gave up, and on Wednesday, October 8, we came home. For the following ten days, Hope's strength gradually returned and after a few days, she was allowed to have visitors. What was of paramount importance to her at this time was being normal, and trivial issues like chemo were not going to slow her down.

Reflections of a Mother

It was so good to see Hope have an appetite again; when she indicated that she was hungry, I was determined to bring all of her favorite foods: chocolate and vanilla pudding, applesauce, Snicker bars, Skittles, chocolate Swiss rolls (her favorite), Goldfish snack crackers, and, of course, Gummi Bears. Hope loved Gummi Bears and would put them on top of her ice cream. This always made her father gag.

"You are messin' up perfectly good ice cream by doing that," he would tell her. She would just grin at her dad, usually with several of the Gummis stuck in her teeth for effect.

By the time I got through shopping, I had two bags full.

Once I arrived at the hospital, I got the famous preteen, know-it-all eye roll. "Gee, Mom, we can feed the whole floor with all that food!" she said sarcastically.

I didn't care. She was hungry and I was going to feed her any-thing and everything she wanted.

From the time Dr. McMahon had started her treatments Hope had kept reminding him of her social calendar. Now she was focused on her cousin Thomas and Bonnie's wedding in late October. (Thomas was one of the three "fireheads," and she was not going to miss it.) Believe it or not, Hope had never attended a wedding in her life: Thomas and Bonnie's would be her first. She also brought up the Weddington Wildcat games, the Weddington High School home-coming game, the Panther games, and, of course, Halloween.

Dr. McMahon finally said, "Hope, why don't we wait until next year to start your next chemo treatment since your calendar is so full."

"Works for me," Hope said.

Dr. McMahon realized how important these events were to Hope, and he made every effort for her to experience each and every special event on her agenda in the days ahead.

29

"Drop the Hammer!"

F riday, October 17 was homecoming at Weddington High School, and Hope was bound and determined to be there. We prayed that the weather for the Friday night game would cooperate. As much as we wanted Hope to go, if it was rainy or too cold, we were not going to chance it.

Fortunately, the weatherman hit the forecast out of the park. Friday night turned out to be a perfect fall evening to be outside and watch a football game. We got to the stadium about twenty minutes before kickoff. Wendy and Tom knew we were coming and managed to save some seats for us, which was good because the stands were already packed.

Despite the long walk from the parking lot to the stands, Hope refused to ride in a wheelchair; instead she was determined to use her crutches. We entered the stands on the home side of the stadium and began to make it down to where Wendy and Tom had saved our seats. It didn't take long for all of her buddies to see Hope. One of them screamed her name, and when the rest of the gang saw her, they all rushed up the stadium steps toward her, going against the people trying to get to their seats.

Hope had a huge grin on her face but also looked a little embarrassed at all the attention. She watched the whole football game sitting with her buddies and got to see Holly named to the sophomore homecoming court. Hope was also the recipient of a stadium blanket that someone bought for her and about three boxes of Krispy Kreme doughnuts, which are sold at all the home games.

When we got home, she was exhausted but couldn't stop talking about how much fun she had at the game. It was obvious to us that Hope enjoyed something that had been lost since June 27: just being a normal kid again. We were so happy that Hope could finally enjoy moments with her buddies on her own—without us.

The next day, Shelby, Holly, Hope, and I drove two hours north to the Boone, North Carolina, area. This was the peak weekend for the fall leaf colors, and the weather again cooperated. We had a great time looking at all the scenery and also made a visit to one of Hope's favorite places, Mast General Store, an old-timey store that carries virtually everything, including candy of every description, which, of course, was Hope's main reason for going there.

Hope walked through the aisles on her crutches, examining the huge barrels of treats. She loaded up on all her favorite candies: Gummi Bears, Snicker bars, and Skittles. Then she took her basket to the front counter where we paid for her candy like the old days—by weight, not by individual items.

We almost had to take out a second mortgage to pay for all the candy Hope bought that day. And we would have been all too happy to do it.

After a full day of shopping, we went to dinner. Appalachian State University, which is located in Boone, had a home football game that had just ended and there was a long line. We took our seats in the waiting area, and when our name was called, the gentleman with whom we had been chatting stopped us.

"Excuse me, but are you Hope Stout?" he asked our daughter.

I suppose that hearing our name and seeing a redheaded girl on crutches kinda gave it away. Hope replied that she was, and he told us he was the associate pastor of Weddington United Methodist Church, the very church that had held the prayer service for Hope back in July. "I am continuing to pray for your recovery," he said.

As we took our seats at the table, Hope, using her best aristocratic voice, said, "You know, it is hard being famous. You just cannot get away from all the common people. I hope all these people will let me eat in peace. Autograph seekers can be so annoying when you are trying to eat."

"We will make sure nobody interrupts your dinner, O Great One," I said as the waiter arrived and soon the two girls' attention turned to him. More food was ordered than was needed; Hope's appetite had returned and she had a big time with her sister Holly, even flirting with the cute waiter by asking for his cell phone number for Holly. This thoroughly embarrassed her big sister, which was the plan.

As if the previous two days weren't enough to keep Hope busy, the next day we attended the Carolina Panthers/Tennessee Titans football game. Jim Jacobs, a family friend who is a Charlotte police officer, had arranged for Hope to get club seat tickets to the game from the Panthers organization. Jim handles security at most of the Panther games and even managed to get Hope a field pass. The Tennessee game worked out perfectly because the lull in Hope's treatment allowed her to go.

Our family tailgate parties at all the Panther games are legendary. We go to most of the games with the Reeder family and on this day, because Hope was able to come, we had a massive soiree planned. All of Tom and Wendy's children came along with Bruce and Janet Mullan, and, of course, Hope's friend Emily. There was plenty of good food, the weather was perfect again, and Hope wore a new Carolina Panther jersey featuring Julius Peppers's number 90.

At that time, two members of the Panthers organization were also battling cancer: Mark Fields, #58, a linebacker, and Sam Mills, an assistant coach who had played with the Panthers and whose #51 had been retired by the team. A year earlier during training camp, Sam had been diagnosed, and after cancer struck the Panther family a second time, the organization created a fund-raiser for cancer research called "Drop the Hammer on Cancer" in honor of the two men. For a donation to the fund, you were given a wristband that said "Drop the Hammer!" Hope had painstakingly worked on a poster that featured "Drop the Hammer on Cancer" for several days beforehand and had brought it to the game.

"Maybe the camera guy will see this poster and we will get on TV," Hope had told Shelby.

After parking the car near the stadium, we helped Hope get to the place where we were to meet the Panthers' representative. As we were waiting, Mark Richardson, the president of the Panthers, walked by us with one of his assistants. He was clearly in a hurry to get where he was going, but he spotted Hope's poster and gave her a thumbs up.

"That is what we are going to do," Mark said to Hope. "We are going to keep on fighting cancer." He smiled and continued to walk away.

"Yes, we know. And so are we," Shelby added. Hearing her words, Mark stopped, turned around, and came back, much to the irritation of his assistant. He knelt down and asked Hope her name.

When she told him, he said, "Hey, I know who you are. Listen, I have to be somewhere right now, but I will see you on the field in a few minutes. I want a picture of you and me with that poster."

"Thanks. It took me a couple of hours to draw it," Hope said matter-of-factly.

"Well, it is really good," he said and then he left.

Hope immediately started in on Shelby and me. "You see *the-ah?*
If you fine people will just stick with me, I will introduce you to
him inside. If *the-ah* is time and I feel like doing it, that is," Hope
said with her British accent, which brought the standard giggle
from Emily.

Finally the escort arrived, and we were taken through the tunnel into Ericsson Stadium.

Just as we were about to walk onto the playing field, the
Tennessee Titans came rushing down the tunnel from the visiting
locker room, so the security guards motioned for us to stand aside.
The players' metal cleats on the stadium concrete made such a
racket it sounded like a herd of buffalo. Hope and Emily's eyes
were as large as pie pans as the immense athletes ran past them out
onto the field.

"Geez, those guys are huge! I would hate to get hit by anyone
of them," Hope exclaimed to Emily, who was too amazed to say
anything. After the Titans made it onto the field, we were escorted
out of the tunnel into the sunshine of Ericsson Stadium.

We had never been on the playing field before, so we were overwhelmed by the sheer size and energy of the place. It was about an
hour before kickoff, and the stadium was not yet half full as the
players went through their warm-ups. Yet there was an electricity
in the immense arena as the fans anticipated the upcoming battle
between the surprisingly undefeated Panthers (6–0 at the time, versus previous years where the start of the season wasn't so good)
and the strong AFC Titans, who were picked by many to be in the
Super Bowl.

Hope did not know the surprise that had been arranged for her.
In fact, we didn't know much, except that one of the Panther players
was going to meet Hope. Offensive guard Kevin Donnalley had been
made aware of Hope's diagnosis and what she had been facing over
the past few months, so when he had heard her name mentioned as
one of the guests for the upcoming game during a team meeting, he

volunteered to be the one to meet her. Later on, Kevin told us that he rarely did something like this. Like a lot of athletes, his pre-game ritual was very important, and Kevin was admittedly very superstitious, right down to how he taped his hands. In fact, if he started to tape his hands and got it wrong, he started over. To him, it was a big deal to change or augment his pre-game warm-up routine.

As Hope stood there, leaning against her crutches, taking in the sights and sounds on the sun-drenched field, a gigantic shadow began looming over her. She turned to look up and there stood Kevin, all six-feet, five inches and three hundred pounds of him. "Hi, Hope. My name is Kevin Donnalley. How are you doing?"

After a few seconds, Hope finally managed to mumble an answer. Kevin then asked if she was having a good time at the game. Hope just stood there with a grin on her face, but she said very little, which was really odd. Finally he handed her something.

"Hope, these are the gloves I wore last week. They are kinda stinky and sweaty, but I signed them for you," he said as he handed them to her. "I also have a hat signed by Jerry, Mark, and Jon Richardson. They are pretty important guys. They own the team."

Fortunately, the Panthers photographer showed up about that time and took some pictures of her and Kevin and other photographs with Hope and Sir Purr, the Panthers mascot. Kevin then got ready to resume his warm-up.

"Hope, if it is okay, I will call you next week to see how you are doing. I love your poster and I want you to do the same thing: just keep on fighting and getting better. I will be praying for you."

Then this gigantic professional football player leaned over and gave her a gentle hug before he trotted back to resume his preparation for the game. We had no way of knowing how much seeing Hope had affected him. But later on we found out, and so would millions of other people watching a nationally televised NFL play-off game on January 3, 2004.

Reflections of a Mother

Hope had a great day at the game, despite the Panthers' loss that day. (As we would see, the team rarely lost much after that as the Cardiac Cats forged onward toward the Super Bowl.) She got home and soon was sitting on the couch.

"Mom," she said, "I bet I could get Kevin to take me out to dinner in a limo."

I told her she was getting too big for her britches, that it was quite enough for him to have taken the time to meet her before the game. "Just be happy with today," I said.

Of course, the next day Kevin called to ask if he could come to visit her.

"Sure, Kevin, anytime you want to," Hope told him. After hanging up the phone, she looked at me and said with that smart-alecky smirk on her face, "See. Told you I would see him again. He is coming over on Halloween before all the trick-or-treating starts. Once again, Hope is right and Mom is wrong."

It began to occur to me that maybe Hope did have an unusual influence on people. The way she affected Kevin Donnalley turned out to be just the tip of the iceberg.

30
Wedding Bells

As the cancer progressed, it became harder for Hope to enjoy one of her most favorite pastimes: "Shop till you drop." October 27 was the big wedding of her cousin Thomas, and she was getting worried about what she was going to wear, as most females do.

Just before the wedding, Shelby and I got a chance to go out for dinner. Everything was okay on the home front, Holly had agreed to stay with Hope, and we would only be gone for an hour or so.

Like every other man on earth, I hate to shop. But after dinner I agreed to a trip to the mall to see if we could find Hope something to wear to the rehearsal dinner and wedding. Hope didn't want people to see or even notice her knee and the swelling above it. The contrast between the huge upper part of her leg and the naturally small calf of a slender girl made the devastation of the disease so evident.

At the store I picked out a black-and-white-striped blouse and black slacks. I was just grabbing outfits and putting them together to hurry Shelby along, but what I picked out worked, Shelby thought. She also selected a pink outfit (Hope's favorite color) from Limited Too, one of her favorite stores. When we got home, Shelby showed her the outfits and told her that her dad had picked out the black one.

"My dad picked this out?" she asked, wide-eyed. She was obviously amazed at the image of her father shopping for women's clothes. The black outfit looked gorgeous on her. She would wear it to the rehearsal dinner and the pink outfit to the wedding.

On the day of the wedding, as she moved from the ceremony to the reception the pain in her leg became more intense. Hope quickly found a seat and tried to get comfortable. She was eating and visiting with her cousins when the bridegroom came up and whispered something to her.

Thomas wanted to dance with her.

Hope was very hesitant to do so. How was she going to be able to dance with her crutches? She'd relied on them for a couple of months now, ever since our last trip to the beach. And what about the pain in her leg? Would she make it worse? I knew all these thoughts must be going through her mind.

As Shelby and I were visiting with the other guests, I turned around to see a wonderful sight.

The two fireheads were on the dance floor. Thomas, who was a former all-American baseball player, was holding all of Hope's weight so she did not have to use those stupid crutches.

And they were dancing!

Soon everyone was looking at the two cousins. Women and men alike were crying at the touching scene. The two redheads were simply dancing, but no one missed this overt symbolization of Hope's determination to live her life as normally as possible. Cancer might make some things difficult, but not impossible. Not for Hope Stout.

After the 9/11 attack, Hope had written a poem for her fifth-grade English class, "In a Heartbeat," which ended "And not to let your heart fade out. Do what your heart leads you to do." As she said in this poem, she was still willing to challenge life and make the best of what happened to her.

In a Heartbeat
By Hope Stout

In a heartbeat, a person is gone.
And another, brought into the world.
Life, Death, Happiness, Sadness.
To me it's all a big twirl.
Should we expect death? Challenge life?
Make the best with what we have?
Should we accept our mistakes?
In every way?
And sometimes
Just laugh?
What is this thing called "hate"?
In the September 11 attacks?
Do we all stand up and face our fears?
So we can all fight back?
In a heartbeat, every thing can change.
Every thing can happen in a blink.
This is why I wrote this poem,
For you!
And not to let your heart fade out.
Do what your heart leads you to do.

Yes, Hope got to go to her first wedding.

And Shelby and I watched our daughter dance—and forget the cancer for a little while.

Reflections of a Mother

What is more exciting than turning sixteen years old? You get your driver's license, start going out on dates, enjoy having more freedom, and don't have your mom or dad taking you wherever you need to go.

Turning sixteen is an important step in growing up, a milestone to be celebrated, and Holly was very excited about her sweet sixteen birthday on October 30. She was also pleased that Hope was feeling well enough to celebrate at a restaurant. That night was going to be free of the raging storm of Hope's cancer.

We made plans to go to the Cheesecake Factory. We knew they did not take reservations, but we called, telling them about our situation, and they made an exception. The manager told us to come around seven o'clock and he would seat us immediately. Hope loved playing the "cancer card," because it gave her some control and power in certain situations, which happens so infrequently once cancer strikes.

We were all excited and looking forward to a special time to just focus on Holly. But as the day went on, Hope's leg began to hurt. The pain medicine was not doing the trick. She stayed on the couch most of the day, the pain increasing by the hour. Hope knew going out to dinner meant so much to Holly, but the pain just became too unbearable. Stuart was out of town for the day, and the last time he called, plans were a go. But by the time he stepped in the house from his trip, Holly and I were sitting on the couch with Hope, all three of us crying.

Holly just wanted us all to go out and celebrate her birthday, Hope included. Hope knew she couldn't go because the pain was more than she could bear. And then she saw the disappointment in Holly's face, which hurt as much as the leg pain.

And me? I had no control over the situation. In a heartbeat everything can change.

31

A Hammer

As I entered our neighborhood on Thursday, October 30, the day of Holly's birthday, I had no way of knowing what the next few hours would mean for us. I walked into the kitchen to find my three girls sitting in the den, crying.

You would think Mr. Cool would be able to comfort his wife and children, right? Fathers are supposed to be calm in the face of tears and offer some soothing words that will help everyone over the rough spots in life.

That stuff only happens on TV. A calm, cool, and collected father sure didn't exist that day.

After quickly evaluating the scenario in the den, the frustration of what was happening and the long day I had experienced reached its boiling point. I had been up since before dawn, sat through a boring continuing-education seminar, and had driven through traffic for four hours. I suddenly possessed this overwhelming need to hit something.

Realizing that breaking stuff in the house would be stupid, I quickly walked back out into the garage and slammed the door just hard enough to placate me somewhat, but not hard enough to alarm my family. I looked for something to throw or break, anything to vent this smoldering, pent-up anger.

And then my eyes found the hammer.

Grabbing it, I searched for something to bash, but again stopped as I eliminated the extra refrigerator, the water heater, the tool bench, and the girls' bicycles. Whaling away at that stuff in the garage would get ugly and expensive and would surely upset Shelby and the girls. I opened the garage door and ran into the October night.

Our subdivision is rather unique; each home actually has quite a bit of land around the house, unlike some other developments, and an abundance of trees. Our neighborhood is typically very quiet, and we live on a cul-de-sac so there is not much traffic.

Finally outside of the house and the earshot of my family, I ran to the middle of our heavily wooded backyard. The only light came from inside our house. When I was far enough away from the house, I *let go* as never before. All of the frustration that had been building up for the past four months came spewing out. I was angry, but not at a person or situation.

I was angry at God.

I began screaming at Him; the hammer in my right hand slamming time and time again into the trunk of a pine tree.

"I have had it, God! You and me are done, do You hear me? You aren't listening, are You? Why aren't You healing this kid? Just exactly what has she done to deserve this? It is time for You to start listening to us; we are praying constantly and so is everybody else! Enough of this. Heal this child!"

Admittedly, I know some other things were said that I will not repeat. The point is I was pretty much out of control.

My rant against God and His insufficient handling of our situation continued unabated for several more minutes. I challenged

God to show Himself to me so that we could *have at it*. I wanted to physically struggle with Him, in a literal way, as Jacob did in Genesis 32.

Had this scene unfolded in a typical neighborhood with houses close together, the police would have been summoned and I would have been taken off. In fact, I am still surprised my next-door neighbor didn't hear me.

Finally, after the bark of the pine tree was beaten into a gooey mess, I threw the hammer far into the woods, slumped down, and began sobbing. I was out of options and completely helpless to do anything about Hope's situation.

And now I had pretty much told God off. It began to occur to me what a brilliant move that was.

You know those moments when you wish the words that just tumbled out of your mouth could be reeled back in? This was one of them.

Maybe God hadn't heard me.

Turns out He heard me all right—and so did someone else.

I picked myself up off the cold ground and trudged back into the house where I expected to find crying and pain.

Instead, what I found was peace.

Three pairs of eyes were staring at me as if I were some kind of weird alien who had just landed on earth. There were no tears, just very curious looks.

Reflections of a Mother

When Stuart came home that day, I could tell that he needed to yell, cuss, scream, or all of the above, so I knew to leave him alone. My concern was consoling Hope and Holly. That is a mom's job. I had already given Hope all the pain medicine she could take, so I did not know what else to do. So I said, "Let's all three pray for the pain to go away."

With tears flowing, we pleaded with God for a short time. Then all of a sudden, we felt this sense of peace. The God Pump had kicked in again. We all three stopped crying. I turned and looked at Hope and asked her if she was still hurting.

She said no! The pain had stopped along with the tears. God had heard and answered our prayers once again. This time Hope and Holly saw it firsthand. We actually started laughing about this relief when we heard this yelling coming from outside.

Hope looked at me and said, "What is Dad doing?"

"It sounds like he is yelling at someone," I replied. About that time we heard the back door open and shut. Stuart came in and saw us all smiling. He looked at us very curiously, and we looked kinda funny at him too.

As he sat down beside Hope, we told him Hope's pain had gone away when we started praying. Hope then asked her dad who he was yelling at.

"Oh . . . that. I was in the backyard yelling at God!" he said.

Hope stared at her father for a second. Then she said, "You better watch out who you are yelling at—especially when it's God."

We all laughed at that comment, and then Stuart began to explain about a father's love for his child.

"Hope, you know you yell at me sometimes, but I still love you, and I understand your frustration. It's the same with God. I am His child, and if I yell at Him, He doesn't love me any less."

Stuart had put God's enduring love into terms Hope could understand. She loved her daddy so much, yet she and Stuart argued all the time. Hearing that example, she started to comprehend the depth of God's love; she realized that God was willing to listen to and accept our anger and frustration—and still love us more than we could ever imagine.

Even though the pain had mostly subsided, Hope decided that she couldn't chance overdoing it. But she insisted that Stuart and Holly go to the Cheesecake Factory together and celebrate Holly's sweet sixteen birthday—with one condition.

"Only if you bring me and Mom a piece of their famous cheesecake."

Stuart and Holly did that; however, I didn't get a bite. Hope ate both pieces herself.

Now that shows how deep a mother's love flows!

32

A Halloween Treat

H alloween has always been a big deal around our house. Hope, in particular, would spend weeks getting her costume ready for trick-or-treating. Thankfully the previous night's events were beginning to fade away on the morning of Friday, October 31. And right away the day became brighter.

Early that morning we received a phone call from Kevin Donnalley, who wanted to know if it would be okay to visit Hope around three o'clock that afternoon. The Panthers were scheduled to play at Houston on Sunday, and Kevin had the day off prior to the trip to Texas.

Although Hope had been in quite a bit of pain, she spent much of the day resting so that she could go out trick-or-treating that night. She and Emily had decided to go as nerds, complete with pocket protectors, thick, black glasses, and fake "Bubba" teeth that protruded much like Jerry Lewis's teeth in the old movie *The Nutty*

Professor. The pair had auditioned their costumes for us earlier in the week, and they were a hoot. We just prayed she would feel like going.

Before Kevin Donnalley came over that afternoon, Shelby suggested that Hope change clothes. Her shirt, in particular, hadn't been changed in a day or so and had food spills and cat hairs all over it.

Hope just looked at Shelby and said, "Mom, this is a man who rolls around in the dirt for a living. Do you think he cares if I have a little food on my shirt?"

Despite Little Miss Smarty Pants's comments, Shelby made Hope change the shirt anyway.

Around three o'clock, Kevin Donnalley came into our home. I am not a small guy at six feet two inches and about 230 pounds, but Kevin's enormous size made me look tiny. Kevin, the father of three children, brought Hope a bag of lollipops, and soon he and Hope were watching the popular cartoon *SpongeBob SquarePants* and sucking on lollipops.

Hope told him what Shelby had made her do, and, of course, he took her side. "You didn't have to do that for me. I don't care what you wear."

She looked at Shelby with that "I told you so" look.

Kevin stayed for an hour or so and then had to go home to get ready for Halloween with his kids. We took some pictures with Kevin and Hope, and then Shelby and I walked him to the door.

When we opened it, the whole front yard was full of kids along with several women. For a second, I thought word had spread through the neighborhood that a Panthers player was visiting Hope, and I became concerned that Kevin would be stuck here signing autographs.

But then Shelby spoke up. "Kevin, don't worry. These kids aren't here to bug you. Our neighbor Danette has organized a prayer vigil because Hope has been in so much pain lately. We are supposed to get Hope outside, but if we told her this was going to happen, she wouldn't have come, so we are just going to surprise her."

Kevin looked relieved because there were about thirty-five kids milling around the yard, some of them already dressed in their Halloween costumes. Yet none of the young people stopped him as this large giant of a man walked to his car at the top of driveway. As he turned around to look back at the crowd, the expression on his face was a mixture of relief and curiosity. As a pro athlete (and one you can hardly miss due to his size), Kevin Donnalley rarely waded through a pack of kids without one of them asking for his autograph.

That evening, Hope's pain subsided enough to allow her to go trick-or-treating with Emily. She asked me to take her around in the golf cart, and after loading up Emily and Daisy (who loved riding in the cart with Hope) we headed out into the neighborhood. I drove Hope as close as possible to each front porch, and Emily would take both girls' bags to get candy.

When our neighbors realized that Hope was in the cart, they loaded up her bag, much to her delight. But not to Emily's, who began to complain about the amount of candy Hope was getting.

"Don't worry, Bogeen," Hope said, using her pet name for Emily. "We will split up the candy when we get back to my house."

Hearing Hope call Emily "Bogeen" brought back a fond memory.

About four years earlier, we were heading to a late-season Panthers game, and Hope had invited Emily to go. It was very cold that day, and when we picked up Emily, I noticed she did not have a hat on.

"Emily, don't you have a toboggan or something for your head? You are gonna freeze in this cold weather," I said.

The two girls sitting in the back seat of the car went to pieces, heehawing in laughter.

Evidently there are two meanings to the word *toboggan*. Growing up in the South, I knew only one: *toboggan* meant a knit wool hat worn in cold weather.

After regaining their composure somewhat, Hope asked, "Dad, you want Emily to wear a sled on her head?" That sent the girls into another fit of laughter.

From that moment on, Emily became "Toboggan" and then Hope shortened it to "Bogeen." Go figure.

About halfway through our tour of the neighborhood that Halloween, we met up with one of our neighbors, a seventh-grade boy named Ryan who was trick-or-treating by himself. Surprisingly, Hope asked him to join us in the golf cart. This was really odd because Hope was very particular about whom she wanted around her, especially boys, so when she asked Ryan to hop aboard "Little Ricky," it caught me off guard.

Ryan just said, "Cool," and jumped into the cart. The night was surprisingly warm, and soon Hope announced that she was ready to go back to the house. Again, she surprised me by asking Ryan to come home with them to watch a scary Halloween movie and eat some of their goodies.

I sensed that Hope wanted to have some interaction with someone outside her circle of friends, in this case a boy in her neighborhood whom she only saw during the winter on sledding days. Ryan had the best backyard hill around. She was beginning to accept that cancer did make her different, but she was not ashamed of it.

I helped Hope into the house, followed by Ryan and Emily. As Hope got situated on the couch, Ryan sat down at the other end and Emily plopped into the recliner. The kids started to go through all their candy while Shelby and I looked on.

After about five minutes, Hope announced that she was hot. She had her wig on and because of the warm evening, it was too much to take.

"Ryan, watch out! The wig is coming off . . . Prepare yourself."

And then Hope Stout, the same girl who had fretted over losing her hair two months earlier, reached up and snatched off the wig, revealing her bald head.

Ryan, who had just stuffed a candy bar in his mouth, just stared at her. With a mouth full of candy he paused and took in the sight of Hope's bald noggin. He then said, "Hope . . . that is the coolest thing I have ever seen!"

Reflections of a Mother

The thirty-five people who came to pray for Hope consisted of friends of Hope's, mine and Stuart's, and some of Austin's and Holly's. Hope sat in a chair and everyone surrounded her. I could tell she was very uncomfortable, until her friends joined her in the middle of the circle and took some of the attention off her. Many people prayed individually and several walked around the house, asking for angels to protect our home and all who lived there.

After Kevin had left, Hope had decided not to go trick-or-treating, because she was hurting so badly. But after the prayer service and seeing her friends in costume, she changed her mind and we helped her put on her nerd attire.

Prayers were answered that night, and I was sure they would be answered in the future.

33

Men Are from Mars, Yada, Yada . . .

O ver the past couple of weeks, Shelby and I had had a long discussion with Dr. McMahon about Hope's future treatments,
and it was decided to conduct Hope's next chemotherapy treatment
at home rather than in the hospital. This decision came after Dr.
McMahon told us about a clinical study with a drug called Gleevac.
This particular cancer treatment had been very effective on some
leukemia patients, and Dr. McMahon was going to try to get Hope
into the study for osteosarcoma. He was enthusiastic about the
results Gleevac had been getting on other types of cancer, and he
felt there was a decent possibility that this drug, which acts as a cell
inhibitor, might be effective in reducing some of Hope's tumors. He
also suggested we continue with the VP-16, but to do it at home by
taking a pill instead of intravenously through her port.

When Hope was told that she could do her chemo treatments
at home, she was very happy—and amazed.

"You mean they sell chemo at Eckerd's?"

We were somewhat skeptical at how effective oral chemo treatments would be, but Dr. McMahon felt that we would keep working on shrinking the tumors, while at the same time allowing Hope to enjoy a better quality of life. He knew how much she hated the hospital and felt this was a good compromise. So in late October, Hope had begun home chemo treatments, which consisted of a pill a day for a week. Getting the chemo into Hope this way lessened the side effects such as nausea and lack of appetite. Unfortunately, Hope's condition continued to worsen, little by little.

During the weekend of November 7, Shelby and Margot Smith took their two daughters, Holly and Mallory, to Holden Beach to celebrate their sweet sixteen birthdays. Hope and I both encouraged Shelby and Holly to go. It took Shelby a while to be persuaded, but she knew this was important to Holly and she finally agreed.

And I got to stay at home with Hope.

That Friday night, after the girls left for the beach, Hope and I were watching TV when the local sportscast came on, and, of course, the major topic was the big game on Sunday against Tampa Bay. When Shelby and Holly had decided to go to the beach, I had known I would not be able to attend so I had planned to give my tickets away but hadn't called anyone yet.

After the sportscast ended, Hope asked me if I was going to the game. When I told her no, she insisted that I reconsider. I told her to forget it, but she became resolute.

"Dad, I know how much you want to see that game. It's okay. Wendy can stay with me. It's only for a few hours. Please go."

I could see she was serious.

"I will think about it," I told her, and we watched a late movie together and then went to bed.

Saturday morning Wendy stopped by to check on us. She hadn't been in the house ten minutes when Hope asked her if she would mind staying with her while I went to the Panthers game on Sunday. Despite my protests (which admittedly were much milder now), Wendy said she would be glad to do so. Since both of them were so adamant, I decided to go.

On Sunday morning, both Wendy and her daughter, Liz, came over to stay with Hope, and I went to the game with Tom. Hope's appetite had returned after her chemo treatment had ended, and one of her favorite foods was Eggo waffles. She would eat them anytime of day or night.

As they were watching the Panthers game, Hope asked Wendy to fix a batch of waffles for her. Wendy jumped right on it, and even went so far as to cut up the waffles for Hope.

Later on, Hope told us she had never seen waffles cut up so finely in her life. "I practically had to drink them. Wendy chopped 'em up so much I might as well have used a straw."

In a report to her subjects on CaringBridge, Hope invented a new word to describe this waffle: *mutalized*.

My poor cousin never lived that down.

As for me, well, it was one of the better games I have ever seen, with the Panthers winning 27–24, stopping a furious Buccaneer comeback in the final seconds. Late that afternoon, still on a high from the game, I returned home and saw that Shelby and Holly had also returned from the beach. Wendy and Liz had gone home.

And that is when my trouble started.

Shelby Stout was standing in the kitchen seething. "How could you leave Hope just to go to the game?" Shelby hissed at me. "I cannot believe you made Wendy come over here while you went out and had a good time."

"It didn't happen quite like that," I told her, but there was not much I could say that would help my case. She was furious.

This was another of those times when Shelby and I would disagree on how we should respond to Hope's illness. John Gray, the author of the book *Men Are from Mars, Women Are from Venus,* portrayed the differences in men's and women's approaches to life. Let me verify that this includes our response to illness.

Despite the fact that Hope loved her parents and needed them around, a little change of facial scenery was good for her, I believed, although that is not what she could say to her parents. Shelby and I needed breaks too, although we didn't feel comfortable admitting that either.

"You have no right going off to some ball game with Hope here like this. How dare you do that? Somebody needs to be here with her all the time. What if something had happened?" my wife said hotly.

"Okay, now settle down," I said, hoping to soothe things a bit.

After all these years of marriage you would think I had learned to *never* tell my wife to settle down. It has the opposite effect.

I then tried logic.

"First off, Hope suggested that I go, and secondly, Wendy *is* family. They had a good time, and I called them several times during the game. I coulda been home in forty-five minutes if they needed me," I replied.

If only I would have stopped there. Instead I went on to remind Shelby: "You weren't here either. You were at the beach, right?"

That helped a lot, kinda like throwing gas on an already-burning fire. Shelby reacted as you would expect—she exploded.

For the next half hour, the two of us went back and forth arguing about . . . just what exactly? Perception? How we should both react to coping with Hope's disease? The longer we fought, the further we strayed from what we had started fighting about in the first place. The bottom line is we both felt we were right.

The argument continued until Hope yelled from the upstairs in the playroom. "You guys just chill out and quit yelling at each other. You are giving me a headache."

And that did it.

As mad as we were at each other, we both calmed down. Later, after we apologized to each other, we realized that we were both right.

Once Hope ended the fight, she announced that she wanted to call her buddy Kevin Donnalley to congratulate him on the big win. I dialed his cell phone number expecting to get his voice mail, but surprisingly he answered.

"Kevin, great game today! You guys had us on the edge of our seats! . . . Hey, somebody wants to talk to you. You got a minute?" I said.

"Absolutely. Put her on," he replied, and I handed the phone to Hope. She and Kevin talked for about thirty minutes. Hope told Kevin the Panthers played great but almost let the game get away at the end.

"Stop doing that," she said. "You nearly gave me a heart attack. Are you trying to kill me or somethin'? You will have to play better than that if you want to keep winning," she said matter-of-factly. She went on to suggest that he come by sometime this week so they could talk more.

After hearing her give Kevin her unsolicited counsel, it occurred to me that maybe Hope should call the White House to see if the president needed any advice on world matters.

34

Make-A-Wish

The fact that our family was enduring this hardship did not make us immune to other problems. I really didn't plan on confronting the reality that fairly soon we would need a new roof for our house, but the roof had other ideas. As I pulled out of the driveway one morning on the way to work, I noticed that several shingles had worked their way loose and were barely hanging on.

Great. Just what I needed, I thought. When I got to the office, I telephoned Dave Ballard, a friend of ours who is in the construction business. All I asked Dave for was the name of a good roofer. The last thing I wanted was to spend time shopping around for one.

Dave told me he would get back to me, and sure enough, he called back in an hour with a roofer's name. I telephoned the man and made arrangements to have him meet me at home later that day.

Normally this would have been a big decision for Shelby and me. We wanted the roof to look nice, and a lot of time and energy would be needed to pick out just the right type of shingle. Yet when I mentioned that the roofer was coming by that afternoon, Shelby told me, "You pick out the shingles. I really don't care about that right now. Just get it done."

And the shingle selection process didn't take very long. I picked out the shingles to use and inquired about the price.

The roofer gave me a curious answer. "Talk to Mr. Ballard about that. He is brokering this deal. My crew will be here bright and early on Friday, November 21, and, assuming the weather cooperates, we will be done in a day, two at the most. For two days though, it is going to be noisy on the second floor."

That was on Wednesday, November 19. As I went in to show Shelby what I had selected, she reminded me that the Make-A-Wish Foundation was coming over that night, a fact that had completely slipped my mind. In fact, I had planned on returning to my office to work.

So much for that plan.

Shelby also had to remind Hope of the visit. She was very reluctant to have the folks from Make-A-Wish come over, but Holly and the students at Weddington High School had already raised over eight thousand dollars for Hope's wish.

One night Holly and Austin had suggested that we look on the Make-A-Wish Web site to see if we could get ideas for Hope. We saw a picture of the cutest little three-year-old boy who wanted Ronald McDonald to come to his house for a party. Hope had thought this was the sweetest wish.

Yet she was not in a particularly good mood when the doorbell rang at seven o'clock that Wednesday evening.

I opened it to find Lynne Allen and Kelli Breaux, who were volunteer wish granters from the Make-A-Wish Foundation. Holly had met Lynne the previous year when Weddington High School had funded their first wish child. When Lynne found out that Hope was Holly's sister, she had insisted on being her granter. After we exchanged greetings, I escorted the two women upstairs to the playroom.

Lynne and Kelli sat on the couch opposite Hope. Holly sat on the floor and Shelby sat on the edge of the futon with Hope. I sat behind the futon at the computer desk, a perfect vantage point for me to see everyone's face, which would be very important in about twenty minutes.

It must be noted here that I *did not* want the Make-A-Wish folks there. When Holly told me that Weddington High School had already raised the money for Hope's wish, and that Make-A-Wish wanted to meet with us, I told her to forget it.

"Make-A-Wish is only for terminally ill kids. Hope is not going to die. Tell them, 'Thanks, but no thanks.'"

And then Holly enlightened her ignorant father about Make-A-Wish: their mission is to grant the wishes of children with *life-threatening* medical conditions, not just terminally ill children.

"Dad, a lot of the kids survive. A former wish kid talked to our student council earlier this year, and he was amazing. He had cancer when he was in his teens and is now twenty-five or so and completely healthy."

Since Weddington High School had raised the money for Hope's wish and because Holly had been so active in doing so, I relented and agreed to let Make-A-Wish come over. The staff at Carolinas Medical Center had suggested that it would be good for Hope to concentrate on something else beside her treatments. Still I wasn't too sure about these people as I watched the two volunteers greet my youngest daughter.

"Hope," Lynne began, "it is so nice to finally meet you. I have heard so much about you. I understand that Holly has been talking to you about your wish, so I am sure you have given it a lot of thought. We are here to do everything we can to grant your wish; whatever you want.

"So tell us. What do you want to do? What is your wish?"

Hope was very uncomfortable at this point and did not answer right away.

So her mother replied for her. "Well, Hope said something about being on a sitcom, or a modeling shoot, or—"

And that got an immediate reaction from Hope. "Ahem, Mom, if you don't mind, I will answer that. It is my wish, you know!"

"Well, you were just sitting there not saying anything so I thought I would make some suggestions," Shelby explained, which brought nervous laughter from all of us. This exchange did break the ice, however.

Kelli, a strawberry blonde whose hair was nearly as red as Hope's, then spoke for Make-A-Wish. "Really, Hope, what would you like to do?"

"Well, my mom is right. I would like to be on a TV sitcom. I would like to have been on *Lizzie McGuire* with Hilary Duff. I really like her but it is off the air now. I only watch the re-runs . . .*That's So Raven* might be fun to be on too. I also would like to do a modeling shoot in New York. I have never been to New York before.

"But I want to do all this when I am better," Hope said as Pudge made his appearance by jumping on the futon. "I want a walk-on role in a TV show."

"Hope," Shelby injected, "don't you think it would make more of an impact if you did it now, in a wheelchair? It would show people that anything is possible."

This comment brought "The Look" from Hope, which was directed at her mother. "No, not until I am better and can walk," Hope replied firmly.

Then she turned back to the two wish granters sitting on the couch in front of her. "My mom has been trying to get me to tell you guys that I want to be on Oprah's show. You know the one where they have all those new gadgets and stuff. For me and thirty of my 'closest' adult friends."

"Oprah's Favorite Things," Kelli and Lynne said at exactly the same time.

"Yeah, that one. Well, that ain't happenin', Mom." Hope reached down and scratched Pudge's head. Then she said, "What I really want is to be famous."

Now Lynne, a dark-haired woman whose brown eyes revealed her empathy for our sick daughter, spoke up. "Well, Hope, you kinda already are. I saw the article and pictures of you in the paper last week," she said, referring to the recent article "I Don't Let It Get Me Down," which had appeared in the *Charlotte Observer* on November 13. "That was a great story."

The conversation turned to the article briefly and then Lynne directed our attention back to Hope's wish. "Okay, Hope, let me suggest some things. You can go to Disney World or maybe swim with the dolphins . . . Or how about the Bahamas? Just name it. Your wish has already been funded by Weddington High School, so it is up to you."

Hope looked at Lynne intently. "Well, I am pretty lucky, you know? I have been to Disney World; me and my mom went a year or so ago when Holly was cheering in Orlando. Our family went to Cancun last summer and swam with the dolphins while we were there."

"Hope, how about going to Pebble Beach, California? Or maybe Pinehurst. Or how about the Super Bowl?" I suggested.

That brought a snort from my youngest daughter, who suspected her father might have ulterior motives. "Thanks for that, Dad. Now just be quiet, okay? I will let you know if I need any more suggestions from you."

So Shelby spoke up. "Hope, there is always the Oprah show. If you are confused, that is."

Hope looked at her mom and then cocked her head to one side. "Forget it, Mom. Nobody can get on that show. And again, I remind you, whose wish is this anyway?"

She turned to face Kelli and Lynne. "You say my wish was funded by Weddington High. What does that mean exactly?"

Lynne began: "Each wish costs a certain amount of money. In your case, that is not an issue because the money has already been raised by the high school and—"

"Yeah, I get that," Hope said. "What about the other kids? Isn't there, like, a pile of money sitting around?"

"Uh, no, not exactly," Kelli said. "Each wish has to be funded with money or with something we call 'in kind' donations, like when a kid goes to Disney World. They give us tickets, hotel rooms, and stuff like that."

"So other kids are getting wishes too . . . right?" Hope asked the other Make-A-Wish volunteer, looking Lynne squarely in the eye. The questions and answers were going back and forth between Hope and the two volunteers like a fast game of ping pong.

"Well, ah, yes, we are working with other children. We get a wish request and then we fund the wish. But in your case, that isn't a problem. Your wish is already paid for."

"Right, you said that already." Hope then looked back at Kelli and asked her, "Are any kids waiting on money for their wishes?"

Kelli Breaux and Lynne Allen looked at each other very uneasily. You could see the question on their faces: *Where is this kid going with this?*

"Hope," Lynne began, "here is how it works. Our organization gets a wish request, usually from a physician, like the one Dr. McMahon did for you. It is processed and then people like Kelli and I come and see you. We are wish granters. Once you tell us what you want, we start to work on getting the money raised for the wish."

"So, what about the other kids? Who funds their wishes?" Hope asked. Her blue eyes were locked on the two women.

"Uh, well, you see, we try to raise the money when the wish

comes in. Sometimes it happens quickly, and other times, depending on the wish, it, ah, takes a while," Lynne stammered, clearly befuddled at the nature of the questions coming from this kid.

"So there are some kids waiting on their wishes, right?"

"Yes, there are."

"And some of them have been waiting longer than me, right?"

"Uh, yes, Hope, they have. But that is okay," Kelli said. "Your case is somewhat different because Weddington raised the money for—"

"Yes, I know that," Hope interrupted, clearly annoyed. "Just how many kids are waiting for their wish to be granted?"

This brought another puzzled look from Kelli and Lynne. Neither spoke for a few moments until Lynne decided to tell Hope what she wanted to know.

"As of right now, there are, I think, 155 children waiting for their wishes to be granted in our chapter, which covers central and western North Carolina."

Hope Stout looked at Lynne for a second or two after hearing that. She then reached down and stroked Pudge a few times, stopped, and looked squarely at the two wish granters.

What she said next changed the lives of everyone in the room.

"Then my wish is to grant all the wishes of the 155 kids on the waiting list—every single one of them!"

And then she resumed stroking her cat.

Kelli Breaux and Lynne Allen's eyes registered the same look as a deer in the headlights of an oncoming car. They didn't move or know what to say or even know how to respond. They just stared blankly at Hope.

And, as I found out later, for good reason.

The Make-A-Wish Foundation does everything in its power to grant the wishes presented to them, unless the wish is to travel to the moon or something crazy like that. This organization moves heaven and earth to make wishes come true for these kids.

And Hope's wish *was* achievable: it wasn't a trip to the moon. But the wish granters knew it would be extremely difficult to accomplish.

Kelli, who is a banker, quickly began crunching the numbers on the pad of paper she had brought for note taking.

With an average wish cost of around $5,500 times the 155 wishes the figure came to $852,500. She showed Lynne the number.

What Lynne Allen said next was truly priceless. In a very small, breathless voice, she said, "Uh, Hope, let us try and get you on Oprah's Favorite Things . . . It might be a lot easier."

We found out later that the fund-raising budget for the local Make-A-Wish Foundation chapter was around $800,000. For the entire year.

Hope had just requested one wish that would mean raising more than that.

"Definitely this wish is what I want. I have been really lucky. I have been to Cancun and to Disney, but some of these kids haven't. They deserve a chance to do so and I want to make that happen." She then paused, commanding everyone in the room's attention.

"That is my wish."

As the reality of the situation began to sink in, Lynne finally found her voice. "Well, Hope, if that is your wish, let us get to work on it."

Lynne and Kelli then began to suggest ways to raise that kind of money. The discussion soon centered on the idea of a large, grand gala as the most likely event. The idea of selling charms was also discussed. One of Holly's friends had bought a round, silver charm that had *Hope* inscribed on it, and from that, Holly came up with the idea to sell Hope charms. She had even gotten a local jewelry store to donate three hundred of the charms for Weddington High School to sell for their fund-raising efforts. Lynne suggested that a new Hope charm could be developed to help fund Hope's million-dollar wish. Soon all the women were discussing what the charm should look like and where they could sell it.

After a few minutes of kicking around these various ideas and how they could be implemented, Lynne said, "Hope, I have to take this back to our board. They are not gonna believe this, but we will do everything we can to make it happen. I am not trying to be rude or anything, but I need to ask you one question." She turned and faced Hope directly.

"Are you sure that is what you want?"

Hope did not hesitate. "Yes, I am sure. Let's grant all 155 wishes—as soon as possible," Hope Stout said to the two women. And then she added this comment which I will never forget.

"What? Is that a problem?"

And to Hope Elizabeth Stout, it wasn't a big deal.

Armed with Hope's decision, Lynne and Kelli announced that they had to leave. But Lynne stayed behind a moment, talking to Shelby and Hope.

Later, as all three of us walked outside onto our front porch, Lynne said, "Stuart, I don't even know where to begin. Granting this wish means raising nearly a million dollars! We have never come close to that amount before."

Lynne and Kelli then told me they had to notify the Make-A-Wish board executive committee, since any wish that is over the "average" amount allocated needs their approval. This was standard operating procedure and occasionally occurred with special wish requests.

But never with a wish that would require nearly one million dollars to fund it. I was telling Lynne and Kelli to drive carefully when Lynne turned around suddenly.

"Stuart, has Hope always been like this?"

"Yes, she has, Lynne. Welcome to our world."

Reflections of a Mother

During that moment after Stuart and Kelli left the room, Holly mentioned that Hope might become famous if all 155 wishes were granted. And Hope agreed.

She asked, "Do you think I need an agent?"

Lynne and I started laughing and brushed her comment off. "Well, let's just work on this first," I said, "and see how it goes."

When I came back into the room after telling Lynne good-bye, I found a very upset Hope Stout. She glared at me and said through clenched teeth, "Why did you laugh when I said I might need an agent?" Her blue eyes were piercing into me like a spear.

I tried to make up some excuse for my reaction, but it didn't help. Hope was livid and didn't speak to me until the next day. I have thought about that question many times since then and realized that she was right.

Over the next few weeks, as we got to know Lynne Allen better, we discovered that meeting Hope Stout had a tremendous impact on her, even though she had been a wish granter many times and met many wonderful children.

"Hope had this 'force' about her that was hard to miss," Lynne said. "When I first met her, I knew her prognosis was not that good. But after meeting her, I was mesmerized by her: those blue eyes were so clear and her skin was flawless, kind of like ivory. Her presence seemed angelic to me, almost like she had already gone to heaven but was still here physically. It created a sense of urgency in me to make sure we got this wish done for her. And yet, as daunting as the task was, Hope seemed unfazed by it. It was like she knew it was going to happen."

I can see why Lynne and Kelli were surprised by Hope's wish, but Stuart and I really shouldn't have been so astonished. Two years earlier Hope had made the following list of her dreams:

Better handwriting

To be a marine biologist
To be president
Make the world a better place
Be an English actor
Be an FBI agent.

All of these dreams are the typical aspirations of a fifth-grader, except the one in the middle: make the world a better place. And truly, she did.

35

A Million Dollars?

That weekend Tom Reeder, Bruce Mullan, and I returned to Holden Beach for a couple days of golf. Because Hope was doing pretty well, and because we had arrived at a mutual understanding after our fight two weeks earlier, Shelby had insisted I go.

The three of us were planning to leave Friday morning, but I wanted to make sure the roofers arrived to begin work on the house. They showed up all right; at dawn they were on our roof scraping off the old shingles. After getting assurances that the roofing job was under control, we left later that morning for our golf weekend.

It is funny how little things become so important. This weekend would produce the first steps of a journey nobody could have predicted.

After our round of golf on Friday afternoon, Tom, Bruce, and I, along with Don Brafford, retired to the front porch of Tom's cottage. The setting sun was creating sparkles of light on the Intracoastal

Waterway. There was not a cloud in the sky and the warmth of this beautiful Indian summer day was giving way to the chill of the night. The four of us were recounting the day's golf adventure and remembering all the good (and mostly bad) shots. Soon, however, the conversation turned to Hope and her condition.

I could tell that the guys were concerned, and they were trying to broach any conversation about her condition subtly. They really wanted to know what was happening with Hope. You know, the kind of question where you want to be blunt and just ask, but cannot.

I recognized what they were doing so I recounted the last month and what had happened: we were facing a disease that just wouldn't go away despite throwing everything at it.

Bruce heard my concern and quickly spoke up. "You know, we have to do something really big to help Hope. The golf tournament in August was good, but now we also have to do something for others as well. And it needs to be big."

My good friend then made a suggestion I will never forget. "We just have to tug hard on God's robe and get His attention. We have to get Him to heal Hope."

Soon my three friends began to brainstorm about ways they could raise money not just for us but for others as well. All kind of ideas were brought up: another golf tournament, a telethon, or some other kind of fund-raiser. I could see that these guys were serious, but they were beginning to get frustrated at not being able to come up with a fresh idea. About this time God nudged me to make this suggestion.

"Guys, I appreciate what you are doing. But let's just let it lay for a while. The desire to do something big is there, and I can't tell you how much that means to me.

"Let's just leave it in God's hands. He will put something in our path, I promise that. Just let Him work on what that is."

Why I said that still baffles me to this day. At the time, I didn't know why God put that thought in my noggin.

But I found out on Monday night.

After Lynne and Kelli had left our home the previous Wednesday night, they had made a report to the Make-A-Wish board. Because of the sheer magnitude of the wish request, the board felt they had to make 100 percent sure that this was truly what Hope wanted, so Lynne Allen, along with Amy Laws, who is the chapter wish coordinator, came to our home to meet with Hope on Monday night, November 24.

During the visit, Hope once again reiterated her desire to have a walk-on role on a sitcom or a New York modeling shoot. But again she said she wanted to do all that when she was better.

"My wish is to grant the 155 wishes of the kids waiting—that is what I want," she told Lynne and Amy.

After getting this assurance from Hope, we began to brainstorm about how the money could be raised. It was decided that the best way would be to hold a large gala. A calendar was soon produced and a date chosen.

Friday, January 16, 2004, would be the date for the gala, which would be called The Celebration of Hope.

That date was chosen mainly because of Hope's physical condition. While we were praying nonstop for Hope to be healed, we wanted to set a date close enough that it would allow her to go. The speed with which her disease had struck taught us a lesson: we didn't make too many plans down the road. We took things day-by-day. Also, although Make-A-Wish wanted to grant this wish, the sooner the better, a lot of preparation had to be done. Everyone in the room agreed that seven weeks planning time should be sufficient. So January 16, 2004, was chosen as the date.

Hope loved the idea, and she and Holly started to talk about possible themes for the event. She quickly announced that she would ask Kevin Donnalley to be her escort. After doing so, she immediately turned her attention to me, fearing that my feelings would be hurt. "Dad, you understand, don't you? I love you and all, but Kevin would probably get me a limo and stuff."

I assured my daughter that I would survive.

Lynne and Amy spent another thirty minutes or so visiting with Hope and then announced that it was time for them to go. As they were leaving, Lynne said, "Hope, I have a feeling this gala is going to be huge. I am going back to the Make-A-Wish board tomorrow to report on what we have decided. It is going to be amazing to see this happen!"

Both Lynne and Amy told everyone good-bye, and I walked the two women outside into the cool evening. We stood on our front porch for a few minutes talking.

"Stuart, listen," Lynne said. "We are going to make this gala happen, but we are definitely gonna need some help. Do you know any company we can contact that might be willing to get behind this? We need something big to get the ball rolling."

And then I remembered the conversation I had had with Tom and Bruce last Friday at the beach.

So, these guys wanted to be involved in something big to help Hope and other people as well, did they?

I guessed helping raise a million dollars to grant the wishes of 155 kids might fit the bill.

"Ladies, it just so happens I was talking to some guys this weekend who might want to help out. They work for a company here in Charlotte and actually put together a golf tournament for us back in August that raised about thirty thousand dollars. Let me make a call to them tomorrow."

The next day, I called Tom Reeder and filled him in on the visit from Make-A-Wish and what we had planned. I asked him if the company he worked for, Swisher Hygiene, might be interested in helping out. After getting an enthusiastic response from Tom, I suggested a meeting with him and the Make-A-Wish representatives for that afternoon.

I was not involved in that first get-together, but what took place was the beginning of a phenomenal fifty-three days. In less than ten minutes, Tom and Bruce agreed to be heavily involved in The Celebration of Hope. In fact, Tom's first phone call after the meeting that afternoon was to the owner of his company. Very quickly, he secured a large financial commitment from Pat Swisher and his wife, Laura. Later that day they wrote a check for twenty-five thousand dollars, and The Celebration of Hope (COH) was off and running. Swisher made available their information technology department to help design a Web site, and Bruce, who was the director of purchasing, basically agreed to take a leave of absence to work on nothing but COH.

After the meeting concluded, Tom called to tell me what had happened. I was completely overwhelmed at what Pat and Laura had done, and the extent to which Swisher had gotten involved in this effort. Tom then told me a funny story.

"When the meeting ended, I went back to my office to return a few phone calls," Tom said. "About five minutes later, Bruce blows into my office and flops down in a chair across from my desk. He takes a deep breath and says, 'Tom, do you realize that we just agreed to raise *one million dollars*?! In just seven weeks? Are we nuts or what?'

"Stuart, I told him, 'We asked for something big at the beach last weekend . . . And here it is, handed right to us.'"

And that is how The Celebration of Hope started. We could not have predicted how it would end.

Reflections of a Mother

As the girls were growing up, animals of all varieties ended up in our home. We have had the standard array of cats, dogs, mice, hamsters, hermit crabs, and fish. But we never had a pet bird. That changed when Bubba arrived on the scene the spring before Hope was diagnosed. Bubba was a gorgeous red cardinal who announced his presence by pecking and banging on our front windows.

At first we thought the bird was nuts, but later found out that the males will do this if they see their reflection in the glass. They think this image is another male cardinal and try to fight off the adversary. Since it was spring, the mating season was in full bloom, so we would watch this bird hitting the window day after day. Summer came along, and he was still living in the front bushes, banging on the window every morning.

After Hope's diagnosis, I naturally began to worry all the time. I looked to the Bible for comfort and found a verse that addresses worrying in Matthew 6:25–27:

"Therefore I tell you, do not worry about your life, what you will eat or drink; or about your body, what you will wear. Is not life more important than food, and the body more important than clothes? Look at the birds of the air; they do not sow or reap or store away in barns, and yet your heavenly Father feeds them. Are you not much more valuable than they? Who of you by worrying can add a single hour to his life?" God said the birds don't worry about food or anything, so why should we? Are we not more important than the birds? So I got it in my mind that every time the bird hit the window it was saying, "Don't worry. Just don't worry."

After the cardinal decided to stay at our house for good, we named it Bubba, in memory of our friend Bubba Smitha who had died six months earlier. After his death we had gone over to see his wife, Suzanne, and his two daughters, and Suzanne told us he loved cardinals (Bubba being redheaded also). The day he died she had looked out in her backyard, and there was a blanket of red. Cardinals were everywhere. She had never seen so many before or since. Thus the name Bubba stuck.

After a while though, this Bubba, unlike the real Bubba, started to get on our nerves. On one occasion I found myself so annoyed,

I grabbed Stuart's BB gun and actually started shooting at Bubba.

The Red Rider BB gun was a gift from the girls for Stuart. Like a lot of families, we watch *The Christmas Story* during the holiday season. The center theme in the movie is Ralphie's desire to get a Red Rider BB gun for Christmas, so a few years ago the girls insisted we get one for their daddy for Christmas. They even hid it behind the desk on Christmas Day, just like in the movie. Stuart, who is definitely not a hunter, rarely used it except to scare off stray dogs that meandered through the woods in our backyard. His aim is not that good.

As for my aim, that bird had as much chance of being eaten by a lion as being hit by one of my shots. Later, I actually found myself apologizing to Bubba! It appeared to me that the cardinal was laughing at my aim.

We tried everything to get the cardinal to stop pounding on the windows. We even had some friends buy a bird feeder to lure him away, but to no avail. Bubba continued to hit all four front windows.

As if we needed something else to challenge us and our faith, our roof needed replacing. Since the roofers were to start around seven on Friday morning, we blew up an air mattress the night before so Hope could sleep downstairs in the den.

At around 6:00 a.m., even before the roofers arrived, Hope woke me up, fussing and complaining. I just knew the pain had worsened. She had not taken any pain medicine all night, and I figured what I had given her at bedtime had surely worn off. After quickly jumping up to attend to her, I asked if she needed more pain medication.

"No, I am fine, but would you get Dad's BB gun out, and shoot that bird? He has been pounding on that window for about thirty minutes and woke me up!"

Soon the roofers arrived and the commotion scared Bubba away. But even with all the pounding on the roof, Hope did manage to go back to sleep.

In the next days another prayer was answered by good friends who helped us with a new roof. Every time Stuart asked Dave Ballard about the cost, Dave would offer some cheesy excuse like, "Gee, I don't know . . . Let me get back to you." Stuart never could convince Dave to give him a bill for the roofing; we were told that it had been taken care of. What a blessing that was to a struggling family like ours.

And Bubba continued to watch over us the whole time. In fact, we didn't pay the cardinal much attention after that. He was part of the family. That is until about two weeks after Hope passed away. We then noticed that Bubba was gone. We never saw him again.

From the end of November through early January as Hope's condition worsened, she needed me much more than she needed Stuart. He so wanted to help his daughter, but she needed her mother to attend to her physical needs. I hated to see Hope lose her independence and dignity, but this was a mother's job. So I will relate the rest of our journey from here on, and Stuart will provide the Reflections of a Father.

36

Just Five More Minutes

Stuart and I noticed that despite the oral chemotherapy Hope had been taking, she was becoming more and more immobile as the tumor in her right leg kept getting bigger. And the pain was getting worse, which kept her from going anywhere but to the bathroom and back to the futon. She would come downstairs only if we had to go to the doctor or to Core Club, which she still wanted to attend. Finally, the girls in the club began to come to our house to make it easier for Hope. But try as she might, it was getting harder and harder for her to manage the pain, so she stopped attending Core Club meetings altogether. The girls in the club continued to pray for Hope and stayed in touch by phone, e-mail, and cards.

Hope got cards from everywhere: from church members, family, friends, and even strangers she had never met. Some of these cards were very heartwarming for Stuart and me and provided a lot of motivation for Hope. One card that arrived at least twice a month had particular impact on Hope and our family.

When this special card first arrived, we were getting mail that would literally fill half our mailbox most every day. (I kept all of the cards in a 122-quart Rubbermaid box, which was finally filled to the top.) That afternoon Hope began opening her mail, reading each card or letter and tossing some aside as fast as possible as she looked, in typical "kid fashion," for money, coupons, or gift cards. Then she opened one and asked, "Mom, who is Mary Wheeler?"

Hope handed me the card, and I couldn't believe it. Mary Wheeler had been my Sunday school teacher when I was five years old. She loved all the children at Sharon Baptist Church and always hosted the annual Easter Egg hunt. Mary also gave her Sunday school students little surprises or treats when we learned our Bible verses. She was not wealthy by any means, but always shared what she had.

I was not surprised that Mary had sent a card to Hope, since everyone in my church back home was aware of Hope's illness. I told Hope about my memories of Mary, and then she held up a one-dollar bill that was in the card.

"Wow! She sent me one whole dollar!" Hope said sarcastically. Hope was accustomed to opening her mail and receiving gift cards or cash for twenty dollars or more. So to her, a dollar was practically nothing.

Very gently, I told Hope that this one-dollar bill was probably all Mary could send, but the love Mary was showing counted just as much as twenty dollars or more.

Every two weeks these cards kept coming with one dollar inside. Soon Hope began looking forward to that one card and, instead of sarcasm, her attitude changed.

She would open the card and say, "Oh, Mom," and hold up the dollar, waving it in the air. I would say, "It is from Mary, right?" and she would answer, "Yes." And we would both smile at God's love, which was represented in these cards and dollar bills from Mary. After that, Hope never again looked at the amount of money being sent, but rather at the thought and love behind it.

Hope used that money for many things. Unfortunately, shopping, which was her favorite pastime, now had to be done by me or her sisters. Before she became immobile, however, she loved to go to Dish It Out, a pottery painting store near our home. She and Austin, who is very much into art, would go together and create pottery pieces, using Hope's money.

When the time had come to get Hope's cats Peanut and Pudge spayed and neutered, Hope had accumulated quite a bit of money, which was burning a hole in her pocket. When she found out that there was a new, less-invasive way using a laser, she volunteered to pay the extra money. Her cats would have less pain and "down time" and to her, this was money well spent.

Hope's lack of mobility finally forced us to bring her downstairs onto the air mattress all of the time. When she was upstairs, she was disconnected from everyone and couldn't stand that, so a move to the den took place.

Since she was now in the middle of all the activities in the house, we spent a lot more time together talking. During one of our discussions, Hope asked me to take some of her money and buy a devotional at the Christian bookstore. She really liked the book I bought, *Quiet Moments with God*, which had a devotion on one side and a blank journal page on the other.

With the cancer now reaching into her shoulder, it was getting nearly impossible for her to write, so Hope only wrote on three separate days: November 26, 27, and 28.

On these days, Hope wrote:

November 26
I am thankful that God has matched me with my completely wonderful family. Without them in my life to help me carry on I would

never have the faith to fight this cancer. Believe me when I say my
family is the best gift I could ever have.
(Below this entry she drew hearts with "Mom," "Dad,"
"Aus," "Hol," and "me' on them.)

November 27
I would like to give more to my parents. It is countless all the things
they have given me. And about everyday they tell me how much
they want to take my cancer from me and suffer for me. To me, my
parents are like a mini version of God, and I would give anything
for them.

November 28
My being different is good because since I have my cancer which
has made me different, I can show others back to their faith and
inspire others to be closer to God. I am very grateful to be different.
I have changed peoples' lives.

Before getting cancer, Hope was just a normal teenager living
the good life. Now, as she was battling this horrible disease, she
began to experience a newfound support system in God's love, in
her family's support, and in being different. She saw being different
as a gift that went beyond what she had ever experienced in her
twelve short years.

Family traditions mean so much to us. Stuart and I learned to
follow the same traditions every year so the girls would be happy.
But this year, as Thanksgiving approached, we knew things would
have to be different. Normally we would have Thanksgiving dinner
with my parents and then drive immediately to Holden Beach for
the remainder of the holiday weekend. But it was evident that
Hope could not travel far away from home due to the pain.
However, as she pointed out to us, that didn't mean we had to scrap
all Thanksgiving plans. She insisted on going to my mom and dad's

for Thanksgiving Day, which was only one hour away. My brother, Jeff, told us he had an air mattress ready for Hope along with a surprise: he and his wife, Jane, had just gotten a tiny kitten.

That's all I had to say to Hope. She couldn't wait to go.

We got Hope in the car pretty easily, drove the hour to my mom and dad's house, and had a wonderful day of parades, food, football, and more food. Hope enjoyed the whole day lying on the air mattress, occasionally playing with the kitten. But later in the day we could see it was a little too much for her. As we were trying to leave, she was truly unable to walk. Finally, Stuart had to pick her up and put her in the car. As we left, I saw my mom looking out the door waving good-bye, her face clouded with the tears in her eyes. I knew exactly what she was thinking.

Is this the last time Hope will ever come to my house?

According to our family tradition, we always decorated the Christmas tree together right after Thanksgiving. This year we had to do so before Austin left to go back to NC State on Sunday night.

Normally we put our tree in the living room so that it can be seen from the street. This year, however, Stuart put the tree in the corner of the den. Now the Christmas tree was right beside Hope where she could see, touch, and help decorate it.

Our family tree-trimming tradition involves baking sugar cookies, complete with decorations and hot chocolate, while we put on the ornaments. Well, we did just that, all the while with bittersweet feelings. Since Hope could no longer stand up to put her ornaments on, she placed hers on the bottom branch, which she could reach from her air mattress.

Each year, the sisters took turns putting the angel on top—and there was usually an argument over whose turn it was. After a few years of this, Stuart had remedied that problem by placing a note on the angel, noting which sister had angel duty the year before. Stuart always gave the girls a boost to let them place the angel perfectly on the top of the tree.

This year it was supposed to be Hope's turn. But how was that going to happen with her being so weak and bedridden?

But with Hope, where there was a will, there was a way. When it came time to put the angel on the tree, she took hold of Stuart's left hand and with the angel in his right hand he placed it on top of our beautiful Christmas tree.

They had made a human chain to the top, just like the one I wanted in my prayers.

Sometimes traditions have to change a bit, but they still mean the same. And sometimes they have even more meaning the new way. This Christmas, our new tradition did.

After the Thanksgiving weekend was over, Hope could no longer get comfortable. We used pillows to prop, lift, and support different parts of her aching body, but she was in constant pain. The pain got so unbearable that she could no longer walk to the bathroom, so we had to start handling matters bedside. The cancer was forcing her dignity to be stripped away little by little. Dr. McMahon suggested radiation to help relieve some pain and arranged for Hope to come into the hospital on Wednesday, December 3.

I'll never forget trying to get her out of the house that day for the trip to the hospital. She was in so much pain, she kept asking for five more minutes, and finally I said, "Hope, we just have to do it now or we will never get there." Stuart offered to pick her up as he had at my parents, but she said, "That's out of the question, Dad. That was very painful."

Finally, she rolled over on the air mattress so she could pull herself into the wheelchair (with some gentle help from me), and we made our way out the front door to the car. She was crying in pain, as Stuart and I tried to get her in the backseat as gently as we could. Our hearts were being ripped out as we tried our best to help our daughter. Finally, we made it into the car and drove to the hospital. Not wanting to repeat the scene we had in our driveway, we went straight to the ER entrance.

While Hope and I were getting checked in, Stuart went up to Hope's assigned room. He walked in and saw this video tape lying on the desk beside the bed. The title simply said MIRACLE in big red letters. It was actually the movie Miracle on 34th Street, but we took this video as the sign of assurance we needed. Maybe this radiation treatment would be the miracle we were all praying for.

The staff in the radiation department was wonderful to Hope, but getting her to move from the bed to the gurney was proving to be a major issue, much as we had run into at home. Whenever it was time to go to the radiation department, Hope hit us with "Just give me five more minutes, and then I will be ready to move." That act got old quickly. But we really couldn't blame her. The thought of moving with that much pain was too much to bear.

So a plan was put into action. No longer would the folks down in radiation make her move from the bed to the gurney. Instead, they would simply wheel her down in her own hospital bed. When she got there, they sedated her so that the radiation could be performed. And this solution met with Hope's approval.

The only negative was that she had to go to recovery to come out of the anesthesia, but getting her radiation treatments this way made her more at ease. When we got back to the room after the first treatment, we discovered that Hope had been given a morphine pump, as she had way back in June. Just taking pain pills by mouth didn't work anymore because of the level of her pain.

We also had a lot of visitors while we were in the hospital, but during this visit, Hope was in no mood for any. So she had me put a sign on the door, which showed Hope's spunk and sense of humor. It read:

DO NOT DISTURB UNLESS
YOU ALSO WANT TO BE HOSPITALIZED!

Consequently, fewer and fewer people came in. What could I do? These were Hope's orders.

During this visit, I began talking with the family next to Hope's room. The mother told me her daughter had received a kidney transplant and, so far, was doing great. She was so glad they were making progress on her daughter's illness and told me she was leaving to take care of a few things at work and would be back soon.

One of the Sunday school classes at our church had brought a box full of small Christmas stockings filled with candy so Hope could share them with the kids on her floor. I told Hope about the girl next door, and she told me to get one of the stockings, put in some meal tickets, and give it to the family, which I did.

The next day, when I stopped by to see how they were doing, the room was empty. I asked one of the nurses if they had checked out and was told that the little girl had been moved to the Pediatric Intensive Care Unit (PICU) because of complications with the transplant; it appeared that her body was rejecting the kidney.

I returned to Hope's room and told her what had happened. She became very concerned and said to get another stocking, put in some more meal tickets, and track the family down. Armed with another stocking, I went to the PICU waiting room to find the little girl's mother. When I got there, the nurse's response to my inquiry devastated me. On the same day the mom had received the mind-numbing news about her daughter's complications, this poor woman was also informed that she had just lost her job due to missing work so many days with her sick child.

I didn't know what to say. I left the Christmas stocking with the nurse at the PICU station and went back to Hope's room.

Immediately she wanted to know how the family was doing, and I gently broke the news to her. Hope got very upset.

"Children need their parents at the hospital with them. How could this happen?" she asked me, desperately seeking some kind of answer. I tried to calm her down but to no avail. In a very loud, emotional voice Hope continued to tell me how kids needed their parents to get through stuff like this. When she finally calmed

down somewhat, we made a pact: I promised her that we would do
something to help families like this when she got better.

Hope was very pleased with this, and on that day, the concept
of the March Forth with Hope Foundation was born.

Because we had such a difficult time getting her to the hospital
in our car, Dr. McMahon made arrangements to take Hope home
by ambulance. This made sense because the only way she was able
to get comfortable was by lying down. So we took off for home
with Stuart riding in the back of the ambulance with Hope. I went
ahead of the ambulance to get the house ready.

While I was worried about the ride home and how she was
doing, Hope was only worried about one thing: would any of the
boys in the neighborhood see her coming home like this?

Despite all her difficulties this kid still had moments when she
was a typical twelve-year-old.

Reflections of a Father

On December 3, when Hope's radiation treatments were scheduled, we simply could not get her into the Cadillac, despite the fact
that it was lower and easier to get into than Shelby's SUV. As we
tried to convince Hope that we were not going to hurt her, she
became very upset and started to cry and yell very loudly at us. For
the next twenty to thirty minutes Shelby and I could do nothing
but sit on the side of the car or stand beside our daughter as she
struggled with her fear and pain.

About this time, I saw my neighbor Rick Smith walking down
his driveway, his hands full of mail.

Rick and his wife, Kristi, have four children, and since we moved
into the neighborhood in 1994, our kids have grown up together. As
he walked down the driveway, rage began to churn away inside of
me like a hot acid, not at Rick personally but at what he represented.

His children were at school. They were facing the kind of pressures kids that age are supposed to: getting good grades, staying off the computer when homework needed to be done, not getting sassy with their parents. His kids were healthy.

All around us, life simply went on, and here we were dealing with this horrendous situation.

Instead of sitting in a wheelchair, afraid to get into the car due to the pain it would cause, Hope should have been somewhere else. Like sitting in her classroom at Weddington Middle School, anxiously watching the clock tick toward the end of the school day, something all kids do, particularly when it gets close to Christmas.

I let my mind drift back to our life a year ago. A wonderfully healthy Hope would come home soon. I looked up toward the road and pictured my tall, energetic redhead bounding off the bus and down our driveway, as she had so many times before, stopping off to pet the cats before heading into the house.

She would be getting a snack now and arguing with her mother about getting her homework done.

Or going to basketball practice in the car with me, her shoes untied and her hair pulled back in a ponytail.

At that moment, I would have done anything to make this cancer just disappear. And I mean *literally* anything. Everything would have been on the table. The memory of Hopie bouncing down the driveway faded back into reality the second I looked down to see her frail body sitting in the wheelchair.

How had things gotten so bad? In such a short period of time? It was just not fair.

As Rick made his way down the driveway, he looked over at us and stopped. I could see the pain and tears in his eyes. Clearly he wanted to help, but knew it was not his place to get involved in this situation. Rick told me later that seeing what Shelby and I were facing and how frail Hope had become ripped him apart.

As I stood there unable to help Hope in any way, the rage that had begun thirty minutes earlier threatened to come out. But this time, I held it in check. Exploding in front of Hope and Shelby would do nothing but upset them.

Finally, after about a half hour of waiting, I told Hope that we had to get going or I was going to call an ambulance. She got very angry at me but my deadline worked. She finally managed to get into the car by herself, despite the pain.

On the way to the hospital, my rage over this whole fiasco finally reached the boiling point. My knuckles whitened as I grabbed the steering wheel with all my might. It was a funny time to pray, but I did. It just wasn't the kind of prayer you hear every day.

God, just let me wrench that cancer out of my daughter's body through this steering wheel, just let me get my hands somehow around that disease and rip it out of her.

For several miles I drove like this, bargaining silently with God and nearly ripping the steering wheel from the column.

37

The Power of Hope

A fter Hope's radiation treatments were finished, we made plans
to have a hospital bed delivered to our home, complete with a
trapeze so that Hope could pull herself up rather than having us do
it. She, of course, insisted that the bed be located right in the middle
of the den, so we moved some of the furniture out of the room.

On the morning of Thursday, December 11, the Home Health
Care people arrived right on schedule and the bed was set up in no
time. Stuart had them position the bed so Hope could see the TV,
the Christmas tree, and any other activity that was happening. The
air mattress was not inflated, but the technicians showed Stuart
how to do it. They left and when he returned to the bed, Stuart saw
that Peanut had jumped up on the flat air mattress and was investi-
gating the new bed.

As Stuart walked by the bed, he flipped on the air compressor,
figuring it would inflate the mattress slowly.

He was wrong.

The bed immediately began to rise as it filled up with air. Stuart spotted Peanut, who had her back turned to him. He deduced that her claws would not be a good match for the air mattress and reached over to pick her up.

That was a bad mistake.

The normally docile and gentle cat, already spooked by the bed rising under her, immediately turned into a wild porcupine. It only took Stuart a nanosecond to realize that he had scared her to death. When he grabbed her, she did what cats do, and soon he had a long, deep scratch on his hand. He immediately dropped the terrified cat down on the floor.

Fortunately, the mattress was saved, but his hand didn't fare too well.

There was only one slight problem. The hospital bed was a twin, and there was practically no room for Hope because of the cats that insisted on being up there with her. She had missed them during her hospital stay and clearly the cats missed her too, so there was some catching up to do. Before long, however, the cats returned to their routine and started taking shifts. Either Pudge or Peanut was always at Hope's beck and call.

Hope's wish to help the 155 children on the waiting list was gaining momentum. Elizabeth Leland of the *Charlotte Observer* called, and Hope gave her an interview that ran on Friday, December 19, 2003. The article, which was on the front page, included a picture of Hope holding Pudge.

That newspaper article would change our lives and serve as the catalyst for The Celebration of Hope.

Very early that Friday morning, while Stuart was at the office, he received a phone call from the producer of *The Keith Larson Show*. Keith is a morning talk-show host on WBT, the Charlotte area's largest and most popular radio station. Keith had read the article in the paper and wanted Stuart to talk about Hope, her condition, and her wish on the air.

When I told Hope that Dad was going on *The Keith Larson Show*, she immediately reacted. "Why are they talking to him and not to me?"

This surprised me because for the past few days, Hope had been getting weaker and didn't want to see or talk to any of her friends. But I saw that serious, determined look on her face that I had seen a thousand times. Clearly she wanted to talk to Keith Larson. So I told her not to worry; Dad would take care of it.

At around ten o'clock that morning, Keith Larson interviewed Stuart on WBT, and Hope and I listened. She heard her daddy answer a lot of Keith's questions about her, then Stuart suggested that it might be better if Keith talked to Hope directly. Keith reluctantly agreed and arrangements were made to have him call Hope back an hour later.

Just before it was time for Hope to go on the air, both Stuart and I talked to her, Stuart by phone and me by her bedside. We both said the same thing to her: "Hope, be nice, use your manners, and don't get on your soapbox."

We were concerned about what she might say about the hospital and the situation with the lady who had lost her job. Lately Hope had become almost obsessed with wanting to take care of people, particularly the children in the hospital.

When I was in the middle of telling her the dos and don'ts, she interrupted me. "Gosh, Mom. What do you think I am going to do? Embarrass you or something?"

Stuart and I kinda laughed about it, but we both knew how Hope could focus in on something and not let it go.

When you are talking on the phone to a radio station, you cannot be in the same room with the radio, due to the feedback. All our radios are upstairs, so I was more than a little nervous, since Hope would have the phone all to herself downstairs. I wanted to hear what Keith was asking, and the only way to do that was to go upstairs and listen on the radio. Austin, who was home from college for Christmas break, and Holly were upstairs in the bedroom listening to the interview as well.

When Keith began talking to Hope, I would run upstairs and listen to Keith, then run back downstairs to be with Hope as she answered. The interview began slowly at first but soon, Hope's slight nervousness disappeared.

Keith: Hello, Hope.

Hope: Hello, how are you doing?

Keith: Well, uh, I'm fine . . .Thank you for coming on WBT today. Your dad said it was okay to talk to you. I appreciate you talking to us.

Hope: Thank you for having me on.

Keith: Hope, how, uh, you have a form of bone cancer . . .

Hope: Yes, sir.

Keith: And you have been dealing with this for five or six months now?

Hope: Um, hmm, yes sir.

Keith: The Make-A-Wish people came to you at some point, and ah, you got to have a wish. Exactly where did this thought come from?

Hope: Well, it came from being in the hospital and getting all these treatments and I saw all these other kids, and uh, they were just, uh, they just seemed so happy in there and they just didn't know what was going on. They were just runnin' around with their little IV poles. Then I found out some of them aren't nearly as lucky as me because I had my parents there by me 24/7. And some of them didn't have their parents there because they lived in another state or something. And all they are just asking is to meet Ronald McDonald or just go on a cruise or something, and it just seemed so easy to do, and it just broke my heart that some kids don't get the chance to do all this great stuff. I, I had that an opportunity to go to like Cancun or something and some of these kids just ask for so little and they might not even have the chance to get it and I just had to do something about it. I just couldn't live with myself knowing that little kids are asking for so little and maybe not getting the chance to get it.

Keith: (Rueful chuckle, clears throat.) And some of those wishes—the Ronald McDonald variety—those aren't even so much about big money, uh, are they? That's just about making some arrangements, but, of course, for 155 kids, that would be a lot of wishes and some will run into some money and the Make-A-Wish people figure that can cost a million bucks. But we've heard from a bunch of people here today, Hope, that are just blown away by this thought that you had when given that opportunity for a wish for yourself, to say what I want is for these wishes to happen for these other kids. People here in Charlotte seem to be of the idea that we can commit to and raise this money quickly, immediately, so that these kids can be told that these wishes are gonna happen, maybe even as Christmas presents. So I think you've inspired, uh, a lot of people around the area today. Are you aware of that?

Hope: Yes, I am, and it's just amazing at how many people are so inspired by me, but (a little giggle) all I am doing is really sitting in bed all day just watching TV and just caring about these other kids. And just to, uh, just to see their smile and to know that I made a difference in their life is just an amazing feeling, and it's far better than any other wish like to go to the Bahamas or something, or be famous . . . It's just that feeling that you get that you know you made a difference in some kid's life. It's just amazing.

Keith: (Voice quivering slightly) And, uh, you say you're at home, Hope, and uh, when's the last time you were at school?

Hope: Um, I have not been to school at all this year. I am doing homeschool and um, I have my teachers come and they give me the work and stuff. But as of this year, I have not been in the seventh grade (slight giggle).

Keith: So you are in the seventh grade or would be in the seventh grade at Weddington Middle, but the, ah, the treatments and things have ah, just the totality of that has kept you home all this past fall?

Hope: Yes, sir.

Keith: And you're going through radiation treatments, huh?

Hope: Yes, I uh, recently went through them and stuff and um, just a few weeks ago. And um, I just wanted to say thank you to all the radiationists down there. They were just sooo nice and so caring, and just came over every day to see how I was doing. And the others at Carolinas Medical Center who just took time out of their breaks to come over to see me and see how I was doing. It is just sooo sweet, and I just want to take the time to say thank you. They made the stays in the hospital so much more enjoyable.

Keith: And you're saying you're sort of, uh referencing that you've got your parents and your sisters and your family but you obviously have that source of inspiration and support, I guess, and that helped you in some way to have this thought at this challenging time for you to be thinking of other kids . . . Where did that kind of thought come from, do you think?

Hope: Just, uh, my mom, is just a caring person and when she was staying in the hospital [with me], she would go and find out about the other people who were, um, in the hospital and just see what their story was about. And I just heard that some of the kids were alone in the room and didn't have their parents there because their parents had to work to pay off medical supplies and I just . . . honestly cannot see myself fighting this cancer without my parents there. They just think they do so little but they have no idea how much they do whether it's just handing me the remote or just going down to get me a snack. It just means so much to me—to have them there. And the thought of some little kid who's younger than me who'll be going through something worse *alone* without having their faith is just amazing. I want to do whatever I can to make their stay the best it can be.

Keith: That's a big part of it, faith, isn't it?

Hope: Um, hmm. Yes, it all comes from faith in God. None of this, not one part of this, would be happening if we did not have God in our lives. It's just my relationship with, uh, how I've grown with Him is just unexplainable. How I can just find myself starting up a conversation with God to thank Him for making this day easy for me. And just be with all the other ones in pain who have it so much worse than me and who may not live to see next year and their big wish is to, uh, have a puppy or go to Legoland or just uh, I have to make sure these kids get their wish. It's *going to happen* with the power of God and with all these people who are hearing about this. I know that this can happen—100 percent. I just know we can do so much more but I have 100 percent faith in God, and we are just going to give it all to Him and He is going to take care of it.

Keith: Well, a lot of people are responding to that idea of yours, Hope . . . People are responding to you, and here you just feel like you're really, ah, carrying the message for and just being a champion for God, which is an amazing thing. You're just an amazing person. You've really inspired a lot of people today, and I want you to know that and I really appreciate your time and telling your story. And I am sure you are going to get a lot of response for the Make-A-Wish office over the next few days.

Hope: Yes, I am just telling everybody to just trust in God and just believe in yourself and anything is possible. I have 100 percent faith that we can make these kids' wishes come true, and my wish will come true. My first wish was to be famous and to have a walk-on TV role on a TV show, but that's already happening. I mean from you calling me and wanting to talk. I mean this is all I need right now. Just, and then, just to have these kids' wishes come true, that just. I just know we can do it! Just have 100 percent faith in God and anything can happen.

Keith: (Voice cracking slightly) Uh, the Make-A-Wish phone number is 704-339-0334. The Web sites for North Carolina are www.ncwish.org or www.celebrationofhope.org. We have both of those linked up to the Larson page at www.wbt.com. Uh, Hope Stout, thanks again . . . I know a lot of people, us included, are grateful for what you are doing, and we are praying for these other kids and especially praying for you as well. I really appreciate you talking with me.

Hope: Thank you for having me on the show. It's been a great honor.

Keith: Uh, well, uh, (clears throat, clearly fighting back emotions), uh, well, uh, I don't know about that but, (a pause) hopefully we raise the money, uh, Hope, and thanks for talking with us.

Hope: Okay, thank you for having me.

Keith: (Quickly, with emotion in his voice) Okay, we'll be right back.

Even though I knew Hope's trust in God had grown a lot during the past few months, her faith truly shocked me. Hope had renewed strength in her voice, which resonated with peace and hope, which I knew was coming from someone else. She was being a faithful disciple for what God had planned for her.

I had never been more proud of Hope than at that moment. When she finished the interview, the girls and I came bounding down the stairs and told her how well she had done.

Hope just looked at us with that mischievous twinkle in her eyes and sniffed, "What did you think I was going to do, guys? Say something stupid?"

On Saturday morning, December 20, our house was invaded by the folks from Make-A-Wish and a film production crew. The film crew, complete with bright lights, cameras, and backdrops, arrived to tape the video of Hope and our family for the upcoming Celebration of Hope Gala. Austin, Holly, and I had worked very hard to remove all the dust that had piled up since I had been taking care of Hope, but it didn't matter. All our work was tossed to the wayside as the film crews covered all my windows and furniture with black sheets. Getting the lighting and background just right took a great deal of work and preparation.

While the others were being prepped to be filmed, Hope met with the event coordinator, Mary Tribble of Tribble Creative Group. Mary, who has planned hundreds of corporate and civic functions, began making some suggestions and soon realized that Hope had her own idea about the event theme.

"What I want is a 1950s 'Rat Pack' theme, with long gowns and tuxedos for the guys and stuff like that. You know . . . Hollywood glitzy."

Mary Tribble loved the concept, but was shocked that Hope knew so much about that era, so she asked how she came up with the idea.

"There was an episode of *Lizzie McGuire* where they had a school dance with a Rat Pack theme, and it seemed kinda cool."

Hope had some other plans we had to nix, however. As she thumbed through one of the planning books, she told Mary to include shirtless male waiters with bow ties. "What about some really good-looking guys with perfect six-pack abs?"

Austin and Holly were all for it, but I informed my impetuous redhead, "This is a family event and the shirtless guys are out."

All three girls were disappointed at being overruled by Mom.

The shoot took six long hours as they interviewed Stuart and me, Austin, Holly, and finally Hope's friend Emily and her cousin Liz. As the day wore on, I knew Hope would be beside herself with everyone being there for so long.

But as I periodically went to check on her, I found a different child. Despite the intrusion (we had to be *very* quiet, which meant no TV and, horror of horrors, her cats had to stay outside in the cold December chill!), she showed tremendous patience and had this peace and calm all through the day. You must remember that this kid did not want to see anybody the day before, and now she was allowing complete strangers in her house for a whole day.

Hope was the last one to be filmed. The Make-A-Wish volunteers had gone shopping at Hope's favorite store, Limited Too, and picked out three different tops for her to choose from for her video debut. She selected a turquoise top with matching headband that was very appealing. A professional makeup artist applied her makeup, and when she was finished, Hope looked absolutely radiant.

The whole crew was in the room as she filmed her part for the video. The spot took about twenty minutes, and at the very end, two funny things happened.

When Rick Fitts, the producer for the video, had finished, he asked everyone to be very quiet so that he could get another sound check after the filming. "This equipment is so sensitive, I need to be sure that we have not picked up any background noise," he explained.

However, just before he performed the actual sound check, Hope insisted that Pudge be let in. The poor cat had been watching through the sliding glass door for the last six hours.

As Rick was checking the sound levels, Pudge jumped up on Hope's bed and let out a long, shrill *meow* right on cue. Then Daisy, who had been napping all morning on the couch, yawned loudly and let out a huge groan. Because the room was so quiet, both sounds echoed loudly.

For a split second, everyone tried to hold in their laughter, especially Hope, since the microphone boom used to record her interview was still hanging over her head. But soon a giggle slipped out of her mouth. That did it for everyone else. The whole room broke up.

After the laughter subsided, Rick told us not to worry. "I had enough time recorded before Hope's animals decided to get in on the action. We are fine."

The video crew began packing up all their equipment and soon everyone left. After the house had emptied and silence fell upon us, Hope slept for three hours straight. Stuart and I were both exhausted, and when Austin and Holly left to go shopping, we also fell asleep. I woke up from my nap to check on Hope, and when I did, I realized that her breathing had dramatically changed. All of a sudden, it was hard for her to talk and catch her breath.

I was alarmed, but Stuart told me it was probably because of the exhaustion of the day. Still I couldn't help but wonder. Had something happened during those three short hours of rest?

We called Kid's Path, the home healthcare company that was making periodic visits to Hope to monitor her condition. Jennifer, the nurse who had been primarily working with us, came right over. She checked Hope and her vitals and asked to speak to us in the dining room.

Before she began talking, Jennifer handed us a paper from hospice and told us to read it. Stuart and I looked at the sheet of paper that was telling us how the body shuts down before dying.

We stood there in disbelief. How could Jennifer be saying this to us? She must be wrong. After all, she hadn't seen Hope with such strength only three hours earlier!

Jennifer could see the doubt in our eyes so she began a specific explanation. "Her vital signs have really changed since a couple of days ago. Her breathing is very labored, and that tells me her lungs are filling with fluid from the cancer. She is in no pain, but you should be prepared."

And then she said something that knocked the breath out of me.

"I just hope she makes it through Christmas."

I fell apart. How could she say this to Stuart and me when we just *knew* God was preparing Hope for something big.

It took us a while, but we regained our composure as best we could. We reassured ourselves with the knowledge that God could heal Hope at the last possible second, and we were convinced that would be the case!

Reflections of a Father

The newspaper article on December 19 lit a fire under Keith Larson. When I got the phone call from WBT at work that morning, I was only too happy to talk about Hope, figuring she wouldn't want to. However, when I called home with the news, Miss Hope told me differently, so during my talk with Keith, I suggested he talk with Hope herself.

Keith has since become very close to our family, but at the time, he wasn't sure about talking to Hope. Kids on the radio are unpredictable, he later told me. Also, he didn't know us personally, so he really was taking a chance.

I was scheduled to meet with one of my clients when Hope's interview took place at 11:35 that morning. Just before she went on the air, I called this woman and told her I would be a few minutes late. She said not to worry; she would also listen to the interview.

When Hope Stout went on the air that day, I was in the parking lot of a strip shopping center, listening like so many others. What I heard still affects me to this day. The conviction of her words was so powerful. I had to keep reminding myself that this was my daughter speaking.

To me, it sounded like the voice of God.

The interview is now a Christmas tradition on *The Keith Larson Show*, and the audio clip is permanently on his Web site.

As for Keith, Hope ended the interview with him by causing him to break down emotionally *while still on the air*, something that practically never happens to this tough talk show host.

When Hope's talk with Keith ended, and after composing myself somewhat, I went to see my client. I found her in her office, wiping tears from her face.

"Stuart, that is the most powerful thing I have ever heard."

The interview with Keith Larson created quite a stir. WBT received so many requests to hear the interview that the whole segment with Hope was replayed four more times that day.

On December 20, when we received the devastating news from Jennifer, Shelby went to pieces. My reaction was somewhat less dramatic.

All I could do was give Jennifer a rueful laugh, the kind you give people when they have just delivered ridiculous news.

"You have got to be kidding me" was all I could say.

How could Hope's condition have changed so fast? Three hours earlier, this kid was so strong and positive doing the interviews. Her determination to plan The Celebration of Hope down to the last detail had lifted everyone's spirits.

Now Jennifer was telling us that she hoped our daughter lived through the Christmas holiday? It didn't make any sense.

Despite being a seasoned and dedicated medical professional and one who had seen death many times before, Jennifer just didn't know Hope Elizabeth Stout very well.

Miss Hope had other ideas.

38

A Christmas to Remember

In 2003, our established Christmas traditions flew right out the window—and they were many and truly loved. As soon as the girls had been old enough, they would all sleep together in Austin's bed the night before Christmas. That way, whichever sister woke up first could wake the others. Another tradition was going to my mom and dad's house for a huge Christmas Eve lunch, where we would eat all the Christmas favorites until we were stuffed. My three brothers and their families along with ours made for a houseful. After lunch, it was time to commence opening all of the Christmas presents, which we did in about five minutes flat.

But we never opened presents before the grandchildren had all gathered around the coffee table, lit the Christmas candles on each side of the family Bible, and listened as Maw Maw read from the second chapter of Luke, the story of the Christmas miracle. That chapter describes the hope for the world, born that night over two thousand years ago.

Now many years later we were waiting for another miracle during the Christmas season of 2003.

Because the cancer was rapidly progressing, we knew we couldn't make the trek to Mom and Dad's house. Instead we were stuck at home, and instead of greeting Christmas guests coming over for some Yuletide fellowship, we had hospice coming in. For our Christmas "present," we had heard Jennifer say, "I hope she makes it through Christmas."

But by now, you know that Hope didn't function by the book. Thankfully the difficulty in breathing that Hope had experienced for the past days had eased somewhat. In fact, her condition had stabilized—a small miracle, but one we gladly accepted.

Unfortunately, we didn't have a lot of presents under the tree. Normally I shop for two straight months prior to Christmas; finding the perfect gifts for everyone is something I take pride in. But the thought of shopping for Christmas presents hadn't even crossed my mind.

But Hope was not without presents. Far from it! A few days before Christmas, her boyfriend Kevin had asked if he could come over to bring Hope a present. I warned him that she might not want to see him. However, when we told Hope that Kevin wanted to come over, she quickly surprised me. "Duh, Mom, of course he can come over. 'Specially if he is bringing me presents!"

Kevin arrived with a small blue box from Tiffany's, which immediately got Hope's attention. Inside was a beautiful silver necklace with triple hearts. He also brought Hope a Carolina Panther blanket monogrammed with her name and his. In her eyes you could see how much she loved Kevin and the presents.

On Christmas Eve Hope woke up late. I had already called my family and told them that depending on how Hope felt, they might be able to come for a short visit. I told them I would let them know for sure later, since she didn't want a lot of people around, even grandparents, aunts, and uncles.

When she woke up, I told Hope they all wanted to come, but we understood if she didn't want to see them. She stared hard at me with that typical look of disgust.

Despite having difficulty breathing, she told me in a very strong voice, "What do you mean we aren't having them over? It's Christmas Eve! Are they not bringing food? What's wrong with you, Mom?"

This girl who wasn't eating and hadn't talked much for several days now wanted to have our traditional Christmas Eve family party?

I called my mom and told her to come, although we didn't have a lot of food so she might bring what they had; together we would make do. I also made another phone call to Wendy and told her that Hope wanted to have Christmas and our pantry was bare. That was all it took.

Within two hours, we had enough food on our table to feed fifty people, and that is not an exaggeration. Not one but *two* honey-baked hams were dropped off at our house. I am positive that some of my friends' Christmas tables were a little on the empty side, because they cared enough to give their meal to our family.

Before everyone arrived Hope gave me strict orders: "Everyone will get their food and come into the den to eat with me." She didn't want to be left all by herself.

My brothers—Stan, Kenny, and Jeff—and their families and my mom and dad enjoyed a wonderful day filled with food, presents, and the reading of the Christmas story. And, of course, Hope, despite her frail condition, stole the show.

You know how maddening the noise can be when there is a room full of people and everyone is talking at the same time. That day our den was buzzing with conversation. I was sitting beside Hope in a chair along with Holly. Suddenly, the two of us heard this weak, faint voice.

"Hey, is anybody listening? Mom, I'm dying over here."

Upon hearing that, I turned around quickly to face Hope.

"Well, finally I got your attention. It's about time!"

Thus the queen spoke to her loyal subjects. She thanked everyone for coming and joked about all the food we had eaten. Despite the cancer, she was her old self! We had a great Christmas, not because of traditions, but because we were all together as a family, sharing a Christmas miracle with Hope.

Just after my family left, another family tradition was revised when Stuart's mom, Betty, and his sister, Beth, arrived from Holden Beach. Usually Stuart's extended family gathered on Christmas Day in Thomasville, North Carolina. Now only two of the clan were at our house.

Around six thirty that evening, we were visiting with Betty and Beth when we heard a knock on the door. Immediately Hope said she didn't want to see anyone else; she was exhausted from an already full day. I went to open the door, and what I saw humbled and amazed me.

We live at the end of a cul-de-sac, and our large front yard slopes significantly from the road down to our house. The entire expanse of our yard was full of people! We found out later that over 150 of our friends were there, all holding lighted candles. The darkness of the evening was beautifully illuminated by the light from all those candles!

At first, I couldn't believe that these wonderful people would take time out of their own Christmas Eve to spend this sacred moment with us.

But then it hit me. Of course—yes!—I could believe that. People had been with us all along, so why should it surprise me that they were here now? Even though Hope didn't want to see anyone, we left the front door open so she could hear what was going on as her Core Club friends led the families in Christmas carols and prayers for her and our family. After they finished, I told everyone that this was the best gift we would receive this Christmas. In fact, this is exactly what Hope was teaching us with her wish: to think of others before we think of ourselves.

Isn't that what Christmas is all about, Charlie Brown?

During the entire holiday week we had monitored the news constantly, and Hope's wish was the lead story just about every day. Contributions for Hope's wish were pouring in to the Make-A-Wish office. Over $370,000 had been contributed in just four days! The Make-A-Wish folks told us that it typically takes six months to raise that kind of money.

We were hearing stories of kids who were giving their Christmas money to Make-A-Wish. A little girl heard about Hope's wish and began selling hot chocolate mix door to door. She raised over one thousand dollars. Kids were emptying their piggy banks and bringing their money to the Make-A-Wish offices in brown paper bags. Two sisters who did that were on the evening news. One of the girls gave three dollars and the other sister gave thirteen dollars. One boy asked his parents to take back his Christmas presents and send the money to Make-A-Wish. One family even cancelled their Christmas trip to Disney and gave the money to fulfill Hope's wish.

And these sacrifices filled some of the 155 children's wishes. Hope's first wish went to a girl in Ellerbe, North Carolina, named Amber, an energetic fifteen-year-old softball player. After experiencing shoulder pain, she was diagnosed on August 15, 2003, with osteosarcoma, the same type of bone cancer as Hope. On December 22, a limo picked up Amber and her family, and they were whisked away on a five-day, four-night cruise to the Bahamas. In Nassau, Amber got to ride on a jet ski with her dad, while her mom and brother went swimming and enjoyed the sun.

Then a little boy who lives in Newton, North Carolina, about an hour north of Charlotte, received a pony on Christmas Eve. Because of Hope's wish, he finally got the pony he had wished for!

When Hope heard about these two recipients, she was very happy. She knew what a blessing this pony would be for the little boy, since Pudge and Peanut had been so important to her during her illness. And hearing about Amber's wish thrilled her because she loved the beach and riding jet skis with her own dad.

Yet at the same time that the fund-raising and the publicity from Hope's wish grew, she became weaker and weaker. Before eating some food on Christmas Eve, she had gone a few days without eating anything. She did continue to drink water and, despite her condition, had the amazing ability to make me laugh.

A few days after Christmas I was hovering over her, hoping to help her get into a somewhat comfortable position as she lay in her bed, watching her sisters play PlayStation®. Despite her discomfort, she kept saying, "Just give me five more minutes to think about it."

Like any good mom I would come back in five minutes, and she would send me away again. This went on and on until finally she actually *sang* to me in a labored voice, "Let me sleep in hea-ven-ly peace, sleep in hea-ven-ly peace!"

One afternoon I was sitting with my head resting on the edge of the bed thinking, *Are we getting to the end of Hope's life?* She had been in and out of consciousness with the morphine pump delivering pain medicine as needed. I was praying softly when I realized that Hope was awake and looking at me.

"Mom, I wish you would quit praying like I am going somewhere."

I had no idea she had even heard me.

"Hope, I just don't know what else to do."

And then I asked her a question. To this day, I am not sure why I said this.

"Hopie, do you feel like you are dying?"

Her blue eyes shot open. She looked straight at me and with a very clear voice said, "Gee, Mom. I don't know. I've never done that before."

At a time like this, in the situation she was facing, Hope Elizabeth Stout made me laugh. She went on to say that she didn't know if it was a vision or fantasy, but she didn't feel that she was going to die. And it made sense, given all the publicity of her wish, and the money that was now pouring in for the 155 children.

"Look what I am doing, just lying in my bed. Just think what I can do when I can get up and walk again," she said.

How true that was. She was right in the middle of something big that God had planned for her. He just had to make sure she would survive to tell this great story later.

Right?

Reflections of a Father

I will always remember the Christmas season of 2003 as the best of times, and the worst of times. Often during December I caught myself becoming depressed and angry because of what we were facing. I would hear a Christmas song on the radio and quickly shut it off, being in no mood to hear "glad tidings of great joy."

And yet, as we got closer to Christmas, Hope brought me out of my pity party with her relentless determination to keep on living. I don't know if she had a secret deal with God or what, but something spiritual within her seemed to be much bigger than what was happening to her physically.

Just before Christmas, Pastor Ken Lyon came by to visit. Hope was hesitant to see him, but Shelby and I insisted she spend a few minutes with him and she reluctantly agreed.

Shelby and I sat in the room and listened to this wonderful man talk to Hope—who had her eyes shut the entire time—about the possibility of her physical death, encouraging her to not be afraid. When Ken was finished talking, he said a prayer, and I walked outside to his car with him. He had tears in his eyes as he told me good-bye, and I could see that this was as hard for him as it was for us.

At that moment, Ken brought up a subject I had been dreading. I knew that if Hope passed away, arrangements had to be made, and Ken asked me about that. As a man, I understood what he was saying.

As a father, I did not.

I told him that Shelby and I had not broached the subject, nor would we until we needed to, and he nodded his head in agreement.

Yet I knew that at some point in the very near future, I was going to have to discuss final arrangements with Shelby Stout.

And I dreaded it.

It was just not fair. No parent should have to discuss their child's *final arrangements.* I didn't even like those two words rattling around in my brain.

When I went back inside, I walked over to Hope's bedside, pulled up a chair, and took a seat. I immediately became aware that she was wide awake—and upset. Her blue eyes were blazing at me. Shelby joined me at her bedside.

"Dad, just exactly why was Pastor Ken here today?"

Oh boy, this is going to be fun.

Shelby and I just looked at each other.

I decided to speak first. "Well, Hope, Pastor Ken wanted to spend some time with you. He wanted to make sure you were okay and to see if you had any questions. He loves you very much, you know."

That sounded lame to me and as expected, Hope knocked it right out of the park.

"No, it sounds to me like he thinks I am going to die. Is that what he thinks?"

As she said this, I looked into her eyes and could see that she was really asking *me* if I felt she was going to die. At that moment,

I didn't know what to say, but I knew she needed an answer from her daddy.

"Hope, Pastor Ken, Mom, me—we are all so frustrated by this. We don't understand why you have this cancer, and why we can't seem to get it under control. But the fact is God *can heal you in the blink of an eye* and that is what we are praying for. We are just being straight with you."

She took this in without any hint of emotion. Shelby had tears in her eyes and said nothing. I was also beginning to cry, which is something Hope hated to see.

"Don't worry, Dad. I am not going anywhere. And I don't appreciate Pastor Ken thinking I am dying. What does he know anyway?"

While there were many moments during this journey that stopped me in my tracks, this one really stuck out. Dealing with impending death is hard on anybody; I had this same discussion with my dad in 1996, and although he was only sixty-six, he had lived a good, full life. Even though he accepted his death, it was still difficult.

Hope, on the other hand, seemed to be taking this in stride. Here we were talking to our daughter about her impending demise, and she was pooh-poohing it. Hope Stout was a very intelligent kid, who had to know what was happening to her physically, yet she did not show the slightest fear of dying.

What does she know that we don't?

At that moment, knowing Hope's penchant for doing things her own way, I wondered if God was taking us to the point where no medical intervention was possible so that He could really get everyone's attention.

I envisioned almighty God rolling up the sleeves of His robe, spitting into His hands, rubbing them together, and saying, "Watch this, boys and girls!"

And Hope Elizabeth Stout would be miraculously and mysteriously healed from a horrible disease that medical science was powerless to stop.

Would there be any doubt that she would be famous then?
I thought back to the sign I had seen in the mountains.
Hope Thou in God.
Since Hope seemed unfazed by the possibility of her own
death, why should I worry about it?

39

Minutes to Hours

Our family began an emotional roller coaster ride, constantly going up and down, up and down, as Hopie's condition would worsen, then stabilize. When we got so low in the valley and I thought there wasn't a way out, she would pull one of her surprises on us. One of those unexpected moments took place on New Year's Eve.

That morning Jennifer came to check on Hope. She told us Hope's blood pressure was very low and her heart rate was high.

"This is not a good sign," she whispered. As she looked at us with hurting eyes, we could tell how upset she was to have to tell us this news.

Suddenly we noticed that Hope was trying to speak. Jennifer turned her attention to Hope and asked her very affectionately what she was trying to say.

Jennifer couldn't make out what Hope was asking because of her very frail condition. But after listening to her mumble day

after day for over a week, I could tell what she wanted so I trans-
lated for her.

"Jennifer, she wants to know if you are through, because she
wants to have the PlayStation controls so she can play the SpongeBob
video game."

The hospice nurse just threw up her hands in total amazement.
"I've never seen anything like this! . . . By all means, let her play the
videogame."

And then Jennifer left, still shaking her head as she walked out
the door.

After playing the video game a while with her dad and sisters,
Hope slept that afternoon. But when she woke up, she made sure
we celebrated New Year's Eve right at midnight in our traditional
way, with little confetti noisemakers, party hats, and Welch's sparkl-
ing grape juice. We put a wine glass in Hope's hand and she toasted
the New Year and drank from the glass, which stunned Stuart and
me. Earlier that day this child was barely swallowing water. Now
she was leading us in a New Year's Eve toast!

God allowed the Stout family to say good-bye to the old year
and all the good and bad news it had brought and to ring in the
New Year together. It was easy to say good-bye to the painful year
we just completed and hello to 2004.

In my journal, I wrote:

Thank You, God, for another year!

In that day's journal entry, I also made a note to read Philippians
1:12–26. As I was writing this chapter I looked back on verses 21–24,
and the words have dramatically impacted me. Paul says, "For to
me, to live is Christ and to die is gain." Then he goes on to show
the conflicting emotions he felt as he looked at these two alterna-
tives: life and death. "I am torn between the two," he says, "I desire
to depart and be with Christ, which is better by far; but it is more
necessary for you that I remain in the body."

Was Hope struggling with these thoughts? Did she know that her healing would only come through death—and new life? Yet was she lingering here because she knew how much we wanted her to live?

Hope slept a lot on New Year's Day, and when she woke up, she didn't respond to much of anything we said. After a while, her lack of response got to me and I broke down, thinking that she was not able to hear me crying.

Then Hope suddenly opened her eyes, turned to me, and said, "Mom, why so gloomy?"

Really, what twelve-year-old uses the word *gloomy* these days? To me that is a word mentioned more frequently in the Bible.

I stared into those crystal blue eyes that were looking at me inquisitively. What could I say to her at this moment?

"Hope," I said, "I am so sorry you have to go through this. It is not fair! I am crying because I want God to heal you NOW!" I then dropped my head down on the edge of her bed and began to sob.

Hope put her hand on my head. "Don't worry. I am going to be okay," she told me matter-of-factly.

That put a quick stop to my tears. Was God talking to me through her? Did she and God have a pact of some kind?

After that I received a very comfortable sense of peace. Maybe God and Hope were planning something really big.

However, later that day, reality hit us again. Jennifer came by and checked Hope's vital signs. Her blood pressure was 90/50 and her breathing was now very shallow.

The hospice nurse took Stuart and me aside. "I am afraid it is minutes to hours now."

Minutes to hours?

We started to panic again. After Jennifer left, I watched Hope's breathing, praying very hard for God to heal our child. I prayed constantly over her and even went so far as to put anointing oil on her head. Even though I am not Catholic, I found a Mother Teresa medallion someone had sent to us and prayed over Hope with that. I felt as helpless as I ever have in my life. Jennifer's news was leaving me no choice but to totally depend on God to heal our baby. And we still believed He would.

But when was God going to step in? It was so hard for me to sit there and watch her take each breath as if it might be her last. Hope was now in a semiconscious state. At one point she started having a conversation with someone. I asked her who she was talking to and she pointed to the end of the bed.

"Ask her."

"Ask who?"

"Her." Hope again pointed to the end of the bed. I have heard that people talk to angels at the end of their lives, and I am convinced that Hope was speaking to one of them.

Then Hope started saying more things that didn't make a bit of sense. She told me I "had tea in my car," and then said, "It's almost time for my big moment . . . Turn off the cameras. Have you turned them off?"

Then she simply said, "Bye."

I freaked out!

"Hope, are you saying good-bye to me?"

Instead of taking her last breath, Hope Elizabeth Stout balled up her fist at me and accompanied the gesture with the infamous Hope eye-roll.

Right after that, just when I thought she was about to take her last breath, she asked me for a drink of water and not one, but two popsicles! She even asked me to give her a breathing treatment, which was something we had been doing for several weeks.

What was God doing to me, taking me from one extreme to the other? One minute I thought she was dying and talking to an angel and the next she was making a fist at me and wanting popsicles!

On the morning of Saturday, January 3, we made the decision to let Austin and Holly go to the Carolina Panther playoff game against the Dallas Cowboys. Hope had been asleep most of the day, and we assured the girls that there was nothing they could do at the house but hold a vigil. And the way Hope was holding on, we were certain she would make it through yet another day.

The girls went to the game with Tom and Liz, and Wendy joined Stuart and me at home where we watched the game on the TV in our den.

Kevin Donnalley had told us that ABC-TV, the network broadcasting the game, might run a feature on Hope. Sure enough, during the broadcast, Lisa Guerrero, ABC's sideline reporter, said, "Panthers offensive guard Kevin Donnalley was very much looking forward to the spotlight of tonight's game, not for himself, not for his teammates, but for a twelve-year-old girl by the name of Hope Stout. He met her earlier this season. She's been battling a rare form of bone cancer and has become an inspiration to him."

Lisa Guerrero went on to chronicle the story of Hope's selfless wish as a picture of our daughter appeared on the screen.

While the piece was being aired, Stuart went over to Hope's bedside to tell her about it.

"Hopie," Stuart said, "you are famous! You are on national TV!" Hot tears filled his eyes. While we both desperately wanted her to open her eyes and see the piece for herself, there was no doubt in our minds that she heard Stuart.

Meanwhile, halfway around the world in Tokyo, Japan, Stuart's cousin Roger Brown sat in a hotel room, preparing for the next day's lectures at a local university. Because the hotel was equipped to receive satellite broadcasts, he stayed up late to watch the Panthers game and soon found himself looking at Hope's smiling face. While the Japanese broadcaster described the little redhead appearing on the screen, tears welled up in Roger's eyes as complex emotions tugged at his heart; deep sadness at Hope's plight and suffering competed with humility in the face of her selfless courage. Likewise, he experienced a sense of amazement and gratitude that her story was being shared on the opposite side of the world as it played out back in Charlotte.

Later that afternoon Austin and Holly returned home from the game and proudly announced that Hope's picture had been shown on the video screen at the stadium, courtesy of the Carolina Panthers, who are big supporters of the Make-A-Wish Foundation. The girls told us that all of the people in Section 551, where our seats are located, stood and cheered when the video clip came on.

We also learned that shortly after this feature, the Make-A-Wish office in Dallas, Texas, was inundated with phone calls and donations. This was significant because Dallas lost the game to the Panthers, 29–10, giving our team its first playoff victory, which qualified them for a trip to St. Louis the following week to play the Rams.

Hope's story also made the *Dallas Morning News*.

On the morning of January 4, the nurses come over two different times: once to change the amount of morphine to a higher dose and another to change the morphine bag since it was running low.

About this time Hope began to do something that deeply disturbed all of us.

She started to moan.

The nurses assured me that the moaning was not from pain but from her body pushing the air out of her lungs, which was part of the dying process.

Despite their reassurances, the sound made everyone extremely uncomfortable. The girls simply could not take hearing these sounds coming from their baby sister and stayed upstairs. As tough as the moaning was to hear, I could not stay away from her bedside for any length of time, because I was afraid she would leave without me being there.

Poor Stuart had been going crazy the past few days as Hope's condition went up and down. Our house was pretty much bare of any food, so that evening Stuart made a quick run to the store for some chicken. He had to do something for his family, so he grilled the chicken and called us into the kitchen to eat it.

We all just stood around looking at each other. Then we all turned and went in different directions.

Bless his heart for trying, but who could eat at a time like this?

I felt as if the walls were closing in on me so I headed upstairs. I went into Hope's room and fell to my knees at the foot of her bed, screaming out to God.

God, You said You would never give us more than we could handle. Well, Stuart and I are there now!! It's time to heal her if You are going to—or take her to heaven!! I cannot stand seeing her like this.

I sat there for a minute, crying even harder. Then, realizing that I needed to be with Hope, I pulled myself together as best I could and went downstairs to her bedside.

All was quiet. She had stopped moaning! She looked very peaceful. God had heard my cry.

But I also realized that her big moment had arrived. I felt the change, saw the slowing of her breathing.

I screamed at Stuart, who was covering the grill outside, to come in quickly. We both stood there holding her hand. We told her to run to Jesus, that we loved her very much, and that we would be okay.

At 8:35 p.m. on January 4, Hope Elizabeth Stout experienced the greatest moment in her life, passing into perfect life in heaven with her Savior. And God let us know she was okay because she had a smile on her face.

As one father passed her off to the other, I knew that God had her in His arms, keeping her safe until her mom and dad and her sisters could join her.

Reflections of a Father

As a man and a father, my reaction to Hope's condition was very different from Shelby's. As cruel as it sounds, at this point, I was ready for God to take Hope home. No father wants to see his child suffer, and I had come to grips with letting her go. A conversation we had had back in November 2003 gave me a good reason for thinking that way.

Hope and I had been sitting together on the couch at home, watching a rerun of *The Cosby Show*, the popular sitcom from the late '80s that starred Bill Cosby. That particular episode featured two special guests: Dick Vitale of NCAA basketball fame and Jim Valvano, former coach of the NC State Wolfpack basketball team, which had won the 1983 national championship. The show featured these two as goofy Italian movers.

Watching this rerun had scared me, because Jim Valvano had died of bone cancer in April 1993.

Almost immediately, Hope asked me a question. "Dad, who is that guy? He looks familiar." Hope's blue eyes were focused on the TV.

"Who, that guy? He is Dick Vitale. You know, that crazy bald guy that does college basketball. He just has a horrible-looking toupee on."

"Yeah, I know him. I am talking about the other guy. He looks familiar too. Do you know who he is?"

Uh, oh, I thought. *Here we go.*

"Oh, that guy . . . That is Jim Valvano. He coached basketball at NC State back in the '80s before you were born. He even won a national championship," I said, hoping that would end the conversation.

But, of course, that didn't satisfy the redhead.

"Well, what is he doing now?"

"Uh, well, Hope, he died a few years ago."

"What happened to him?"

"Well, uh . . . he died of cancer."

When I said that, Hope turned and looked at me. "That is so sad. What kind of cancer did he have?"

I tried my best to ignore the question, which, of course, did not work.

"Dad! . . . Did you hear me? What kind of cancer did he have?"

"Well, Hope, he died of bone cancer. It was in his spine really bad when they found it. It was also a long time ago. A lot of strides have been made since then," I said reluctantly, praying that this revelation would not depress her.

"Well, that's comforting. He had the same thing I have and he croaked!" she said sarcastically. "That doesn't sound too good."

"Hope," I began, "as I told you, that *was* a long time ago, and he *was* much older, *his* cancer was in his spine, and yours is in your leg primarily. Don't read into that, okay?"

Hope didn't respond right away, but I could see her mulling this information over. Thankfully, about that time, a McDonald's commercial came on. But I quickly realized it was about the Ronald McDonald house and a very attractive sixteen-year-old girl . . .

Who had lost a leg to bone cancer.

God, what are You doing? I asked. *First I have to explain to Hope about Valvano and now this.*

I reached for the remote control but Hope quickly told me to drop it; she was riveted on the commercial.

The girl in the feature was getting ready to go snow skiing, and the camera showed her putting a prosthetic device on her right leg and then *shooshing* down the slopes at breakneck speed as if nothing was wrong with her.

I started to speak about how terrific and courageous this young lady was, when Hope cut me off.

"Dad, I want you to listen to me. There is *no way* you are going to let them cut off my leg. Do you hear me? *Never!*" she said hotly, her blue eyes piercing me.

I pondered what I could say to her.

Unfortunately the pragmatic, male side of me came out, not the loving daddy.

"Hope, I will tell you one thing . . . If amputating your right leg would cure you of this cancer, you would be under the knife tomorrow. Look at that girl. She is as cute as a button and a terrific athlete. Losing a leg didn't stop her."

"Dad, there is no way that is happening . . . Do you hear me? *No way!* I want you to promise me you will never let that happen!"

The rest of the conversation was not pretty. In fact, it was one of the few arguments Hope and I had during her illness. We finally let the topic die. The point was really moot anyway. Hope's cancer was not just confined to her knee; it was all the way up her leg into her hip, so amputation was not an alternative.

But I could see that Hope wanted to get completely better and just be a normal kid again.

Now, on the night of January 4 that seemed impossible. Knowing Hope's feelings, as much as it pained me to admit it, I was simply ready for God to take her home.

As you would expect, Hope's last moments here on earth are hardwired into my memory. Like any traumatic moment a person experiences, you remember exactly what you were doing and what was going on around you.

When I heard Shelby's voice imploring me to come quickly, I knew this was the moment we were dreading. As I got to Hope's bedside, I was able to see that she was not suffering.

At that moment, all I wanted to be sure of was that she knew how much her daddy loved her. I told her she was my baby, and it was okay to let go, that I would take care of the family. I knew that was important to her because she loved her family so much.

Reaching down, I stroked her face, and as she took her last breath, she smiled ever so slightly. I wished that God would have let me pop my head into heaven for the briefest of seconds to see what made Hope Stout smile that way.

And then, just like that, with her family around her, she left her cancer-ridden physical body behind and went to heaven.

Despite our tears, a wonderful peace filled the room. Austin and Holly came over to say their good-byes to Hope, and very quickly, God sent me the strength to become the comforting father to my two oldest daughters.

As I held Austin and Holly and watched Shelby kneeling by Hope's bed, something struck me. It was a little thing, but I will never forget it.

Hope's hair had started to grow out again because of the lack of chemo. The tuffs of hair were just beginning to get long enough to show that her red hair was going to come out even more striking than before cancer struck. And then it hit me.

Her hair looked exactly as it did on March 4, 1991, when a nurse announced her birth with "Well, hello there, little red!"

Through my tears, I smiled, knowing that God had answered our prayers and the prayers of so many others. Hope Elizabeth Stout didn't die! She was truly born again and in the presence of her heavenly Father.

Hope had been healed—and had been healed 100 percent.

And I'm sure within twenty minutes of arriving in heaven, Hope looked around and told God, "This is wonderful. This is really as I pictured it would be . . . But I have a few suggestions . . ."

40

Flipping the Switch

The night of January 4 Shelby and I finally went to bed around midnight. We weren't sure if sleep would find us, but after putting about five of Hope's stuffed animals in the bed with us and crying together for a while, we fell asleep.

When I awoke to the first strands of light filtering in through the windows on Monday, January 5, it occurred to me that this was the first time in weeks that Shelby and I had slept in the same bed together. Rather than wake my exhausted wife, I slipped downstairs very quietly, started some coffee brewing, and walked outside to get the newspaper.

The news of Hope's passing literally hit me in the face when I opened the paper, because her story was on the front page. This shocked me at first, but then I remembered that the night before I had given Tom Reeder permission to inform Don Hudson, a reporter for the *Charlotte Observer* who had been following Hope's story, about her passing. As Don told me later he had the story already prepared, but hoped he would never have to use it. The reality of seeing it in the paper took my breath away and brought hot tears to my eyes despite the early morning chill.

I didn't realize it then, but this would be my first step in the journey back to normalcy. Or what would count for normal without Hope physically present in our lives. The stark reality of the newspaper article provided the first of many occasions where we would be reminded that Hope was gone. They even continue to this day. Every so often we hear a Backstreet Boys song on the radio, which brings back memories of the fifth grade when Hope, Gina, Emily, and several other girls went to see the then-popular band. My ears are still ringing from all the preteen girls screaming that night!

The hardest jolt for me came when the plaque at Hope's gravesite was completed two months later. Although it was very beautiful, seeing Hope's name on a grave made me cry about as hard as I ever have in my life.

But every journey, even one toward healing, begins with a first step. Mine came that morning.

Early Wednesday afternoon, January 7, 2004, a limousine arrived to take us to Matthews United Methodist Church for Hope's service. As I rode in the car with my family, Shelby's parents, and my mom and sister, I felt dread beginning to creep in on me the closer we got to the church.

How in the world will I be able to get through this?

As a boy growing up, my father had always told me, "You just have to be man enough to handle some situations." For six months, I tried to do that as father to the girls and husband to Shelby. However, on this day, I wasn't sure if I could handle the next few hours. Generally speaking, I hate funerals. Who doesn't? Going to a child's funeral who died way before his or her time is especially difficult.

For some reason, the most important thing to me at that point was to be strong. The last thing I wanted to do was lose control of my emotions during that service. I knew that everybody attending the service was heartbroken, just as we were. If I lost it, what would that do to everybody else? All of these thoughts were spinning around in my mind.

The drive from our house to Matthews United Methodist Church is about seven miles. As we approached the church at about one fifteen, we all could see that the parking lot was packed, and several news crews from local TV stations were set up in front of the church. When we pulled into the parking lot, two uniformed police officers honored us with a salute. Their gesture was very unexpected and moving, and they even escorted us into the church.

We joined the rest of our family in the chapel of the church, many of whom had driven several hours to be in attendance. All of our cousins, aunts, and uncles from both sides of our family were there. As I was greeting everybody, one of my friends who was helping with the service pulled me aside and told me the church had been completely full for about an hour and that every available chair was being used, including Pastor Ken's own personal chair from his study.

After a brief service for just the family, we followed Pastor Ken down the hall to the sanctuary. I was walking in between Austin and Holly, with my arms around both girls, and Shelby walked beside Austin, their arms locked together.

And none of my girls were doing well at all.

Austin had been crying very hard for most of the morning and seemed incapable of holding her emotions back. Shelby had also started to tear up and looked as if she could burst into sobbing at any minute. And Holly, the emotional rock of our family, was also beginning to crumble. Tears formed in her big blue eyes and rolled down her cheeks.

This was not what I wanted to see happen.

And so, at around one fifty-five that sunny Wednesday in January,

I held a quick pow-wow with God. Only this time I didn't yell or rant and rave at Him. I just very quietly made an appeal.

Okay, God, You now have Hope there with You, and I know she is fine. But we are not. There are about three thousand people sitting in the sanctuary down the hall, and how we do emotionally is how they are going to react. My family is crumbling and I ain't too far from breaking apart either. I need You to give us the strength to get through this.

Please God, help!

About two seconds after I finished that quick petition to God, we arrived at the narthex. I could see rows of folding chairs full of people, lined up at the back of the sanctuary, which immediately told me the church was now overflowing.

And then I spotted three people.

The first was Mike Schaefer, my friend from Knoxville whose family had vacationed with us at Holden Beach for about ten years. We had watched each other's kids change from year to year. Mike had been visiting family in Columbus, Ohio, for the holidays when he had found out about Hope's passing only twelve hours earlier. He had driven straight through the night and hadn't even bothered to change his blue jeans before he left.

As I quickly hugged Mike, I noticed two close friends of mine from high school: Jean Lancaster and Terry Groseclose. I had not seen them in years, but here they were at our daughter's funeral.

Seeing these friends of mine, from two different stages of my life, immediately calmed me somewhat as I realized how lucky I was to have people who cared so much about me and my family.

What happened to me next is one of the most powerful emotions I have ever experienced. In a heartbeat, just as Hope said in her poem, everything can change. It was then that God showed up yet again. As my family and I left the narthex to begin the walk down the aisle of the sanctuary, I saw Hope's sixth-grade picture grinning at me from the front of the church. Pastor Ken always said this was his favorite: "Her expression in that picture looks like she has just dumped a bowl of spaghetti on somebody's head and has completely gotten away with it."

When my eyes found that picture, after seeing my friends in the narthex, God gently nudged me—or maybe He hit me upside the head. Either way, it was crystal clear.

This is not a time for mourning. This is a time for celebration! Hope is perfect now; she is 100 percent healed, just as we had prayed for. There is no need for tears. She is with her heavenly Father and no longer suffering from cancer.

Just like that, God calmed His adult child by simply flipping my emotional switch from despair to celebration.

And it wasn't just me either. As we took our seats, I stole a quick glance at my family. Shelby was smiling, as were Austin and Holly. There were no tears.

For the rest of the service, I did not shed one tear. Incredibly, Shelby, Austin, and Holly didn't either. People later marveled at how well we "controlled" our emotions.

Not so.

Just as in the past six months, we couldn't control anything. We just let God handle it. All during this journey, He was there for us in our darkest hours, always providing comfort. He never once let us down, and today was no exception. He took our grief away and let us know that Hope was okay.

After all, she said it best: "We are turning it all over to God, and He is going to take care of it."

And take care of it He did.

Hope was *alive* again. Why shouldn't we celebrate?

41

Wishes Can Come True

S tarting on Monday, January 12, we began to get feedback from the folks at the Make-A-Wish office that the Celebration of Hope was going to be much bigger than anyone could have imagined. As of Wednesday, over nine hundred tickets to the gala had been sold. Extra staffers were brought in to the Make-A-Wish office to help with the preparation and to handle ticket sales. Donations were also pouring in; everything from envelopes filled with cash and coins to donations made by businesses.

On one occasion, the owner of a relatively small privately held company walked in and wrote a check for $100,000.

All he asked in return was to remain anonymous.

One afternoon that week, a man walked into the Make-A-Wish office in downtown Charlotte. His clothes were worn and dirty and he had an unkempt beard. At first the staff became alarmed, because the office did contain a lot of cash that had come through the mail.

"Is this the Make-A-Wish office?" the man asked.

"Yes it is," one of the volunteers replied, still cautious.

"I want to make a donation to help that little girl, but I don't have much to give . . . But I got to do something.

"Here." The man handed over a small handful of change. "It isn't much, but I have to help out that little girl."

The staffer told him to keep the money for himself, but the man was resolute in giving the money for Hope's wish. After taking his donation, the Make-A-Wish staff member gave him a Hope charm, which was a small star with Hope inscribed on the back.

The man left holding the charm in both hands, like it was gold.

The Make-A-Wish folks told us other stories. One child came in with her mother and her piggy bank and emptied it on the spot.

Teenagers brought in their baby-sitting and Christmas money. Schools began arranging walk-a-thons. One in particular was very special to us. The elementary school Hope had attended from kindergarten through fifth grade, Wesley Chapel, organized a walk-a-thon. They hoped to raise $5,500, enough to grant one wish.

Instead they collected over $25,000, the donations coming from pledges for kids who walked around the school gym for Hope.

One child named Evan went door-to-door in his neighborhood and raised $9,000. That was significant by itself, but Evan accomplished this despite being confined to a wheelchair. He made his parents, Betsy and Steve, take him through his neighborhood to help raise money for Hope's wish. Neighbors found it hard to say no to him, since his wish had been granted a year earlier: he got to meet Michael Jordan.

On Wednesday we received a phone call that totally floored us. Charlotte mayor Pat McCrory had officially proclaimed Friday, January 16, "The Day of Hope." A pep rally was scheduled for downtown Charlotte at noon, which would serve a dual purpose. The Panthers were traveling to Philadelphia for a Sunday game to decide the NFC championship with the winner going to the Super Bowl.

And the city of Charlotte would honor Hope. Our family was invited to attend the pep rally as guests of the city and to accept the honor from the mayor onstage.

Now we began to eagerly anticipate the pep rally and the Celebration of Hope. Austin arrived on Thursday afternoon, and she, Shelby, and Holly went through the major female preparations needed prior to the formal affair: nails had to be done and hair cut just so. I did my best to stay out of the way. On Friday morning, we were packed and ready to head downtown. We were to travel in style in a limousine that Make-A-Wish had graciously provided.

The girls were thrilled to ride in a limo again; and this time it was for a good reason as opposed to the limo ride we had taken on January 7 to Hope's memorial service. The car was huge; in addition to the four of us, Austin's boyfriend Matt rode with us. We could have taken eight other people along with no problem. The looks we got from pedestrians as we drove down Independence Boulevard toward downtown were the fodder for some comments from all of us.

"I bet they think there is some big celebrity in this car," Shelby said. "If we popped out, they would be asking, 'Just who is that?'"

About halfway to the pep rally, my cell phone rang. A buddy of mine had closed his business at lunch and taken his staff downtown to the rally. He was also attending the Celebration of Hope that night.

"You are not going to believe this, Stuart. There must be ten thousand people down here with more pouring in. "Where are you guys? Are you already down here somewhere?"

When I told him that we were en route, he wished me luck. I assured him that I thought we would make it there okay.

As we arrived in the downtown area, several of the streets were blocked off. The weather was gorgeous: a crisp, cool, sunny January day with very little wind. The limo drove slowly up Trade Street and arrived behind the stage where we were greeted by several of the Make-A-Wish staff who informed us that a police officer had been assigned to us as a bodyguard.

Austin and Holly cackled at that. But Hope would have loved it!

The officer escorted us to the back entrance of the raised stage platform where we waited until it was our time to be introduced. From our vantage point, we really couldn't see much of the crowd, which was probably a good thing. The emcee was leading the crowd in Panther cheers, and I could tell from the deafening noise that a lot of people were out there.

About this time, Kevin arrived with Brad Hoover, the Panthers fullback. They had been excused from part of their practice session to attend the pep rally and were still in their practice uniforms. When they arrived, the emcee was notified and because of the time constraints the two players were under, they were immediately escorted up on stage. The emcee also told our family to come up with Kevin and Brad.

When we walked up the small flight of stairs, I could not believe my eyes. As far as I could see, people were packed into the downtown area. The sea of faces was dotted with signs and placards. While many signs supported the Panthers, there were just as many about Hope. One man held up a sign that said "Wishes Do Come True in Carolina," an obvious tie-in to both Hope's wish and the Panthers' success.

As we took our place on stage with Kevin and Brad, Pat McCrory stepped up to the microphone. Just before Mayor McCrory started to speak, Kevin leaned over to me.

"Do you believe this?" he asked incredulously.

"No, I don't. I knew a lot of people were coming out but this is nuts," I replied as I took in the incredible sight. We found out later that over fifteen thousand people had jammed the streets, way more than the police had counted on.

The rally continued and then Kevin was introduced to a loud roar. He immediately got the crowd going by leading a "Let's Go

Panthers" cheer, which continued for a minute or so until Kevin quieted them.

Then he told them about his relationship with Hope. Again, the crowd began cheering as loudly as before. As I took in the scene, it was fortunate that my sunglasses were on to hide my tears, which were flowing unabatedly. The outpouring of support for Hope from this throng of people was overwhelming. Hope had gotten her first wish all right: she was truly famous!

Both Shelby and I thanked everyone for their support, and after getting the Day of Hope proclamation from Mayor McCrory, we went backstage where many people told us how Hope had impacted them. One person in particular got to me.

This very well-dressed woman approached me and introduced herself. I don't remember her name but I remember what she said.

"Mr. Stout, I just want to thank you. Hope was wonderful! She has reminded me of what really matters. I was caught up in my job. I even worked on Christmas Day. I was so into my work, I didn't even know about Hope and her wish until I slowed down long enough to read the paper. When I saw her picture, I felt like I was looking into the face of an angel. Suddenly, in an instant, I realized my job wasn't the most important thing in my life. What really matters is helping others.

"To be famous for being on a television show is okay, but to be famous for bringing people hope is even better." —Hope Stout

"Your little girl changed my life."

The sincerity in her voice and face was so evident I could not do anything but hug her and tell her thanks.

As we were getting ready to leave, one of the Make-A-Wish volunteers came up holding a box. "Stuart and Shelby, look at this!" he said excitedly.

The cardboard box was about twelve Hope Stout inches deep and two feet square.

It was completely full of cash and checks!

"One second I was holding this box with a Make-A-Wish Celebration of Hope sign on it. The next thing I knew, it was full of money," he said breathlessly.

Thank goodness he had a police officer with him for security. There was so much cash in that container that he looked like a bank robber.

Finally we were pulled away from the well-wishers for the short trip to the Westin, where the Celebration of Hope would take place a few hours later. After checking into our suite, we got to spend a few hours relaxing.

Around five thirty, we began to get ready for the big evening. Pictures of our family were made, which seemed strange because there were only four of us.

At six thirty we went downstairs, dressed as they say to the nines. As we exited the elevator into the grand ballroom, nothing could have prepared us for what we saw.

The large ballroom was exquisitely decorated with 155 large silver balloons, one for each child on the wish list. There was an ice sculpture with *Hope* written in it, which had been brought all the way from Richmond, Virginia, by Dan and Donna Kelliher, our best friends when we first got married. A red carpet led guests to the escalators to the ballroom where a photographer captured the moment. As the guests entered, they saw Hope's name written on the floor along with Frank Sinatra, Sammy Davis Jr., Dean Martin, and Marilyn Monroe, a miniature Hollywood Walk of Fame. Hope's "Rat Pack" theme was evident throughout these Academy Awards decorations.

Although the event wasn't scheduled to begin for thirty more minutes, one hundred or so people were already sitting at their tables or milling around the ballroom. Very quickly Shelby and I were separated by all the guests coming up to talk to us. We were not reunited at our table until the official program was about to begin.

Keith Larson, the emcee for the evening, asked the guests to take their seats. Realizing that we had to speak, I found Amy Laws and asked her about the running total of the money being raised. She informed me that it was still being counted.

"Are we close?" I asked.

"I am not sure," Amy said vaguely.

When I told her that I wanted to mention how much had been raised, Amy told me, "Don't worry about it" and hustled off, leaving me without an answer. I concluded that we must not be anywhere close to the million dollars.

But whether we got the million dollars or not didn't matter. Seeing so many people dressed in tuxedos and long gowns here to honor Hope was enough for me.

Shelby and I were soon escorted to the podium, and we both got a chance to speak. In my line of work, I occasionally have to do some public speaking, so it didn't bother me too much. Shelby on the other hand was terrified. She had fretted over what to say in the room earlier and had a handful of notes as she took the podium first.

When she began speaking, it was evident that her nerves were gone. She thanked all of the people who had supported us and in particular pointed out the Core Club girls, who were sitting on the floor (despite their long gowns!) just to the right of the stage. Her brief talk was warm and from the heart, and she did great, taking about fifteen minutes, much longer than was budgeted.

When it was my turn, I joked, "Now you see where Hope got her gift of gab!" I also thanked everyone and then introduced the video that was filmed on December 20. Hope looked absolutely radiant in her turquoise sweater and matching bandanna. Seeing and hearing her brought tears to our eyes, but we noticed something.

Her crystal blue eyes simply grabbed you. Despite having seen the video before, I simply could not take my eyes off Hope Elizabeth Stout.

When the lights came up after the piece ended, there was not a dry eye in the place. Everybody—men, women, and children alike— was either dabbing at their eyes or crying outright.

Very slowly, applause started, building up to a standing ovation. Soon the whole room was shaking from the noise. Try as I did to hold back my tears, it was futile. The ovation continued for several minutes, the love contained in it for Hope and our family clearly evident.

Our emotions make us different from every other living creature. Unquestionably we live in an evil world; individuals become so twisted that they kill children in schools and fly planes into buildings.

But this was all about one little girl caring about others. On this night, January 16, it was all about doing something to help others.

After that ovation ended, I felt there was nothing that could top it. I was wrong.

At that moment Keith Larson started the auction. All of the donated items were very special, but the last one was the biggie. Kevin Donnalley had gotten a football autographed by each Carolina Panther.

The bidding started at $2,000 and began escalating quickly. The amount reached $5,000. Then $7,500. The crowd, at first murmuring about the bidding war, soon began to gasp as the number climbed higher and higher. When the $10,000 figure hit, a loud cheer went up. Soon, $11,000 and then $12,000 was reached. When auctioneer Ernie Perry asked for and got $15,000, the crowd roared its approval.

The bidders were now down to two men, each on opposite sides of the room. As Ernie waited for the crowd to settle down so the auction could continue, Kevin Donnalley walked toward Ernie and took the microphone out of his hands.

"If these two gentlemen will each agree to pay $15,000, then I will get another ball autographed by the entire team. Each man could have a ball, and we will have raised $30,000, rather than $15,000."

Each bidder readily agreed and $30,000 was paid for two footballs. Or to put this in more appropriate terms, five wishes were granted.

Two very sane men paid $15,000 each for a football that probably cost about $75. But it really wasn't for a football; it was to help a redheaded girl's wish come true.

After the auction was over, Keith Larson asked Shelby and me and our family to join him in front of the stage.

"We are getting ready to announce the total amount of money that has been raised toward Hope's wish," Keith said, and the room began to buzz. Everybody was on their feet as our family walked to the front of the stage where we were joined by Shelby's parents and my mom, and, of course, Kevin. We all held hands as Amy Laws handed Keith a piece of paper.

Unbeknownst to me at the time, God was getting ready to provide another memory that will never be forgotten.

"Ladies and gentlemen, as you know Hope challenged us to raise enough money to grant the 155 wishes of the children on the waiting list for the central and western North Carolina chapter of the Make-A-Wish Foundation," Keith said. "I have been handed the final total, and in just a second we are going to show it on the video screens. However, it would only be fitting if we could have a drum roll please . . ."

We turned to face the large video screen, which had been set up for the event. After the drum roll ended, something appeared on the screen.

The "something" was just a number.

We use numbers every day. Numbers tell us how much money we have in our bank accounts (or don't!); numbers guide our speed as we navigate through traffic; numbers identify our favorite athletes on the playing field. Numbers are consistent and universal; they tran-

scend all religious and ethnic barriers. While numbers may be written in different languages, they mean the same. The number 1 signi-
fies the same amount in China as it does in Brazil.

The number we saw on Friday, January 16, 2004, at about 9:30
p.m. in the Westin Hotel ballroom in Charlotte was . . .

$1,160,761.

At that moment, a roar unlike any I have every heard at any
sporting event was unleashed! The sound was ear-splitting. That
moment for me is frozen in time. I see the exuberance present in
the faces of my family and of Kevin. People around the stage have
their mouths wide open in mid-scream; then their hands begin to
make the quick journey to try and stifle the already-emitted sound.
Flashes are going off and confetti is flying through the air from the
poppers that have just exploded. The crowd is beginning to hug
and high-five each other.

I don't recall how it happened this quickly, but the band that
had been hired for the event, appropriately named Peace and Love,
began playing "Celebration" by Kool and the Gang. There could be
no other song played at that moment.

Scores of people began storming the dance floor and we were
soon engulfed by them. Hugs were the language of the moment.

I have thought many times of that second when the total was
announced. As more time passes, one thing becomes evident to me.

This *was* Hope's purpose in life.

This is what God created her for. Not just to raise a million dollars but to raise the awareness that life is all about people.

Yeah, $1,160,761 was raised, which meant granting around
200 wishes, not just 155. But another legacy was born: the legacy
of giving. As the event was ending, many of the people in attendance threatened me with my life if we didn't have a Celebration
of Hope the following year.

So that is exactly what we have done. The Celebration of Hope to benefit the Make-A-Wish Foundation is now an annual event, taking place in January of each year. All told, the Celebrations of Hope have raised over $2,000,000 and have granted close to five hundred wishes in North Carolina and other states.

Early the next morning, I woke up just before dawn, the excitement of the previous night's events still rattling around inside me. Shelby was still asleep and I quietly went into the sitting area of our suite. Our rooms at the Westin were located on the corner of the building, affording us a panoramic view.

The sun was just beginning to peek over the horizon. The January morning air was crystal clear, the kind of sky you only get in the winter. All the impurities in the air were gone and I could literally see forever. As the sun began its journey west, the rays played on the buildings, setting off quick sparkles of light in the windows. The North Carolina mountains to the west were beginning to become visible in the rapidly growing sunlight; I could even see the upper peaks snowcapped in white.

After the incredible events of the night before, this was a very fitting sunrise. Six months earlier, a view like the one in front of me would not have been as vibrant. Yes, I would have noticed the beauty; I just wouldn't have seen it in such splendor.

At that moment, I thanked God for giving me the blessing of being Hope Stout's dad.

It is the greatest privilege any man could ever have.

Reflections of a Mother

The Celebration of Hope could not have been more magical. Mary Tribble, the party planner who was in charge of the event, told us she felt Hope there from the very beginning. "If I put a vase of flowers in the wrong place on a table, I swear I could hear Hope say, 'Nope, not there.' Her spirit was very much there."

The event was oversold, and we won't mention the wall-to-wall crowd of people and all the fire codes we probably broke that night. The support of family, friends, and strangers alike came together once again that evening. Some of the Panthers—most of the offensive line, dressed up in tuxedos to honor our girl—even showed up despite the fact that they were leaving the next day for the NFC Championship game in Philadelphia.

When we saw that Hope's wish had come true, I could feel her smiling down on us and hear her beautiful sweet voice say to her mother:

"I told you I would be famous and would need an agent!"

And this time I didn't laugh.

Wendy summed up the past year in a poem she wrote for us. We want to share it with you so you will always keep this same hope in your heart.

What I Learned from Hope

Red hair is an asset.
Refried beans can turn around a bad reaction to chemo.
SpongeBob rules!
A Jerry Springer moment can help you laugh again.
Shoes are optional, even in doctors' offices.
Cats are as good as medicine.
In fact, you cannot have too many cats.
To sneak a cat into the hospital, don't get stuck in the elevator.
(If you do happen to have a cat in the bed, be sure Holly,
Austin, and Liz divert attention and hide it in the bathroom.)
Nurses are like angels.
Handmade quilts and blankets are priceless.
Paul Walker is cute, but Kevin Donnalley is the man.
There is a right way to cut up a waffle. (I'm working on it.)
You can be grown up at twelve.

It is all about faith.
Have 100 percent faith in God.
Get right with God.
Look around for ways to help others.
Pray and always, always give thanks in all circumstances.
Find the silver lining.
Teach by example.
Appreciate family.
Treasure time.
The only difference between $1 and $1 million
is faith and hope.

42

Signs of Hope

Shortly after the emotional high of the Celebration of Hope, Shelby and I found ourselves returning to a "normal" life. Right off the bat, we took different paths on the grieving trail. I found that the best way for me to deal with my grief was to stay busy; I threw myself into the business of writing this book and into my work. Shelby perceived my busyness as an improper way of grieving, and she let me know it.

Shelby spent a lot of time at Hope's gravesite; I still find it difficult to go there.

I needed to be around people, but it took several months before Shelby would allow herself to have a good time.

Austin and Holly needed their mother, and it took a knockdown, drag-out fight between the girls and their mom during Mother's Day weekend (of all times) before Shelby began to understand that.

Both of us were in uncharted waters, and we just didn't know how to react to one another. There was a lot of resentment on both of our parts, which created friction in our marriage.

Once during this period of time, I thought about what that guy had told me back in July 2003 when I took Austin to orientation at NC State:

"I can almost guarantee you that your marriage will not survive this."

There were times a few months after Hope's death when I wondered if he wouldn't be right.

However, both our marriage and our faith got stronger for one reason: gradually we came to understand that we were not supposed to go through our grief *alone*. Instead, we did what a little red-head said she was doing in that now-famous radio interview with Keith Larson.

We just turned our grief over to God and let Him take care of it.

Reflections of a Mother

You will remember that before we started Hope's chemotherapy in July, my friend Nina Wheeling gave me a small, silver prayer box to wear around my neck. Inside the prayer box I wrote that I wanted Hope's 100 percent complete healing. Well, the prayer in my prayer box was answered: Hope did receive 100 percent healing. It just wasn't the way I expected. I thought that at the last possible second, God would lay His mighty hand on Hope and *bam!* she would have no trace of the cancer whatsoever. Today she would be on a national speaking tour about her courageous story of hope and perseverance.

But sometimes prayers aren't answered the way we want them to be. In August 2003 I had failed to notice all the details of that stained-glass window in the hospital chapel. The girl was dressed in a flowing white gown, not jeans and a T-shirt as Hope often wore. And she was standing with the Great Physician, before the gates of heaven. God answered my prayer in this way.

Stuart and I and the girls are still feeling God's presence—and His God Pump—through signs of hope. I asked Him to send me a sign on Hope's thirteenth birthday, always a special time in any kid's life, to help me make it through that day. The "firsts" after someone passes away are very hard, and her birthday on March 4 came so soon after her death. A few days earlier some of Holly's friends had brought by a present that their Bible study leader had purchased months before Hope's birthday. I told them that it was good timing, because tomorrow was her birthday and I would open it then.

The next morning I unwrapped the present: a redheaded angel with Hope's hairstyle and long lanky legs, holding a sign that said, "Hope Is Reborn." As I held the angel, God reassured me that Hope was with Him and not to worry. That sign would have been enough for me but that wasn't all. As Paul Harvey says, here is the rest of the story.

We knew Pudge was special because he never left Hope's side during her illness. About four months after her death, Pudge was lying on Holly's bed early one morning.

"Uh, Mom," Holly said as she entered our bedroom with her eyes wide and her face slightly pale, "you are going to think I'm crazy, but Pudge's stripes spell Hope's name in them."

Obviously Stuart and I were confused by what she was saying, so we walked into her room. As we looked at the gray-and-black-striped cat stretched out on the bed, we did see H-O-P-E in the waves of his gray fur. Because we had never noticed this pattern in Pudge's stripes before, I immediately found the many pictures we had taken when Pudge was a kitten. There was only one of him lying on his right side, and sure enough, we see H-O-P-E in his fur. We just didn't notice it until that moment.

The three of us just stood there in shock, not believing our eyes. Then we realized that only our Hope could pull this off. I could hear her saying, "Hey God, let's really freak them out."

Well, you get the picture. Pudge struts around the house showing off his stripes and reminds us there is a God and our Hope is with Him.

There have been many more signs, but one is most important because it shows that God does listen to us and respond in ways we can't imagine. When school started in the fall of 2004 Danette said that the Weddington Wildcat yearbook was doing a full-page spread in Hope's memory. The school asked me to pick out pictures of Hope and her friends to go on this page.

As honored as I was, I kept putting this off. Late the night before the pictures were due, I began thumbing through the photos under the cabinet where I stored most of Hope's school things. Many of the unhappy memories we shared with you came flooding back. The more I looked, the more distraught I became until my anger finally got the best of me. I began yelling at the top of my lungs.

"God, why did You take my baby? I want her back now! I just want to see her again! I just want to hold her! God, do this for me. I miss her so much!"

My crying was so loud, I thought I was going to wake everyone in the house, at which point my family would have fitted me for a straightjacket. But I was so mad at God, I challenged Him to do something for me and me alone.

After my bout of yelling, I settled down a little bit; yelling always does that for me. And what happened next is one of the most compelling moments I have ever had. As I reached in the cabinet to get more pictures, I pulled out a grocery bag.

What is this doing here? I thought. *What did I put in this bag?* I wondered, and then I opened it.

Inside the bag were the strands of Hope's hair that had fallen

out at the beach in July 2003. An actual physical part of my precious daughter that I could touch and hold, just the sign I had asked
God for.

Now you can see why I look for signs every day; they are there
and I can see them if I make time for God.

We chose Romans 12:12 for Hope's grave marker: *Be joyful in
hope, patient in affliction and faithful in prayer.* We think this verse
sums up Hope's journey perfectly.

Despite knowing how sick she was, Hope never feared death.
Just how could that be? You remember I told you of the verses in
Philippians 1? I feel Hope left verses 20–21 especially for me. As a
matter of fact, I can almost hear her saying those words to me: *For
I live in eager expectation and hope that I will never do anything that
causes me shame, but that I will always be bold for Christ, as I have been
in the past, and that my life will always honor Christ whether I live or I
die. For to me, living is for Christ, and dying is ever better* (NLT).

When you look at Hope's life that way, sharing her faith is the
greatest legacy she could have left behind. With the childlike faith
of no worries, no doubts, no concerns, and with love and compassion for others less fortunate than her, she was able to experience
the most beautiful moment we all desire as followers of Christ: to
see Jesus face-to-face and hear Him say, "Well done, my good and
faithful servant."

When faced with a horrifying illness that unfortunately cut her
physical life short, Hope Elizabeth Stout showed us how to have a
childlike faith and trust God in every circumstance. She knew God
would take care of it.

So why shouldn't we?

Notes

Life Is Precious
1. Isaiah 11:6
2. Michael Yaconelli, *Dangerous Wonder* (Navpress: Colorado Springs, Colorado, 2003), 14.

Eight
1. James 1:2–4

Acknowledgments

There are so many people who encouraged and supported us through this journey whom we need to thank: First and foremost, to our dear friend and book editor Janet Thoma. Janet is truly a blessing and an answered prayer from God. She believed in our writing ability and believed in us. She allowed us to write the story of Hope and kept us focused on this precious project. This book is blessed because of her.

And if we left somebody out of the story, it is all Janet's fault!

To Carl Etzel for his help in capturing the true essence of Hope in designing the pictures in this book.

To Sharon Whitby whose care and devotion to this book was truly a blessing.

To Shelby's parents: Bud and Dean Shull. Dean left us on November 10, 2005, and Bud passed away on November 21, 2006; we miss them both terribly. To Stuart's mom, Betty Stout, and Bill

Stout who passed away in 1996. Thanks for loving us and being great examples of Christ's love.

To Shelby's brothers: Kenny Shull and his wife, Cheryll; Jeff Shull and his wife, Jane, and Stan Shull. To Stuart's sister Beth Stout (and her evil cat Gizmo!), thanks for being great aunts and uncles to our girls.

To our many aunts, uncles, and cousins who gave us support and love our whole lives and especially through the most difficult time a parent could ever face.

To all of Hopie's friends: Zachary Tompkins (Hope's first true friend), Emily (Bogeen) Rutherford, Gina (Ginta) Wheeling, Erin (Cheese Babe) Kiffmeyer, Kelsey Hawthorne, Lara Plattenberger, Meredith (Myrtle) Cook, Ashley Sietz, Emily Buffie, Kelsey Campbell, Allie Ballard, Caitlyn Holton, and Chelsea Leander and so many others that we can't name them all. Thanks for your friendship with our daughter; it meant everything to her.

To "T" Johnson, for loving Hope and taking her under your wing through Rainbow Express Camp and Confirmation and being with her through her journey. She had the biggest crush on you. You made her feel so special. I know she has your back always.

To our church family at Matthews United Methodist that was there for us in the midst of the storm and beyond and especially to Pastor Ken Lyon, Madeline Kamp, and Laurie Little who taught our girls about God's love for us all and how to serve others.

To all of Hope's "Hovering Hens": Danette Rutherford (Hope's "other" mother), Nina Wheeling, Margot Smith, Cornelia Price, Jeannette Coggins, Mandy Hawthorne, Brenda Seitz, Cindy Wood, Lucia Johnson, Kim Ballard, and especially Wendy Reeder, who took care of us, our house, and our family through Hope's illness. We could not have done it without you all.

To Keith Larson and Kevin Donnalley who loved Hope like one of their own.

To the Make-A-Wish Foundation® and all they stand for.

To Robyn and Ali Spizman for honoring Hope's memory by creating the Handbag of Hope for Make-A-Wish during the summer after her death.

To Weddington United Methodist for their Friday morning prayer group where they prayed for Hope's healing.

Finally, to all the people who continue to keep Hope's legacy alive. The Zach Ramsey family; Jim and Lisa Wright and Abby; Dan and Beth Meyer and their children David, Jason, and Lauren for their care and nurturing of "The Hope Oaks"; for all the birthday parties kids had in support of the March Forth with Hope Foundation. Sandy Buffie for the "Crazy Crutches" outreach, Jeff Fowlkes and company (you know how much you do for us!).

And especially to all the people who share the story of Hope with others in letting them know that we can all make a difference and leave a legacy in this world.

Stuart and Shelby Stout
March 1, 2008

THE MARCH FORTH WITH HOPE FOUNDATION

was established in 2004 by Stuart and Shelby Stout to provide financial assistance to families who have children who are battling life-threatening illnesses or injuries. Additionally, a portion of all proceeds goes to support the Make-A-Wish Foundation®.

For more information about the Foundation,
visit www.marchforthwithhope.org.

ABOUT MAKE-A-WISH FOUNDATION®

The Make-A-Wish Foundation® grants the wishes of children with life-threatening medical conditions to enrich the human experience with hope, strength, and joy. Born in 1980 when a group of caring volunteers helped a young boy fulfill his dream of becoming a police officer, the Foundation is now the largest wish-granting charity in the world, with sixty seven chapters in the United States and its territories. With the help of generous donors and more than twenty-five thousand volunteers, the Make-A-Wish Foundation® grants a wish every forty-one minutes and has granted more than 153,000 wishes in the U.S. since inception.

For more information about the Make-A-Wish Foundation®,
visit www.wish.org and discover
how you can *share the power of a wish*®.

Memories of Hope

A page from Hope's fifth grade project, My Life after 11 Years. Hope clearly had big aspirations.

Stuart's "FOURCHIX," which is the license plate on the family car: Hope, Holly, Austin, and Shelby.

Big sister Austin and Hope relaxing in a bubbly Jacuzzi in Cancun, Mexico.

Hope's sixth grade picture. It was the last school picture taken of Hope.

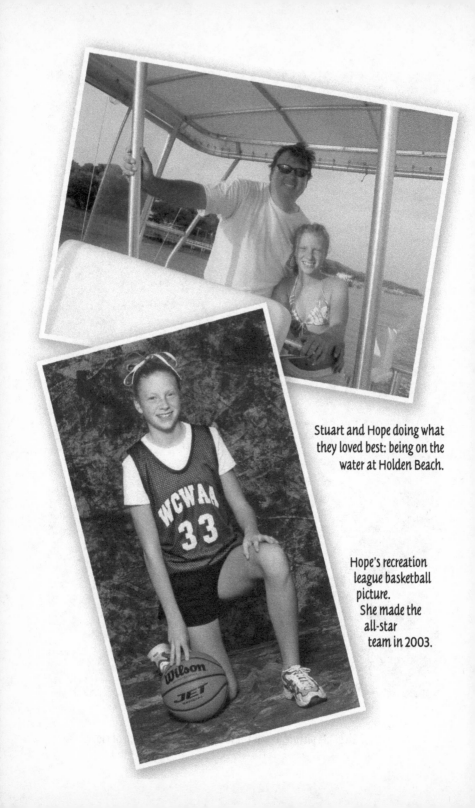

Stuart and Hope doing what they loved best: being on the water at Holden Beach.

Hope's recreation league basketball picture. She made the all-star team in 2003.

Hope and her kittens: Tuffy, Peanut, and Pudge.

This blanket was with Hope always and was a great source of comfort.

Hope and her Weddington Middle School cheerleading team. Hope worked extremely hard to make the team and was very proud to be on the squad.

Hope and Dr. Daniel McMahon, a gifted and compassionate physician.

Holly, Hope, and Austin clowning around before Austin left for N.C. State.

We received a lot of comfort in the chapel at Carolinas Medical Center,
especially from this stained glass window of Hope.

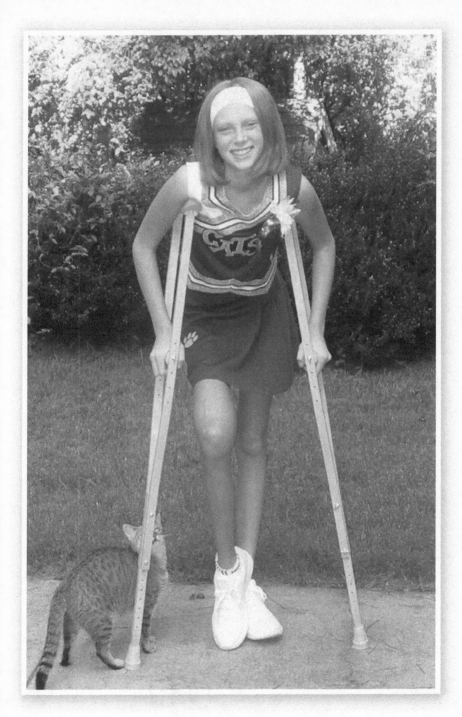

A very proud Weddington Wildcat cheerleader.

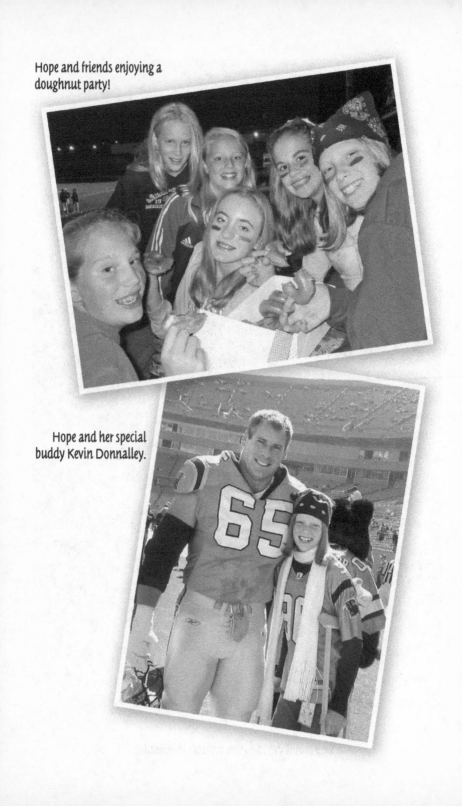

Hope and friends enjoying a
doughnut party!

Hope and her special
buddy Kevin Donnalley.

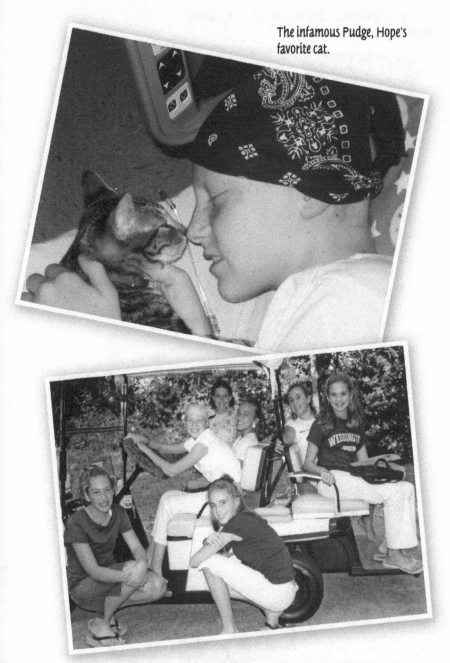

The infamous Pudge, Hope's favorite cat.

Hope, her Core Club, and "Little Ricky," Hope's golf cart.

The trio of "fireheads," the only redheads in our family:
Thomas, Hope, and Chris.

A picture of Hope being her typical self, taken
at her grandparent's 50th wedding anniversary party.

Hope rarely had an appetite during her treatment, but this was one exception!

Pudge is a special cat, for sure. Notice anything in his fur?

The sheer excitement of our family and Kevin when the million dollars was reached on January 16, 2004.

Hope as an angel in the annual Christmas pageant, a role she is playing now!